THE DAUGHTER
A POLITICAL BIOGRAPHY OF AUNG SAN SUU KYI

THE DAUGHTER

A Political Biography of Aung San Suu Kyi

HANS-BERND ZÖLLNER

and

RODION EBBIGHAUSEN

Translated by

VIPASHA BANSAL

Silkworm Books

ABOUT THE TRANSLATOR

VIPASHA BANSAL is an associate professor of law and linguist with degrees from the School of Oriental and African Studies (SOAS) and Columbia University. She first came in contact with Myanmar in 2004, when she worked with refugees from the country at UNHCR in Malaysia. Vipasha currently lives in Tokyo. She is a native speaker of Dutch, English, and Hindi, and fluent in German and Spanish.

ISBN: 978-616-215-146-0
English edition © 2018 by Silkworm Books
All rights reserved

This edition published in 2018 by
Silkworm Books
430/58 M. 7, T. Mae Hia, Chiang Mai 50100, Thailand
P. O. Box 296, Phra Singh, Chiang Mai 50205, Thailand
info@silkwormbooks.com
http://www.silkwormbooks.com

Cover photo: Aung San Suu Kyi in front of a portrait of her father. © Wolf/laif.

Typeset by Silk Type in Minion Pro 10.5 pt.

Printed and bound in Thailand by O. S. Printing House Bangkok

5 4 3 2 1

Mother,

this is the vow your daughter makes,
to stay on the soil of our country
and strive until the end of my life,
along the road marked out by my father,
together with the people of the Union
and all my strength
so that our country will remain strong,
all the people born in our country will progress
and democracy flourish.
May you rest in peace.

Pledge Aung San Suu Kyi gave at her mother's funeral, January 2, 1989
(translated by Jacques Leider)

Contents

Abbreviations

AFPFL	Anti-Fascist People's Freedom League
ASEAN	Association of Southeast Asian Nations (founded 1967)
BDA	Burma Defence Army (1942–1943)
BIA	Burma Independence Army (1941–1942)
BNA	Burma National Army (1943–1945)
BSPP	Burma Socialist Programme Party (1962–1988)
CRPP	Committee Representing the People's Parliament (founded 1998)
JMC	Joint Ceasefire Monitoring Committee
KIA	Kachin Independence Army (founded 1961)
NCA	National Ceasfire Agreement
NDF	National Democratic Front (founded 2010)
NLD	National League for Democracy (founded 1988)
SLORC	State Law and Order Restoration Council (1988–1997)
SPDC	State Peace and Development Council (1997–2011)
UNHCR	United Nations High Commissioner for Refugees
UPDJ	Union Peace Dialogue Joint Committee
USDA	Union Solidarity and Development Association (1993–2010)
UWSA	United Wa State Army
USDP	Union Solidarity and Development Party (founded 2010)

Prologue

Magical moments and unexpected turns are hallmarks of Myanmar's history. The world witnessed one such magical moment on the night of November 8, 2015. Not far from the Shwedagon Pagoda, whose sky-bound golden spire had fascinated so many over the centuries, stood the party headquarters of the National League for Democracy (NLD). Election day had ended. Long before the final announcements by the first electoral districts, supporters streamed to the party headquarters. Traffic came to a standstill in a wide radius around the inconspicuous building. The people squeezed close together to stand on the street and the footpaths. With red headbands, red T-shirts, and red flags parading the image of the fighting peacock—the NLD's logo—Aung San Suu Kyi's supporters celebrated the electoral victory of their "Mother Suu."

A large screen had been mounted on the roof of the NLD building. Songs that had provided vigor to the opposition movement over the years played on the loudspeakers, reminding everyone of the long political struggle that had preceded this point. Video snippets showed Aung San Suu Kyi at speeches or campaign events, surrounded by her high-spirited supporters. The screen switched between different districts, where poll workers had started counting the votes. An old party veteran, U Tin Oo, stepped out on the balcony at a late hour and tried to calm the gathering. He asked the reveling crowd to wait until the official results were known, and to go home. He urged them not to appear too triumphant and asked them to treat the political opponent with respect.

The festive crowds remained on the streets. Some stayed for days. They wanted to savor the victory in full. The ruling party had finally been voted out of office. The injustice of many decades would finally be rectified. Aung San Suu Kyi would finally take her well-deserved place at the helm of the country. A young Burmese man, who had the NLD flag painted on his cheeks and forehead and whose face glowed with exultation, expressed the rapture of the election night like this: "Tomorrow we will wake up in a new country."[1]

Naturally, international media was also present at this historic event. Broadcasting vans of the BBC, CNN, Channel News Asia, and others jutted out like islands between the throngs of people. They sent images of the pre-outcome election party around the globe. The media hype was shaped on age-old patterns; the good—in the form of Aung San Suu Kyi and the NLD—would finally prevail over the evil—represented by the military and its artificial political party.

In the euphoria, there was no time for looking behind the scenes, where one would have found lurking shades of grey. Enormous challenges lay ahead for the NLD in the event of a victory, and it was by no means clear whether the party would be able to overcome them. In any case, Aung San Suu Kyi would not be able to solve the country's problems on her own. Even under her leadership, politics would require the military's collaboration. Contrary to the popular mood, it was clear that simply holding elections was insufficient for achieving "genuine democracy," a term often used by Aung San Suu Kyi.

The cameras and journalists' questions still remain directed at Aung San Suu Kyi, as do the hopes and expectations of the majority of Myanmar's population. In Myanmar, she is called "our leader" and "our mother." Over the years, she has come to embody a dream of a better future, a life of freedom, and values that combine the structures of Western democracy with the tenets of Buddhism. Given the painful history of the country, it is understandable that she would have been the one chosen to fill such a role.

That magical November 2015 evening was the zenith of Aung San Suu Kyi's fame. This charismatic individual was already seventy years old on election night and had been an icon, both at home and abroad, for a long time.

Nobody expected that her descent—at least in the eyes of the West—would follow shortly after. Almost two years later, on September 29, 2017, St. Hugh's College in Oxford—where she had studied from 1964 to 1967—took down her portrait from its walls. Three weeks later, the St. Hugh's college students in Oxford unanimously voted to have the Myanmar leader's name removed from the name of their junior common room. The decision was substantiated thus: "Aung San Suu Kyi's inability to condemn the mass murder, gang rape and severe human rights abuses in Rakhine is inexcusable and unacceptable. She has gone against the very principles and ideals she had once righteously promoted."[2] Some weeks later, the Oxford city council also decided to strip Aung San Suu Kyi of the Freedom of the City of Oxford award.[3]

The resolution referred to the events in Myanmar's western Rakhine State that borders Bangladesh. On August 25, 2017, a Muslim rebel group, the Arakan Rohingya Salvation Army (ARSA), carried out a second attack (the first was in October 2016) on several police stations near the border, resulting in the death of eleven people.[4] Myanmar's security forces retaliated immediately. The clashes caused more than six hundred thousand Muslims in the area, who are referred to as Rohingya, to flee to neighboring Bangladesh. This constituted more than half of the population living in the three townships near the border. Reports about atrocities committed by the Myanmar security forces spread.[5] Zeid Ra'ad al-Hussein, United Nations high commissioner for human rights, said that the military operations seem to be a "textbook example of ethnic cleansing."[6] Such reports were denied by the Myanmar government headed by Aung San Suu Kyi.[7]

Soon there was growing criticism against Aung San Suu Kyi from the West and various Muslim countries, including neighboring Malaysia and Indonesia. The allegations against her ranged from failing to act to being complicit. The tone of the criticism sharpened and the accusations increased by the day.

In Myanmar, however, there was a unity of voices supporting her stance. The slogan "we stand with you, Aung San Suu Kyi" was quickly created and circulated through various meetings between her supporters. People sometimes went so far as to extend their support to the very army they had voted out of politics in 2015.

Placard shown at a demonstration on September 17 in Yangon on the occasion of a live broadcast of Aung San Suu Kyi's speech on the Rakhine crisis. (Photo: Alexej Yusupov)

In contrast to international media, Myanmar's national media refuse to refer to the situation in Rakhine State as a "Rohingya crisis" because Rohingya as a designation of an indigenous group in Myanmar is acknowledged by neither the majority of Myanmar's population nor the government. The two divergent international and national reactions on the crisis in Rakhine State have resulted in a sharp decline in Aung San Suu Kyi's reputation abroad while winning her near unanimous support at home.

◉ ◉ ◉

This political biography addresses the rift between the perceptions of Aung San Suu Kyi's political achievements abroad and at home. It does so by shedding light on Burmese political culture that has shaped her political career from the very beginning and made her popular in her home country before she was elevated to the status of a global icon through the Nobel Prize. The country's political culture was and still is shaped by her father, the national hero Aung San, who led the country to independence. It is thus very much part of her heritage, as are a number of great challenges, such as the country's ethnic diversity, religious variety, and the popular rejection of real or alleged aliens.

Aung San Suu Kyi decided to take on a heavy political burden in 1988 after the former general Ne Win unexpectedly stepped down after twenty-six years of rule. At that magical moment, almost thirty years ago, she addressed half a million people at the foot of the holy Shwedagon Pagoda while standing beside a large picture of her father. She made a promise then to step into his shoes and fulfill his legacy.

Yet it was her mother, Daw Khin Kyi, rather than her father that had a lasting impact on her. It was from her mother that Aung San Suu Kyi adopted her unyielding, disciplined, and dutiful character. Discipline and determination have shaped her political struggle and awed people around the world. From both her father's and her mother's sides, Aung San Suu Kyi is very much a daughter of Burmese soil and traditions. But she is also a child of the world. She studied and lived in India, the UK, the US, Bhutan, and Japan. Many thus saw her as someone who brings together Western democratic and human rights principles and Asian spirituality. However, her international reputation's recent decline suggests that such expectations were illusory from early on in her political career.

The first chapter recalls the mass meeting on the grounds of the great pagoda in 1988. Chapter 2 takes a look at the life of Aung San, a role model for Burmese politicians. Aung San Suu Kyi's political life is set out and analyzed in several chapters arranged in chronological order (chapters 3–11). The last part of the book surveys Aung San Suu Kyi's first two years in government, her role as Myanmar's key civilian politician, and her handling of the humanitarian crisis in Rakhine State (chapter 12).

Aung San Suu Kyi's biography reflects recurring themes within Myanmar's political culture: the strong, if not dominating, influence of Buddhist thinking in politics; the focus on eminent personalities; and a weak culture of compromise. These markers raise the question as to whether different political cultures—as embodied in Aung San Suu Kyi—might result in a stable political system for Myanmar. In other words, will it be possible to transform the promise of a happy life for all people living within the borders of Myanmar into reality? Will the idea of the nation include that significant Muslim community that is left in Rakhine or has fled to Bangladesh?

Hamburg/Bonn, November 2017

CHAPTER 1

Peacock from the Ashes

When I first decided to take part in the movement for democracy, it was more out of a sense of duty than anything else. On the other hand, my sense of duty was very closely linked to my love for my father. I could not separate it from the love for my country, and therefore, from the sense of responsibility towards my people.

Clouds clustered over the Bay of Bengal just days before the big event. Following the age-old rules of the rainy season, the southwesterly monsoon winds dutifully pushed them over to the mainland, where they finally unburdened their load over Rangoon. At around ten o'clock in the morning, these clouds were still spread across the skies. Yet on this special day, the heaviest of downpours would not have stopped the people from making their way to the Shwedagon Pagoda, the holiest place in all of Burma. It was Friday, August 26, 1988. Since the break of dawn, the people had been streaming in from all corners of the city. They made their way to the square in front of the western passage to the podium on the hill, from where the pagoda perforates the sky like a golden needle. There was great curiosity and expectation. Leaflets were being distributed and the message printed on them circulated through the many hands: The daughter of the national hero Aung San will give a speech.

Dramatic weeks had preceded this day. It all started at a run-of-the-mill teahouse near the renowned Rangoon Institute of Technology. At the beginning of March, a scuffle had broken out here between students and other young people. The latter managed to evade punishment because one of them was the son of a member of Burma's single party, the Burma Socialist Programme Party (BSPP). This party had been leading the country on a "Burmese Way to Socialism" since 1974. Outraged

Shwedagon in the rainy season. (Photo: Hans-Bernd Zöllner)

by the authorities' blatant bias, the students burst into protest. Their demonstrations evoked drastic responses from the security forces. The protests escalated, with increasing numbers of the population taking to the streets all over Burma. The people were rising to air their frustrations and disappointments with the political mishandling of their country.

Party Chairman Ne Win had come to power after a military coup in March 1962. Since then, he and his government had kept the country isolated from the rest of the world.[1] In 1974, Ne Win, then the longstanding chief of staff of the army, put away his uniform to continue to rule the country as a civilian. The people felt poorly governed and bullied by this only nominally civilian government.

Weeks of protest led to a wholly unexpected turn of events in the rainy season. In July 1988, the "old man" Ne Win, now seventy-seven years old, stepped down from his last post as chairman of the single party. He did this at an extraordinary party congress, at which he also recommended a referendum for the people to decide on the country's political system. All at once, the dissolution of the government and the demonstrators' goals seemed attainable. With the party leader stepping down, the BSPP government lacked direction. It accepted the resignation of the former Number One but rejected his proposition on the referendum. Instead, in a move towards the opposite direction, the party elected Sein Lwin—a former general detested by the population—as Ne Win's successor.

The new party chairman and head of state would come to be known as the "butcher of Rangoon" for his brutal response to the student protests. One of his first official acts was to declare martial law on August 3. Scores of demonstrators were killed in the follow-up. The demonstrators themselves were also involved in some revenge attacks against supporters of the former regime.

The continuous eruption of protests and violence unleashed a dynamic that had not been seen in Burma for a long time. Uncoordinated ripples of its energy spread in all directions. Despite the repression, a countless number of new associations and unions formed in this protest period. Each association and union had its own program to lead Burma into a new and successful future.

Authors' note: Burma/Myanmar

The military government that came into power on September 18, 1988, changed the name of the country in English texts from Burma to Myanmar by a law enacted in 1989. In the Burmese language, the country was always called Myanmar. It was further established that from that point on, "Myanmar" would be used for the entire country and its population, regardless of ethnicity, whereas the word 'Burma' and its derivatives would be used for the ethnic majority of the country. Until this day, Aung Sang Suu Kyi and her supporters have not fully accepted this change of name, as it was put in place without the approval of the people. In the meantime, "Myanmar" has become commonplace internationally.

Other name changes followed alongside the name of the country: cities (Rangoon became Yangon), rivers (Irrawaddy became Ayeyarwady), and ethnic minorities (the Karen became the Kayin).

Both forms are used in the text that follows. We use the past forms especially when the subject matter relates to the time before 1989 or when it is in relation to Aung San Suu Kyi.

So, by August 26, a colorful collective stood together in front of the Shwedagon Pagoda. There were artists, students, public officials, workers, journalists, nurses, and many more. A gay alliance was present which called itself Promoters of Beauty. Individuals and groups made themselves recognizable through placards or work uniforms. What they lacked, what had in fact been missing in the entire country, was a unifying bond, a banner under which this diverse coalition could gather as one. Also missing was a person who could represent the much longed-for "new Burma." Historically, such a figure had always existed in Burma, ever since the days of the kings. During the struggle against the British colonial rulers and after independence, this figure was the national hero Aung San. Aung San had fought for the country's freedom but did not live to experience it. He was murdered at the orders of a political rival just six months before the country celebrated its independence. His friend and successor, U Nu, had then gone on to set up a Buddhist welfare state. In contrast, the "old man" Ne Win—hailed initially but despised finally in 1988—had stood for a Burmese socialism under the reins of a one-party system. A new leading figure was needed to fill the political vacuum created with Ne Win's departure.

The list of potential candidates in the year 1988 was short. Ne Win had not tolerated competitors and consequently left no successors in his wake. Any such successor would have been discredited anyhow, as was the case with the "butcher" Sein Lwin and Dr. Maung Maung, the state and party leader who followed shortly thereafter. Dr. Maung Maung had tried to pacify the situation, but his efforts had been in vain. The lawyer, historian, and journalist, who had served in different posts in Ne Win's regime, could not appease the angered, protesting masses. The people distrusted the system that he represented. Even the lifting of martial law, two days before the gathering at the foot of the great pagoda, was not accredited to him. On the contrary, it was ascribed to the success of the demonstrators. In the same vein, Dr. Maung Maung's promise to hold the referendum on a new political system after all, which had been rejected by the party congress earlier in July, was seen as tactical sidestepping.[2] In the eyes of the people, Dr. Maung Maung and his government were no more than Ne Win's puppets. They, too, had to go, and they had to go immediately. And with them, the entire old system.

A Risky Choice

Who would be the face of the desired new beginning? There were three individuals with political experience in the country who were generally well known and had not lost credibility as a result of their proximity to Ne Win. All three had once worked with him but had been ousted from their posts by Burma's Number One. All three had political experience and were already quite old.

There was Nu, age seventy-nine, Aung San's companion and after his death the first prime minister of Burma. Ne Win had toppled him from this post in March 1962. Then there was Aung Gyi, ten years younger than Nu and a soldier who, after the 1962 coup, had occupied the place of Number Two in Ne Win's Revolutionary Council, which took over the government after the coup. One year later, owing to differences with the Number One, he had resigned. At the initial stages of unrest in March 1988, Aung Gyi had articulated the population's dissatisfaction in open letters to Ne Win. Finally, there was Tin Oo, sixty-two at this point, who had become commander-in-chief of the armed forces in 1974 under Ne Win. He had to step down two years later, only to subsequently be sentenced to long-term imprisonment for high treason.

None of these candidates really made the cut. The choice of the student protest leaders fell not on a man but on a forty-three-year-old and thus relatively young woman. Aung San Suu Kyi, the daughter of Aung San, was the one chosen to speak on this twenty-sixth day of August, flanked by the spiritual and political core of the country, the Shwedagon Pagoda. She was the one who was expected to rein in the forces unleashed by the protests and transform them into a new Burma. The student protesters wanted a genuinely new beginning. They wanted a beginning that in some way would turn back time to that moment in history when Aung San had succeeded in expelling the British and colonial rule had ended. There was a whiff of resurrection in the air—the resurrection of a peacock from the ashes that could give wings to a people and fill them with hope. This "resurrection motif" that was felt in Burma, however, was not echoed in the Western coverage, which was largely skeptical that this political novice's symbolic stature in the country would enough to counter her political inexperience. In this way, in the beginning the Burmese political scene was seen through Western political lenses stressing "hard" politics over "symbolic" politics, whereas in Burma this was reversed. Soon the Western view would come to parallel the Burmese approach.

The students had carefully set the stage for Aung San Suu Kyi's first big appearance. A larger-than-life portrait of Aung San hung on the left side of the podium. The image summoned the dead hero, whose name shone at the beginning of his daughter's name—a singular prefix reserved for the children of the country's national hero. Demonstrators had taken his image from its usual spot on office walls around the country and

Aung San Suu Kyi on stage beside her father's portrait on August 26, 1988.
(Photo: Onasia)

marched with it during these preceding weeks. The image of Aung San acted as both shield and message. It was a shield against the security forces, of which Aung San was the founding father. It was a message that the moment for something new had come and that the legacy of the slain hero could now be filled with new life.

The student protesters had ordained Aung San Suu Kyi as the messenger before it was even clear that she would be prepared to follow in her father's footsteps and bring down the crumbling regime. The concrete preparations had started exactly one month before August 26 and three days after Ne Win's resignation at Pangyi Soe Moe's (*pangyi* means "painter") studio. Soe Moe was a renowned artist and film director who was born in 1944.

The painter started with his assignment on July 26: a portrait of Aung San that a month later would stand next to Aung San Suu Kyi during her speech and make it clear that she had stepped in to fill her father's shoes. He chose a special technique for the picture, distinguishing it from his otherwise realistic images. The image was composed of the three colors of the revolution that had accompanied Aung San on his rise to becoming the country's leader: yellow, green, and red. Yellow stood for Buddhism, green for the agricultural backbone of the country, and red for the traditional bravery of its people. These were also the colors of Dobama Asiayone or "We Burmans Association," the organization that had fought for independence under Aung San's leadership. A peacock danced in the middle of the tricolored flag of Dobama Asiayone. The

Soe Moe painting Aung San's portrait on July 26, 1988. (Photo: Soe Moe)

bird commemorated the times of the kings, who had adopted the image of the dancing peacock in Burma's first national flag. Now, in August 1988, demonstrators took to the streets carrying flags of these colors. The symbolism of the revolution was obvious long before the question as to who would lead it was answered. When Soe Moe started his painting, he could not have known that Aung San Suu Kyi would accept the role attributed to her. She *was* the students' first choice, but she only accepted after some hesitation and cautious reflection.

Students carrying the tricolor Dobama flag in 1988. (Photo: Htein Win)

It was not only the students—artists, intellectuals, journalists, and politicians had also pushed for Aung San Suu Kyi's acceptance of the role. Many of them would go on to become her advisers or colleagues. U Htwe Myint, a supporter of U Nu in his attempt to topple Ne Win's government in 1969, for example, was among the politicians who now turned to Aung San Suu Kyi. It was together with him that Aung San Suu Kyi went on to write to the State Council on August 15. In their letter, Suu Kyi and U Htwe Myint proposed that a committee be set up in accordance with the 1974 Constitution to find a way out of the crisis in consultation with the public.[3] Such a committee did indeed follow but remained without consequence as it found no resonance with the public.

It was a time when various prominent and unknown individuals walked to Aung San Suu Kyi's house on University Avenue in order to see her and offer support. Among them was Thaw Ka, a Muslim author and former major of the Burmese marine corps.[4] Together with several Buddhist friends, he wanted to speak to her and see if she would be capable of taking part in the uprising. Thaw Ka had great doubts to start with. Would she be able to speak Burmese adequately? After all, she had mostly lived abroad since 1960 and had only returned to Burma in April of this year to care for her ill mother. During the private visits, it quickly became clear that she had an excellent command of her mother tongue. Yet one doubt remained: would she be able to engage such a large audience?

A Symbolic Place

All these doubts were dispelled after Aung San Suu Kyi's first public appearance. On August 24, the day that Dr. Maung Maung lifted martial law, Suu Kyi spoke in front of the Rangoon General Hospital. The hospital was poignantly located on Bogyoke Aung San Road, a street named after her great father. Alongside the American embassy, the hospital was one of the favored final destinations for the demonstrations and protest marches. It became a meeting point after August 10, when a male nurse was shot there and three female nurses injured during clashes with security forces. Aung San Suu Kyi gave a short speech, flanked on one side by a famous Burmese actress, Khin Thida Htun, and on the other by the aforementioned prominent Muslim author Thaw Ka. In a brief address, she spoke in favor of a representative political system and announced that she would hold a longer speech two days later. This first appearance had the air of a dress rehearsal—a performance for which she had expert support and which she delivered with great competence.

Besides Soe Moe's painting, the stage at the foot of the Shwedagon Pagoda was also decorated with large banners. These banners announced

Aung San Suu Kyi on August 24, 1988, at the Rangoon General Hospital, flanked by Thaw Ka on her left and Khin Thida Khun. (Photo: Htein Win)

the keyword for Burma's new program: "democracy." In front of this simple slogan stood students in white shirts and dark longyis. They wore armbands with the revolutionary yellow-green-red colors. From now on they would call themselves the Tri-Color Student Group and serve as bodyguards for Aung San Suu Kyi. On this day their shirts bore the royal peacock—yellow against a red background—in a different pose. It was a fighting bird. This had also been the emblem for students in the past, when the 1936 strike had set off the heated phase of the independence struggle. That strike had also taken place under Aung San's leadership.

The colors and symbols made the objective of this staging clear. Another fight for Burma's freedom was going to take place. The peacock—so the message ran—would tirelessly keep on fighting and with victory would again spread its feathers as in the times of the kings. Only this time, the hoped-for victory would be in the name of democracy. The new flag replacing the socialist one indicated the beginning of a new era and at the same time hearkened back to the time of the independence struggle under Aung San's leadership.

The symbolism of the place chosen for Aung San Suu Kyi's public appearance could hardly have been stronger. The Shwedagon Pagoda's golden stupa glowed in the sunlight and to the crowds appeared to extend the legitimacy of the Buddha's own teachings to the oration. The holy place had been constructed over the Buddha's eight precious hairs that legend holds he sent here himself. Visible from the pagoda was the parliament building, towards which Aung San Suu Kyi would direct her speech. To the left of the stage was a statue of U Wisara. He was a monk who became a martyr after his death in prison following a hunger strike in 1929. He had been imprisoned as punishment for an inflammatory speech he held shortly after Mahatma Gandhi visited Burma. (Aung San Suu Kyi has expressed admiration for Gandhi.) Gandhi had also invited U Wisara to India to recover from an earlier hunger strike. The monk had been holding hunger strikes to protest against the fact that he and other monks were being treated like ordinary civilian criminals.

These evocative surroundings connected the past with the future and indeed hinted at some of what the future was to hold for Aung San Suu Kyi and her followers: the connection with Burma's glorious past, the challenge of democratic governance in parliament, the protection offered through the holy Buddhist traditions of the country, and if was to be their fate, the ultimate sacrificial commitment—as with Aung San and many others—to the point of death itself.

A Standing Acclamation

No one counted the number of people who were present at Aung San Suu Kyi's speech and heard her message. The estimates stand at half a million. The streets leading to the square in front of the pagoda were packed. Aung San Suu Kyi, in whom many were already placing their hope, had traveled the last stretch to the stage on foot, as her convoy of cars could not pass through the crowds. Pagoda visitors curious about why the masses of people had gathered could not make it down the steps to be part of the experience themselves.

More meaningful than the sheer number of people was the fact that they had come together for this speech at the pagoda in spite of their variety and difference. Still it was not a representative collection of the entire population of the country. After all, more than two-thirds of the Burmese population lived, and continues to live, in the countryside. It is worth noting, however, that all religions, classes, and ethnic minorities were represented. In this place, politics and spirituality were inexorably interwoven. The occasion on this day was a traditional festival, a *pwe*, with a particularly special flavor. No puppeteers, musicians, or actors would perform at this celebration, but a star of unique quality.

To announce her arrival, Htun Wai, an almost-seventy-year-old famed actor stepped on to the stage. He introduced the new leader—the one people were waiting for—to the large audience: "General Aung San's daughter, Aung San Suu Kyi, is about to hold a speech about what is desirable and what is necessary under the current conditions. After her speech, we call on you to support her standpoint. We welcome Aung San Suu Kyi for her speech!"[5]

© Photo:Htein Win (1988)

Htun Wai introducing Aung San Suu Kyi to the audience on August 26, 1988.
(Photo: Htein Win)

At the end of this announcement the actor threw up his right arm dramatically to direct the audience's attention to the true star of the event. Shortly thereafter he placed his hands on his chest to commemorate those who had lost their lives in the demonstrations. That is what Aung San Suu Kyi had requested. It was the actor's last great performance. As a result of his commitment to the new movement, he was officially sidelined and his name was banished from the state-controlled media.

The Dawn of a New Era

Aung San Suu Kyi started her speech by greeting those present. The monks were mentioned first, followed by praise for the students. They were the ones who had spearheaded these latest demonstrations and made the mass gathering possible. Dr. Maung Maung had lifted martial law just two days ago, so the gathering had the air of a victory party. It was a win for the people, led by the students, against the government.

In her praise of the students, the speaker indirectly made reference to her father. He had also first come to fame due to his leading role in the student strikes of 1936 as editor of the students' magazine. Two years later, he became a driving force in organizing a large strike as the head of the Dobama Asiayone, through which an alliance of workers, farmers, and students hoped to bring the country's British rulers to their knees. The strike electrified the country; it was a beacon of resistance against the British administration. As in 1936 and 1938, the 1988 protests were organized and led by students.

The role of students as the pioneers of political revolution is a distinctively Burmese feature. As early as 1920, college students had protested against the establishment of a university in Burma. They were not antieducation per se; they were against education installed by the British, which the students referred to as "slave education." The first day of those strikes is still remembered as a national holiday in Burma. On the Shwedagon Pagoda's platform stands a memorial for those students. They had gathered there to take a sacred oath that they would not rest until they were victorious in the fight against their British rulers.

Monument commemorating the student strike of 1920 on the Shwedagon platform. (Photo: Helmar Bischoff)

In both 1920 and 1936, the terraces of the Shwedagon Pagoda served as a base for the strikers. This could happen because both times the students had the monks' approval. The monks provided rooms where students could spend the night and receive food from a population that supported their actions. Since then, the Shwedagon has symbolized the monks' support for the students' fight for independence and freedom. This is one important reason why Aung San Suu Kyi's address to the masses started with "reverend monks." The monks were the ones who had to bless this new movement, giving it legitimacy while withdrawing legitimacy from the former rulers.

Aung San Suu Kyi's speech on August 26 was a sweeping success. The students' strategy had worked, even though the content of the speech could not be heard by everyone. The loudspeaker system was not built for the numbers that had gathered. According to one of Suu Kyi's later colleagues, the majority of the people present did not even hear a word of what was said. Of key importance was the carefully set-up atmosphere. The place, the image of Aung San, the transparent approach, the students' clothing—together they conveyed the message to all present without words: a new beginning lies ahead. The people were captivated by Aung San Suu Kyi's appearance and her manner of speaking. Applause punctuated her sentences. Members of the groups that had come shouted their slogans, and cries of "long live Aung San Suu Kyi!" were frequently heard in the crowd. Many were overwhelmed by the aspect of this forty-three-year-old woman with the appearance of a young girl, who spoke with the authority of a born leader. Many of those present that day took away with them the conviction that she was their rightful leader—that only she was worthy of being her father's successor. In fact, the title "our leader" is used by her supporters to this day when they speak of her. No vote was required to ascertain that she had her listeners' endorsement, which Htun Wai had sought at the introduction of her speech.

Through this mode of popular election she became the leader of, as she herself proclaimed, the "second struggle for national independence."[6] Her father had led the first; now it was her turn. It inevitably followed that a new government should be put in place, one that would promptly organize free and fair elections. A referendum for the people to determine which political system they preferred became redundant. The endorsement of the people present at the August 26 rally replaced any such formal vote. After this day, there was no doubt as to whom the people trusted. The elections that later followed were, in many ways, no more than a formalization of this fact.

Thus Dr. Maung Maung's proposal—as put forward by Aung San Suu Kyi herself on August 15—to resolve the crisis through a constitutional procedure was precluded. A compromise between the government and the demonstrators was out of the question. From this point on, the key question was who could deliver on their claim to leadership. The choice of the people at the foot of the Shwedagon Pagoda was clear. Aung San Suu Kyi was to lead the country.

Yet not all were convinced. Soe Moe, the painter, was not one to remain gripped by Aung San Suu Kyi. He had been drawn into the protest movement by his students at the academy of arts. During this time, he visited Aung San Suu Kyi's house often. He helped to set up the podium and his portrait of Aung San for August 26, and had stayed up all night with other activists on the eve of the speech.

From the beginning, however, he found many of Aung San Suu Kyi's young supporters to be uneducated, and distanced himself from the movement. Politics was not his thing. His name would no longer be mentioned by her supporters even though his painting had made a pivotal contribution to the event's success. Like the actress who had stood alongside Aung San Suu Kyi during the debut speech at the hospital, Soe Moe came to be regarded as a defector.[7] This is because he went on to work with the military junta and made a film about Aung San with the junta's support.[8] He remained an admirer of the man whose portrait he had painted in the summer of 1988. However, he could not summon up the same admiration for the daughter. In 2012 he made the film about his great hero, which failed to draw a great response. It seemed that the only movie about Aung San that people would accept would be one sanctioned by his daughter. They shunned Soe Moe's attempt at a film because of his closeness to junta leadership—in particular Than Shwe, who had opened the Myanmar film archives for him.

On the other hand, Soe Moe's image of Aung San made its rounds through the world without anyone knowing the name of the painter. The portrait was brought to Aung San Suu Kyi's house on University Avenue after the speech and displayed in the living room. It appeared as a background in countless photos taken by visitors to the house, usually together with Aung San Suu Kyi herself (see cover image).

The events of August 26, 1988, kicked off a new struggle for Aung San's legacy. It was a fight that remains unresolved to this day. From its very inception, symbols, people, and the emotions attached to them played a central role.

Aung San Suu Kyi's sudden appearance on the political stage shows how important the element of chance is in Myanmar. She had returned to her home country to care for her ill mother shortly before student unrest turned into a national uprising. Then, unexpectedly, the longstanding ruler Ne Win stepped down as head of state and left a power vacuum. The student leaders invited Aung San Suu Kyi to take over as leader of the protest movement. Meanwhile, the ruling party considered Ne Win's proposal to introduce a multiparty system via elections to end the crisis. However, the protest leaders, including Aung San Suu Kyi, wanted the immediate resignation of the government. The military brought the debate to an end by taking over the government through a coup. Unpredictability and chance encounters also typify the life of Aung San Suu Kyi's father.

CHAPTER 2

The Incomplete Hero

My father once talked about purity in thought, word and deed. That's what I mean by perfection. Purity.

Aung San is still omnipresent in Myanmar, even if his image no longer appears on all banknotes as it once did. A large market and a central street in Yangon still carry his name, as do the main streets of most other cities in the country. His statue can be found on many larger public squares, especially after more were added on the occasion of his one hundredth birthday in 2015. It is clear that Aung San has been accorded the same significance as the founding kings of the three great dynasties of Burma. In most people's minds, he not only freed the country from the yoke of British colonialism but was also the fourth unifier of the multiethnic state of Burma. The large portrait of him—the "father of the nation"—at his daughter's first major public appearance was thus depicting none other than the founder of independent and modern Burma.

Yet Aung San never truly governed the country. The biggest political challenges still lay before him when he was murdered on July 19, 1947. His premature, violent death is the tragic end of a life that was marked by high political ideals and an unusual intuition for the practicable. With all its contradictions, his political legacy remains ingrained in the country. After all, not just every government since 1948 but also each corresponding opposition has tried to claim itself as the rightful heir to Aung San's political inheritance.

Banknotes with Aung San's image. (Photo: Rodion Ebbighausen)

Unlike his daughter, Aung San had only known the wider world through books prior to his debut in the country's politics in 1938. He had grown up within the Buddhist traditions of Burma. From the beginning, his life's trajectory was directed at ridding Burma of British colonial rule, which had commenced fully in 1885 with the victory of Great Britain over the Kingdom of Burma in the Third Anglo-Burmese War.

Aung San was born on February 13, 1915, in Natmauk, in central Myanmar. His birthday fell on a Saturday. The days of the week play an important role in the lives of almost all Burmese, as the horoscope (*sada*) is essentially based on the day and hour of birth. As a result of being born on a Saturday, his name had to traditionally start with the letters T, Ht, D, Dh or N. He was in fact originally called Htein Lein. His brother Aung Than, who was four years older, later revealed that it was he who first started calling his little brother Aung San, so that the names of the two youngest sons would rhyme. It was this brotherly name that history would remember.

Aung San was the youngest of nine children. His father, U Pha, came from a farming family but had graduated as a lawyer. His mother, Daw Suu, had inherited land and was active in its administration. One of Daw Suu's uncles had fought as a rebel against the invaders from the West, had been taken prisoner, and was subsequently beheaded. Aung San had been proud of this ancestor from a young age.

Aung San's childhood home and family in Natmauk. (Photo: Hans-Bernd Zöllner)

In one autobiographical piece, Aung San looked back and described himself as a sickly and difficult child who started to speak so late that his family feared he might be deaf. His disinterest in clean clothing and daily bodily hygiene was legendary. Even at university his clothes were tattered. One of his close companions stated that every now and then they had to push Aung San into taking a bath.

His unkempt exterior was matched with a rough demeanor. Both attributes are typical in the myths surrounding the perfect Burmese hero. A Burmese ruler works his way up from modest means and distinguishes himself in the early years of his ascent through an untamed wildness. He comes to power by ending the unjust rule of his predecessor through violence. Once in power, he governs with clemency and wisdom, in line with the ten kingly virtues—charity, morality, willingness to sacrifice, fairness, mercifulness, restraint, equanimity, avoidance of violence, patience, and pursuit of harmony. Aung San fashioned himself along these traditional notions and embodied the two stages perfectly. However, he never had the opportunity to live out the second part of the story, that of the benevolent ruler. His incomplete legacy is reflected in the fact that to this day he is referred to by his military title, Bogyoke (general) Aung San and not with U (uncle), although he had later decided to become a civilian politician.

It is reported that as a child, Aung San refused to learn to read and write. It was only at the age of eight that he gave up this resistance. He first attended a monastic school and then a high school in Yenangyaung, a city made into Burma's first industrial center owing to its oilfields. The school, at which an older brother taught, was founded by Burmese nationalists after the first student strike in Burma. Under his brother's direction, Aung San developed into an outstanding student with prizewinning achievements.

After finishing his school education, the youngest of the family enrolled at the University of Rangoon in 1932. At the time, around four hundred thousand people lived in the metropolis, which had been partially destroyed by an earthquake and floods two years earlier. Under British rule, Rangoon had developed from a fishing village near the holy Shwedagon Pagoda into the largest and most important port city in Southeast Asia. Rice, teak, and precious stones were handled here. The city grew also because the British drew in migrants from other parts of Asia, especially India. As a result, the Burmese population in the 1930s only constituted a minority.[1]

At university, Aung San majored in Burmese literature and Pali, the language of the holy scriptures used in Theravada Buddhism. But his passion was for politics. Founded in 1930, the university Students' Union became the first forum where he could practice his passion. One of the key engagements of the union was to work on the art of debate, which the students did in a building erected by a rich Burmese businessman. The debating style was based on the English model and was, of course, conducted in the language of the colonial power. Aung San participated in the debates. At his first attempt, no one understood what he was saying due to his poor English, and he was booed. He did not allow this to deter him and finished his speech as planned. This perseverance—also highlighted by his daughter in a short biography of her father—characterized Aung San. For him, resistance was a welcome opportunity. It was good training for becoming a political leader. This perseverance is ultimately what impressed his audience. He did later successfully sharpen his English language and rhetoric skills. He would go on to use them in the struggle against the British.

Aung San was convinced that politics is what sits at the core of all human life: "In short, after all is said and done, politics means your everyday life. It is you in fact; for you are a political animal as Aristotle long ago declared. It is how you eat, sleep, work and live, with which politics is concerned. You may not think about politics. But politics thinks about you."[2] Dagon Taya, a renowned Burmese author who got to know Aung San during the student years, later described the people's hero by referring back to his political identity: "Aung San was a political animal and politics was his only way of being. Nothing else was of significance. No social obligations, no manners, neither art nor music."[3]

Initial Fame

Two years before seventeen-year-old Aung San arrived in Rangoon to start his studies, a sea change had been signaled in Burma. In December 1930, under the leadership of a member of the leading nationalist movement, the General Council of Burmese Associations, a farmers' revolt had started in a district almost two hundred kilometers north of Rangoon. The rebellion was similar to the one that had led to the decapitation of Aung San's great-uncle. Among other hardships, the farmers were suffering from collapsing rice prices in the wake of the global economic crisis of 1929. Certain of their just cause, the poorly armed farmers attacked colonial officers and colonial infrastructure, including railway and telegraph lines. They wore talismans and amulets to protect them from the adversary's bullets. Eventually, Saya San, the leader, was caught, brought to court, and executed in November 1931. Even after the death of the leader the uprising kept the British busy for a long time. Semiviolent protests flared up again and again. The

Aung San (first row, third from right) in the ranks of the Dobama Asiayone in 1938. In the center, Thakin Kodaw Hmaing, the organization's patron, flanked on both sides by monks. (Photo: U Kwalt)

rebellion—regarded by the British as medieval—made small headlines in the international arena.

Half a year before the outbreak of the rebellion, a young lecturer at the University of Rangoon had founded an association that initially stirred no great public interest. The association was not based on traditions of the old Burma. Rather, it promoted a new beginning. The Dobama Asiayone or "We Burmans Association" was created after violent clashes between groups of Burmese and Indians in 1930. Its manifesto called for employing modern techniques in the fight for Burma's independence. It was this organization that saw symbolic revival in the colors adopted during the 1988 protests and Aung San Suu Kyi's stage on August 26 of the same year.

However, the young author of the manifesto had no talent for organizing a movement. It was only after Ba Thaung, the eccentric founder, withdrew from the association in 1935 that it gathered political momentum. He did, however, write the text of Myanmar's national anthem. He propagated the use of the title *thakin* before the names of the members of the new association. *Thakin* is tantamount to "sir" and until then—like the *sahib* in India—had been reserved for addressing the British colonial rulers. Through the use of this *thakin*, the members symbolically demonstrated that they were the rightful masters of the country, not the British or the strangers brought to the country by them. Thakin Ba Thaung had read Friedrich Nietzsche. His choice of the new title owed partly to his fascination with the Übermensch from *Also sprach Zarathustra*. Aung San also later liked to use the Nietzschean motto "live dangerously!"[4]

Aung San only joined the Dobama Asiayone in 1938 (see photo opposite).[5] The founder had long left the association by then. As of the mid-1930s, Ba Thaung's successors had firmly reorganized the association into radical extraparliamentary opposition. The association held an especially strong stance against any British attempt to introduce a British model of democracy in Burma. Like most other Burmese nationalists, Aung San rejected all aspects of the British parliamentary model. His daughter would go on to lend praise to that same model seventy-four years later in a speech at the British Parliament and recommend elements of it for Burma. That same parliament had separated Burma from British India in 1935 and put a new constitution in place for the now separate colony. U Nu and other young friends of Aung San's from the Dobama Asiayone set fire to a British flag in front of the parliament building in Rangoon on the occasion of the new constitution—which had been adopted in London—coming into force.

Despite all this, the first time Aung San caused a real commotion was in the student movement, which was becoming increasingly politicized a few years after the start of his studies. It was his first post, as editor of the student magazine *Oway* ("The Peacock's Voice"), that made him famous throughout the country and catapulted him to the forefront of the anticolonial protest movement. As in the student strike of 1920, the students criticized the education system as a clear symptom of the cancer of colonialism and hence fundamentally rejected it.

In 1936, a satirical article appeared in *Oway* accusing a British faculty member of chasing after female students and frequenting brothels. Aung San refused to reveal the identity of the author—who had written under a pseudonym—to the rector of the university, J. D. Sloss. Actually, the author's name was generally known. What was at stake here for both the editor and the rector was the principle. Aung San was consequently expelled from the university. Just a few days earlier, Aung San's comrade-in-arms Nu—who at the time was president of the Rangoon Students' Union—had also been expelled. He had made the grave error of criticizing the rector in a speech. A four-month-long student strike followed. The strike even found supporters in Mandalay and received lengthy coverage in the newspapers. With this, the first building blocks of Aung San's popularity and his political ascent were set in place.

After the end of the strike, Nu left university while Aung San was able to return in order to resume his studies. In 1936, he was elected general secretary of the Rangoon University Students' Union and also became vice-president of the All Burma Students' Union. A year later he led both boards as their president.

Aung San (center, seated) as a member of the student council. (Photo: U Kwalt)

In the meantime, the Dobama Asiayone had become a strong political force. Many hopes of the times rested in it. The public increasingly viewed the generation of politicians that was competing for ministerial posts in parliament as corrupt. The appearance of Aung San, Nu, and other student leaders in the Dobama Asiayone in 1938, and them adding *thakin* in front of their names, signaled the possibility of a new alternative for the politically interested public. This was a young generation of selfless revolutionaries who were prepared to sacrifice their careers for the noble cause of independence. They had after all risked their university diplomas, which would have opened some doors for them in colonial Burma. Aung San soon became a member of the association's executive committee and, in April 1939, its general secretary.

The outbreak of war in Europe on September 1, 1939, profoundly changed the political state of affairs in Burma. A so-called Freedom Bloc was founded on October 1, 1939. This political bloc achieved a major feat when they tied war assistance for the British against Hitler's Germany to a binding commitment to an independent Burma. This pact in fact violated the general rule of loyalty to the Crown as well as the requirements of the Defence of Burma Act. The alliance was led by Dr. Ba Maw, who had been elected as Burma's first chief minister under the country's new constitution in 1937. Besides his party, which he had named "Poor Man's Party," the Dobama Asiayone and one other group belonged to the Freedom Bloc. Here, too, Aung San became the general secretary. The activities of this united front were the prelude to the Burmese nationalists' final struggle against British rule.

The Enemy of My Enemy . . .

The Second World War thus became the catalyst for Burma's independence. But first the country had to be twice destroyed by it: once with the invasion of the Japanese and then with their withdrawal from the ultimately victorious Allies. The magnificent royal palace in Mandalay fell victim to British-Japanese fighting. A fire left the wooden buildings a pile of soot and ash. In both military campaigns, Aung San stood on the victorious side. He and his fellow fighters were guided by a practical principle: England's challenges would be Burma's opportunities. This much was known even before the war came to Burma. Once the war came, the principle was modified: the enemy of my enemy is my (temporary) friend.

This was a stance that Aung San had in common with his political guru, the Indian politician and Gandhi's rival, Subhas Chandra Bose. The two men had first met when Aung San traveled to India as leader of a Dobama Asiayone delegation in March 1940. At that point, they may not have known how closely they would work together one day, after Bose set up his headquarters for the Indian National Army in Rangoon in 1944. Both went on underground trips in the years in between.

In India, Bose escaped from house arrest in January 1941, leaving Calcutta to travel to Moscow with the intention of fighting against the British from there. After not gaining admittance to the country, he landed in Berlin. From Berlin he traveled to Sumatra with the help of submarines and finally ended up in Burma in 1944.

In Burma, Great Britain's rule did not yet seem under threat in 1940. Leading members of the Freedom Bloc had been arrested on grounds of making incendiary speeches. The arrests were justified under emergency legislation introduced after the outbreak of war. Aung San went underground. Unlike Nu, Dr. Ba Maw, and many others, he did not intend to have his pursuit of independence ennobled by a prison sentence. Besides, he was allegedly offended by the reward amount on offer for tips that would lead to his arrest. Like his political mentor Bose, he went abroad to organize support for the independence struggle. In August 1940 he traveled to China, which was only possible via sea. According to his own accounts, the trip ensued in the hope that he would be able to make his way inland through a port city and there make contact with the Chinese leadership. Whether this would be with the Nationalists under Chiang Kai-shek or the Communists under Mao Tse Tung was something he left open. Aung San had been present when the first Communist cell was founded in Rangoon in August 1939, and his sympathies certainly rested with the Chinese Communists.[6]

Aung San, dressed as a Chinese passenger aboard the Tan Luang Shung *on the way to Amoy. (Photo: Hans-Bernd Zöllner)*

A freighter brought Aung San and another *thakin* called Hla Myaing in its cargo hold to the southern Chinese port city of Amoy, or today's Xiamen. Aung San suffered severely from seasickness. In Amoy the two revolutionaries avoided arrest only because they were able to pay seventy-five rupees as a bribe. With that their financial reserves were near depleted. They holed up in shabby lodgings, which Hla Myaing financed by working as an English teacher. A trip to the inner part of the country did not take place.

The Burmese independence movement under Aung San's leadership could have seen its premature end here had it not been for Japanese Colonel Keiji Suzuki. He had come to Burma shortly before Aung San boarded the ship. As an intelligence officer, Suzuki was tasked with finding out how the so-called Burma Road could be cut off. This was a route at the eastern foothills of the Himalayas, an extremely mountainous and inaccessible landscape, which opened in 1938, connecting Burma and China. Via this route, the Allies could send supplies to the Chinese Nationalists under Chiang Kai-shek, who were fighting in resistance to the Japanese invasion. The colonel was to find out whether the Burma Road could be blocked with the help of Burmese nationalists. Suzuki had good contacts with Dr. Ba Maw, who passed the Japanese offer of cooperation on to his friends from the Dobama Asiayone.

There are varying accounts of the circumstances under which Suzuki made contact with Aung San in Amoy. In any case, Japanese agents eventually identified the independence fighter in the Chinese city. In November 1940, Aung San found himself traveling to Tokyo to—as he later expressed it—"make the best of a bad job."[7] In the Japanese capital, the Imperial Army charted a secret operation. Aung San was to select a group of thirty Burmese patriots who would receive military training under Japanese command. Eventually this group would return to Burma, recruit an underground army, and fight against the British. Japan would provide the necessary resources.

Aung San duly returned to Rangoon in February 1941 aboard a Japanese ship, made contact with the Dobama Asiayone, and helped select the members of the core contingent of thirty men. One after the other, these individuals were then sent on different ships to Hainan, an island under Japanese occupation at the time. Among these chosen to join the legendary Thirty Comrades was Thakin Shu Maung, who later came to be known as General Ne Win.

Rigid military training followed. The instruction brought the young Burmese nationalists close to physical exhaustion on almost a daily basis. Besides hours of exercise and maneuvers in the jungle, the training included everything from weapons technology and military tactics to guerrilla strategies and the organization of large military units. The Thirty Comrades protested against the harsh Japanese regimen more than once. Yet each time Aung San managed to persuade his fellow soldiers to persevere.

At the end of the year, the young officers were brought to Bangkok, where the Burma Independence Army (BIA) was founded on December 26, 1941. The men chose pseudonyms and participated in a traditional Burmese ritual. A silver chalice was filled with water, alcohol, and a drop of each man's blood. In the end, all took a sip and swore eternal allegiance to each of their comrades and committed their lives to independence. Aung San chose the name Teza—"light"—for himself. He became deputy major general of the army under Suzuki. The former *thakin* Shu Maung became Ne Win—"radiant sun." The command of one out of the three divisions was entrusted to him. The army was reinforced by volunteers living in Thailand. In January 1942, the BIA set foot on Burmese soil near Burma's southernmost city, today's Kawthaung.

The Burmese nationalists' aspiration was to free the capital city of Rangoon from British colonialism before the Japanese got to it. This dream was left unfulfilled. By the time Aung San and his more than two thousand-man strong BIA reached the city, the Japanese had already occupied the most important government buildings.

In the following weeks it became apparent that Colonel Suzuki had made an empty promise. The Japanese had no intention of actually granting independence to Burma. Aung San noted in hindsight that the Japanese broke all their promises. From the beginning, their aim had been to close off the Burma Road and integrate the country into

Painting after a photo of Aung San with Japanese military decorations. (Photo: Hans-Bernd Zöllner)

their own empire, the Greater East Asia Co-Prosperity Sphere. Both the Burmese fighters and Colonel Suzuki were just tools to achieve this goal. With this, the Japanese revealed themselves to be arrogant supremacists rather than liberators. Their institutions, such as the secret service, the Kempetai, employed methods similar to the Gestapo in Nazi Germany. The BIA, which had now grown to tens of thousands of men, was whittled down by the Japanese to seven thousand soldiers and renamed the Burma Defence Army (BDA) in April 1942. In 1943, after Burma formally gained independence, the army was renamed again to the Burma National Army (BNA).

Just before this, in March 1942, Aung San's army—which felt itself to be the new leader of the country—had faced bloody conflicts in the Irrawaddy Delta against the Karen population, which, to a certain extent, was still loyal to the British. Karen guerrilla fighters supported Allied efforts to recapture Burma. So it was not just resentment against Japanese occupation that grew; tensions within the country were also on the rise.

In the midst of these difficult times, Aung San fell ill. Two years of deprivation, immense political pressure, and a spell of malaria took their toll. In May 1942, he had to be hospitalized. In the army hospital where Aung San was admitted worked a nurse by the name of Khin Khyi. Khin Khyi came from Myaungmya, a district in the Irrawaddy Delta, where— as just mentioned—fighting had broken out between the army and the Karen. Aung San, who as a young man had recommended castration to his fellow fighters so that they could concentrate fully on politics and had categorically rejected marriage, fell in love with Khin Kyi, who was three years his senior, and married her on September 6, 1942.[8] After recovering from his illness, the freshly married young man dedicated himself to both the task of freeing the country and the role of a husband and father. Three children were born in rapid succession: Oo (1943),

Wedding photograph of Aung San and his wife Khin Kyi, September 7, 1942.
(Photo: U Kwalt)

Lin (1944), and Suu Kyi (1945). Another daughter was born in 1946 but died soon after birth.

In order to secure support of the Burmese in the face of growing resentment within the country, Japan nominally granted independence to Burma on August 1, 1943. Dr. Ba Maw became supreme leader and Aung San war minister. Ne Win replaced Aung San as supreme commander of the army. Yet the concessions did not suffice. The rumbling continued within the army. Plans were forged for an uprising against the Japanese. These were fueled by the fact that the fortunes of war were changing. In February 1943, the United States had won a decisive victory against Japanese troops on the Pacific island of Guadalcanal. The Japanese advance on India with the support of Subhas Chandra Bose's Indian National Army failed in April 1944. From that point on the Imperial Army found itself in retreat.

In August 1944, on a military base in the vicinity of Bago (Pegu), the Anti-Fascist People's Freedom League (AFPFL) was founded.[9] The AFPFL consisted of Burma's military as well as the nascent Communist and Socialist parties. Their common goal was the full and definite independence of Burma.

On March 27, 1945, after consulting with the Allies, Aung San issued orders for military action against the Japanese. He had previously explained the complex situation to the army in a manner that was later understood as a coded call for revolt:

> Comrades, I do not wish to explain everything in detail. Now we must go to war. We will encounter poverty, hunger and [other] difficulties. Burmans, show your courage. Listen to the orders of the officers, who in their place must demonstrate comradely morale. As I promised, I myself will march with you. Destroy the enemies of Burma! Find the next enemy and fight![10]

The attack by their supposed allies caught the Japanese off guard. Throughout the country, units of what was now called the Burma National Army (BNA) attacked Japanese positions and sabotaged their infrastructure.[11] On May 15, Aung San met with General William Slim in Meikthila in Upper Burma, which had been recaptured by the Allies. Although Slim had guaranteed him safe passage, Aung San ran the risk of being arrested on this occasion, given that many British regarded him as a Japanese collaborator.

To his good fortune, the Supreme Commander of the South East Asia Command, Admiral Louis Mountbatten, had decided to at least hear out the leaders of the BNA, should they—even at the last moment—decide to resist the Japanese. Slim followed his commander's lead. This was the start of Aung San's cooperation with the Allied upper command under Lord Mountbatten. It led to the BNA participating in the victory parade in Rangoon on June 15, 1945, together with its former opponents. Japan had been defeated in Burma. For the second time, Aung San had read the signs of the times and picked the right side as an ally.

From Military Commander to Political Leader

The actual fight for independence still lay before Aung San. Albeit weakened, the formal colonial ruler—Great Britain—was back. Governor Dorman-Smith, who had fled to India from the Japanese and their Burmese allies in 1942, immediately began to reinstall his administration, but it was not until 1946 that he moved back into the Secretariat, a majestic, red government building in the heart of Rangoon. Prior to this, a Burmese delegation had entered into an agreement at the Allies' headquarters in Kandy, Ceylon (today's Sri Lanka), according to which the BNA and the military forces under British command—where many individuals from ethnic minorities also served—were unified into one. Mountbatten offered Aung San the post of deputy supreme commander of this new military entity. Aung San refused, stating that he now wanted to dedicate himself to a civil political career as the leader of the AFPFL. The warrior-king Bogyoke Aung San became the political leader U Aung San.

In this new role he opposed the plan for Burma's future that was set out in a government white paper prepared by Governor Dorman-Smith while he was still in India heading the government-in-exile of Burma. According to the document, the earliest that Burma would be granted independence was three years after the triumph over the Japanese. Aung San aligned the AFPFL against this. He had built the AFPFL into a powerful unified front, which spoke with a single—and ultimately his—voice. It thus presented an equal counterparty to the returned colonial power in the upcoming political disagreements.

Aung San's efforts led to Burma's independence on January 4, 1948. He was successful due to two factors: First, the Labour Party won parliamentary elections in Great Britain and replaced the Conservatives under Winston Churchill. In contrast to the Conservatives, the winning party and the new prime minister, Clement Attlee, were much more open to the former colonies' demands for independence. Churchill would have been more reluctant to grant independence, as later speeches reveal him calling Aung San a traitor. Second, the supreme commander of the allied forces in Asia, Admiral Mountbatten, was a pragmatic realist. As viceroy of India he would go on to leave an independent country behind. The man had not only understood that the era of British colonial rule was coming to an end but also that Aung San would be pivotal in ensuring an orderly retreat for Great Britain from Burma. Mountbatten knew that British forces would not have the capacity to contain a nationwide revolt given that hardly any Indian soldiers could be enlisted for the task. Mountbatten specifically protected Aung San when Dorman-Smith, together with his Burmese allies, attempted to bring the Burmese freedom fighter to court for the execution of a summarily tried local Indian headman. The charges were eventually dropped.

The AFPFL started its campaign with a mass demonstration against a list issued by the governor, which named the members of the executive council. The named individuals would govern the country from then on. Governor Dorman-Smith had not included names of members proposed by the AFPFL. A large gathering took place at the Shwedagon Pagoda in November 1945. At that point, it was the first gathering to be described as the "largest" in the country's history. (Later, this honor would pass to crowds gathered to see Aung San Suu Kyi in August 1988.) One of the resolutions adopted here described the governor's stance as "fascist" and not "democratic."

AFPFL flexed its muscles more and more in the course of the confrontations. Chaos and lawlessness increased in the entire country and could not be controlled by the government without enlisting the help of popular Aung San. Moreover, the governor was attacked in the British Parliament by representatives of the Labour Party who had good contacts in Burma. He eventually left the country in June 1946 "for health reasons" and was replaced by Sir Hubert Rance at the end of August. Rance had led the civilian branch of the British military administration and was a confidant of Mountbatten's.

Shortly thereafter, a strike that had started in Rangoon spread through the whole country. The police and other public officials were striking to demand higher pay. Rance subsequently installed a new executive council. Aung Sang stood at its helm and became the de facto prime minister of the not-yet-fully independent Burma. The protests ebbed as a consequence.

Aung San had secured a critical victory against the colonial government. Now it was about consolidating his power in internal politics. An expulsion of the Communists followed. The Communists were led by Aung San's brother-in-law Than Tun, who had sent a representative to the provisional government. In a long speech at the end of October, Aung San justified the exclusion by stating that the Communist Party only had its own interests at heart and not the welfare of the entire nation. Besides, the Communists were described as morally "dirty." At the end of his speech he compared himself to them:

> To cut it short: what sort of a man am I? Have I ever got myself mixed up in sex scandals? Have I ever tipped-off any of my colleagues to the enemy? I am ready to publicly answer such questions. I ask, in conclusion, are communist leaders and other non-Pha-sa-pa-la [AFPFL] leaders prepared to do the same?[12]

With this morally grounded expulsion, the strongest opposition within the AFPFL was neutralized and Aung San could establish a political order of his own design without much resistance. He built the AFPFL into a unity party. This was not in the manner of a party that is held together through ideology. Rather, it was the sort of single party that is bound together by its political leader. Aung San used the Buddhist stupa as a metaphor for his ideal state of order. The party, like society as a whole, should be grounded on a broad foundation, sharpening hierarchically towards one highest leader who ensures stability and orderliness of the entire structure from its apex. This highest leader was Aung San himself.

The support of the new executive council permitted Aung San to take a more assertive stance against the British. Knowing that India had already been guaranteed independence, he demanded the same right for Burma. On January 27, 1947, the Aung San–Attlee Agreement was eventually signed in London. It provided that Burma was to be granted independence within a year. Two of the members of the executive council and the AFPFL, U Saw and Ba Sein, who had also been members of the negotiating delegation, rejected the signing of the agreement, most likely owing to their envy of Aung San's dominant role in the negotiations. Upon their return they stepped down from the executive council and tried in vain to gain political influence in line with their prewar political ambitions.

Aung San had reached the zenith of his authority. However, this was only within the Burmese core of the country and did not yet include the border areas. The British had permitted traditional leaders to rule over Burma's hilly frontiers. The agreement concluded in London required clarification on a key issue before Burma could be granted independence: Would it be possible for the ethnic minorities and the ethnic Burmans to unite in a new Burmese union? This question has not lost any of its relevance and urgency to this day.

In February 1947, Aung San met with representatives of the Shan, Chin, and Kachin in Panglong in Shan State. He made a humble appearance and set out the vision of a Burmese nation, where all would have equal rights and where there would be no discrimination. "If a

Bamar gets one kyat, a Shan will get one kyat as well" was his central promise and one that would come to be repeated again and again.[13] Aung San was essentially promising justice to the ethnic minorities, but without any specifications as to how this would be achieved.

The Panglong Agreement was signed on February 12, 1947. It is still seen as a milestone in Burmese politics, but one that is interpreted very differently by different sides.[14] The agreement was neither detailed nor definite. As later remarks by the delegates attested, it was largely Aung San's credibility that led the other participants to sign the agreement. With his straightforward and open character, Aung San had won the trust of the ethnic minority representatives. The British had regarded the latter as not yet ready for a modern democratic society. Aung San succeeded in dispelling—at least in part—the traditional distrust between the different groups, which had been fomented by the British as per their divide-and-rule colonial strategy. However, the agreement had its shortcomings. For example, the significant Karen ethnic group was represented at the conference with only observer status and did not sign the agreement.

Elections for a constituent assembly followed in April 1947, after the Panglong Conference. The elections took place in accordance with the framework that had guided the previous elections of 1936. The 210 seats that had to be filled were almost all won by the AFPFL or affiliated candidates. Inhabitants of the "frontier areas," which the British had administered separately and where the Shan, Kayah, Kachin, and Chin lived were allowed to vote for the first time and sent forty-five members to the assembly. Political rivals, such as a coalition led by Saw, Ba Sein, and Dr. Ba Maw had boycotted the elections. The same was true for an organization of the Karen that had hoped to form an independent Karen state.

In his assessment of the elections, Aung San emphasized that the individual candidates had not been elected on the basis of their personal qualities. Rather, they were elected because they had been AFPFL candidates—and, one can add, because they had Aung San's support. He had undertaken a demanding journey through the entire country in order to campaign for the candidates of the league. His daughter would follow in his footsteps and travel through the country in the years 1988 and 1989, 2002 and 2003, and finally in 2015 in order to spread her political message and campaign for her party.

In one of the postelection speeches, Aung San stressed that an abuse of the freedoms granted to the government by the people would not be tolerated. Opposition was only permitted because that was just the way things worked in a modern state. This demonstrates a continuation of a traditional Bamar understanding of leadership. The mere existence of an opposition threatens the ruler's claim to power and thus the entire unity of the kingdom. Aung San warned his opponents, "But if the opposition abuse these freedoms they will be smashed."[15] Aung San also had little regard for a free press that could criticize the government. He expected discipline and military honor from his fellow league members, something that Aung San Suu Kyi also persistently demands from herself and her supporters.

On the other hand, he committed himself to the Buddhist virtue of benevolence (*mettā*) and to forgoing his own benefit to the point of self-sacrifice.[16] This readiness for self-abandonment and the tough stance towards potential opponents were two sides of the same coin. They corresponded to the character of an ideal Buddhist ruler, who had to keep social chaos in check and at the same time be an example for his underlings.

Aung San's Syncretic State Design

A newly elected constituent assembly of AFPFL members convened in May 1947 and adopted a draft constitution, based largely on Aung San's ideas.[17] It contained an aggregate of the political ideas he had collected in his eventful life. In these political ideas, Aung San once again proved himself to be a pragmatist. Political convictions and ideologies were selected for their value in attaining the primary objective, independence under the banner of unity. Aung San's political amalgamation of communist, nationalist, and Buddhist ideas can only be understood in this way. In August 1939, he had been one of the founding members of

Burma's first Communist cell; in January 1941, he drafted a blueprint for his country in Tokyo with a "strong state as in Italy and Germany" under the slogan "one nation, one state, one party, one leader."[18]

When it came to drafting the constitution, he proposed to "proclaim Burma as an independent sovereign republic" as the first of fourteen points drafted by him and adopted at a mass meeting on May 27, 1947, stated. A membership in the British Commonwealth was thus excluded because joining the organization could be regarded as still maintaining close ties with the former colonial power that had been so intransigently combated by all means, militarily and politically. The decision was a shock for many British residents in Burma who left the country because of the decision.[19]

In his last big speech in 1947, he emphasized—as he had done previously—the socialist principle of the relations of economic production as forming the basis of every political system. Hence the desired "true Burmese democracy" could not be one that was based on capitalist ideas. But he recognized that socialist principles could not be put in place overnight. Whenever there was a conflict between the interests of businesspeople and the poor masses, Aung San maintained that the state had to side with the poor. The people's representatives in parliament had to maintain the trust of those who had elected them. Parties were important, but they—as he had stated earlier—were to have a formative mandate and not become beholden to individual interests. The "new democracy" that was established with the constitution in Burma was thus something very particular, it was a "Burmese democracy." He concluded his speech with a quotation from a Pali text—the language he had studied at university: "Unity is the foundation. Let this fact be engraved in your memory, ye who harken to me, and go ye to your appointed tasks with diligence."[20]

There was another way in which he connected distinct concepts together in an original manner. He would cite Stalin when defining a nation, calling it a "historically constituted, stable community of people" determined by all linguistic and ethnic groups striving for economic advancement together.[21] In the Stalinist model, all differences, be they ethnic, religious, or class-based, would dissolve into a uniform, classless society.

Furthermore, Aung San emphasized the need for a strong army. The colonial experience had led him to the conviction that without a strong military, a country's sovereignty could not be preserved. He imagined an army with up to a million soldiers, which in 1947 would have accounted

Aung San with Japanese kendo sword—one of the favorites among the images curated for his one-hundredth birthday in 2015. (Photo: Hans-Bernd Zöllner)

for about six percent of the national population. (Almost five hundred thousand soldiers served in the army in 2014.)[22]

Aung San reiterated again and again that things were in flux and that the revolution that had begun could not be realized in one stroke. It was something that required many steps within a lengthy process of transition, with continuous correction and improvement.

The Murder

Aung San's participation in the nascent process of formulating a constitution saw a violent end on July 19, 1947—a Saturday. Aung San had called for a meeting of the executive council in the Secretariat building, which had been transferred de facto to the independent government by the British governor. At ten o'clock he took leave of his wife and children. He left the house on Tower Lane in a golden longyi.

Half an hour later, his personal secretary Bo Tun Hla heard machine gun fire. He rushed to the meeting room to find Aung San and his associates lying on the floor, hit by a deadly barrage of bullets. In a matter of seconds, the assassins had killed nine people, of which seven were members of the provisional government.

The investigations quickly led to one of Aung San's political rivals, U Saw. The latter had convinced himself that as per the Buddhist-Burmese tradition—under which only the worthiest deserved governmental power—he, and not Aung San, was the righteous ruler. This conviction permitted him, with precedent in Burmese history, to seize the throne by violent means. In addition, he relied on his good contacts to the British, which he had crafted before the war, to guarantee him a top post. Yet he had made a fundamental miscalculation. The governor, who always had the last word during the transition process in relation to all important matters, appointed Nu, not U Saw, to the post of acting prime minister in Aung San's succession.

Although the police investigations identified U Saw as the mastermind behind the assassination, they never uncovered the underlying network, leaving room for rumors to flourish. A special tribunal of three Burmese judges sentenced U Saw to death. He was executed in Insein Prison on May 8, 1948.

Aung San had absorbed the political ideas of his times and tried to apply them for attaining his goal of an independent Burma. After his death he quickly joined that canon of mythical heroes and kings that is so richly represented in Burmese history. Chroniclers called him the fourth legendary king after Anawratha, Bayinnaung, and Alaungpaya, who had each—at least for some time—united the different parts of the country into a great Burmese kingdom. At the same time, he became a Buddhist martyr and an enlightened one. Keeping with the traditions of the kings, almost a year went by before Aung San was buried. Before the burial, his corpse was laid out so that all citizens could pay their respects to the father of the nation.

Funeral procession on April 11, 1948, for the burial at the Martyrs' Mausoleum of those murdered on July 19, 1947. (Photo: U Kwalt)

The mythical elevation was aided by the fact that Aung San's life largely followed the path charted for the ideal Buddhist ruler. He possessed the three central qualities of a king: charisma (*pon*), military aptitude (*letyoung*), and authority (*ana*). In the first phase of his life, he was the wild, untamed warrior king who destroyed the prevailing order of British colonial rule to make space for a "worldly nirvana" (*loka nibbein*).[23] As soon as the war was won, he laid down his arms and oriented his rule in alignment with Buddhist virtues. He was always justified in his actions by the affirmative concept of *kamma*. It accorded legitimacy to the ruler in that he only became ruler in the first place because he possessed the necessary *kamma*. His life was a syncretic mixture of Burmese tradition and "modern" global ideas.

Aung San's premature death kept him from putting his political ideas to practical test. Because his political ideas were an amalgamation of different ideologies, it became easy for succeeding elites of all factions to invoke his legacy. The first prime minister of free Burma, U Nu, based his politics on Buddhist values. He wanted to create the "worldly nirvana" that Aung San had promised the people a reality. As of 1962, the government under Ne Win, too, held itself to be the rightful heir given that as a child of his times, Aung San had again and again been drawn to a socialist paradigm and advocated a secular state. The State Law and Order Restoration Council (SLORC), which took power following the 1988 Uprising, also relied on Aung San. After all, the father of the nation had been the founder of the armed forces. Aung San had always stressed that the army's main role was to maintain the unity of the country. And finally, there was the daughter, who could argue that the freedom of the people of the country was her father's primary aim. The great legacy of the incomplete hero was open to all kinds of interpretation.

Aung San, the father of the nation, was murdered before his time. He never got the chance to translate his vision of a cohesive blossoming Burmese union into political reality. He was a charismatic personality and his incomplete legacy would be too great to fill by any of his successors. He combined the talents of a dynamic military leader with those of a pragmatic politician. His death created a split between the military and civilian politics that remains unbridged to this day. The myth of his person—the incomplete hero—has shaped the history of independent Myanmar and was passed on to his daughter.

CHAPTER 3

A Child of Many Worlds

*A family is very special. So, when a family splits up, it's not good,
it's never good.*

Aung San Suu Kyi has often been compared with other great figures of modern history: Gandhi, Martin Luther King Jr., the Dalai Lama, and Nelson Mandela. Seldom is she mentioned in the same breath as the Asian women who stepped into their father's or husband's shoes, such as Indira Gandhi in India or Benazir Bhutto in Pakistan.[1] In fact, Aung San Suu Kyi personifies a mix that combines both these classifications of people who have made history. This unique constellation of hers shone brightly at her first big appearance in August 1988; it was the daughter of a great father—one who had left behind an incomplete legacy—that stepped into the limelight.

She referred to Aung San multiple times during her first key speech. "I could not as my father's daughter remain indifferent to all that was going on," she explained. This was the reason for her entering into the politics of a country that she was born in but had not lived in permanently since the age of fifteen.[2]

In that same speech, she described the 1988 crisis as "Burma's second struggle for national independence." With that, all that lay between the first struggle led by her father and the day of the big speech was declared null and void. She repeatedly stated that she had refrained from following her father's footsteps and entering politics until now:

> A number of people are saying that since I have spent most of my time abroad and am married to a foreigner I could not be familiar with the ramifications of this country's politics. . . . The trouble is that I know too much. My family knows best how complicated and tricky Burmese politics can be and how much my father had to suffer on this account. He expended much mental and physical effort in the cause of Burma's politics without personal gain. That is why my father said that once Burma's independence was gained he would not want to take part in the kind of power politics that would follow. Since my father had no such desire I too have always wanted to place myself at a distance from this kind of politics.[3]

Her words blend together the dynastic with a substantive central theme. She states that in contrast to his adversaries and successors, Aung San followed a "clean" model of politics, free of any tangible or intangible self-interests. Following this example, his daughter stepped into the midst of the 1988 national crisis selflessly in order to deliver a "second independence" and to then potentially step out again. Aung San Suu Kyi thus invokes the unique family tradition of selfless service for the good of the country. Consequently, the political actors who had practiced politics in Burma alongside and after Aung San are made out to be self-serving and power hungry.

Aung San Suu Kyi was forty-three years old at the time of her key first speech. Is it possible to locate the beginnings of the convictions she expressed during that speech in those forty-three years? She could not have received them directly from her father, as she was only two years old when he was killed. Another question could be asked: would she be able to persevere with and implement the high moral claims that she expressed during the speech? But to be fair to her, her speech was about politics, which can never quite meet the exigencies of absolute ideals.

As with every other politician, Aung San Suu Kyi's stance on politics is the result of her life experience. And life experience is difficult to reconstruct in detail. Even the most accurate account of upbringing and background, important life moments, and intellectual experiences would fail to paint a complete or clear picture. This is especially true in the case of Aung San Suu Kyi, who has never really spoken of her own background in detail. However, certain key experiences and fundamental convictions do emerge from her writings, speeches, and interviews. The contents of these are referred to in her compatriots' testimonials as well as in the narratives of the foreigners who have met her. From all of these, it can be safely concluded that the formative years of her life were the ones she spent in Burma during her childhood and adolescence. She was subsequently intellectually nourished abroad. First and foremost, therefore, she was her mother's daughter. Only later did she decide to pursue her father's politics, which she could only have come to know through the accounts of others.

The house in which Aung San Suu Kyi spent her first years. Today, it is the Bogyoke Aung San Museum on the eponymous street, near the German embassy. (Photo: Hans-Bernd Zöllner)

Childhood and Adolescence as the Daughter of a Working Mother

As with her political debut in Burma, Aung San Suu Kyi was born in June 1945 in the midst of dramatic times. Three months before her birth, her father had announced that it was no longer the Allies but the Japanese that were the enemies of the Burmese army. It was a risky move and Aung San knew it. This is clear from the fact that Aung San had his family moved out of Yangon some weeks before the announcement. Khin Kyi, with both sons and pregnant with the little girl, was accompanied by three soldiers to Hmway Saung, a small town in the Irrawaddy Delta. A wealthy businessman had made his house there available to the family. Today the journey to this place near Pyapon takes about four hours by car, using numerous bridges that have been put up by the military in the meantime. At the time of Khin Kyi and the children's trip, the journey by boat took a number of days. The family escaped disaster twice on this journey. On the way there, the boat ran into Japanese soldiers. It was with great effort that Khin Kyi managed to keep her Burmese guards from opening fire. On the way back, at the end of the Buddhist New Year and water festival Thingyan in April, numerous British bombers flew over the area, threatening to drop their deadly cargo.

Aung San Suu Kyi was later born in a hospital close to her parents' home on June 19, a few days after the British and their new Burmese allies' victory parade. The family home had been built by a rich Chinese businessman, the clinic where she was born had been set up by an Indian man, and her mother's ancestors had been Buddhist Burmans and Christian Kayin. Aung San Suu Kyi's birth personified the various worlds that have coexisted in Burma since times bygone and that conflict with one another every now and then.

There is disagreement as to whether Khin Kyi was Bamar or Kayin and whether she had had a Christian baptism like her father. What is known is that after Aung San's death, Khin Kyi's father lived with the family until his own death and was Aung San Suu Kyi's main male role model. According to one of Aung San Suu Kyi's later accounts of her childhood, he was "very indulgent and loving" and "the most important male figure in [her] life."[4]

Aung San Suu Kyi was born during a time of heightened political violence. This had direct consequences for her family. Her father's murder had been commissioned by a political rival. The violent conflict between the Kayin and the Burmese army during the war affected her mother's birthplace. Later there would be the challenge posed by the Communists under Than Tun's leadership. This companion of her father's, who had been with him during the independence struggle and the Japanese occupation, had married Khin Kyi's older sister on the same day that Aung San had married Khin Kyi. Until the end of the Second World War, the two had been political allies in the united front of the AFPFL. After the war, Aung San expelled the party led by his brother-in-law from the movement. Since then, Aung San Suu Kyi's aunt Khin Gyi lived underground. After her husband was murdered by members of his own party in 1968, she spent the remaining years of her life in Yangon. The aunt passed away in 2001 at the age of ninety-three in Aung San Suu Kyi's house.[5]

Khin Kyi and her three children after Aung San's death. Aung San Suu Kyi is next to her mother. (Photo: U Kwalt)

Aung San's family was afflicted with other private disasters. Aung San Suu Kyi had a younger sister, Aung San Chit, who died shortly after her birth on September 26, 1946, the day that Aung San was given his first post in the Burmese government by the British governor. In

1952, Aung San Suu Kyi's favorite brother, Aung San Lin, drowned in the garden pond at the family residence. After the tragedy, the family moved out of the house on Tower Lane into a building provided by the government at 54/56 University Avenue, which is where Aung San Suu Kyi continues to live.[6] The house on Tower Lane has been turned into a museum commemorating Aung San.

There can be no doubt that this accumulation of political and personal catastrophes had a direct effect on Aung San's children and on their adult guardians. Aung San's widow, Khin Kyi, played a central role. She refused to remarry after Aung San's murder and as a result remained the key figure in her children's lives.

Placard on the grounds of the Bogyoke Aung San Museum marking the place of death of Aung San Suu Kyi's favorite brother. (Photo: Hans-Bernd Zöllner)

In an interview conducted shortly after the release from her first house arrest in 1996, Aung San Suu Kyi stated,

What I have learned in life is that it's always your own wrongdoing that causes you the greatest suffering. It is never what other people do to you.

Perhaps this is due to the way in which I was brought up. My mother instilled in me the principle that wrongdoing never pays, and my own experience has proved that to be true. Also, if you have positive feelings towards other people they can't do anything to you—they can't frighten you. I think when you stop loving other people then you really suffer.[7]

Here Aung San Suu Kyi connects Buddhist thinking with a Christian idea. She draws on the teachings of *karma* or *kamma*. According to this, individual deeds set off a sequence of cause and effect in the cycle of death and rebirth (*saṃsāra*). Suffering (*dukkha*) is thus always self-caused. The effect of the actions of others on oneself is to be accepted with a stance of compassion (*karuṇā*), which in the language of Christianity is referred to as loving one's neighbor. The Christian term does carry an emotional tone that is missing from the Buddhist counterpart. These differing "shades" of terms from Buddhist and Christian contexts—both of which Aung San Suu Kyi has lived in—often make it difficult to adequately interpret her statements. Just as Aung San's political convictions were an amalgamation, so are Suu Kyi's foundational beliefs a mix of Buddhist and Christian, as well as Eastern and Western, values.

Khin Kyi's principled way of being, which she also instilled in her children, is what made the personal misfortune dealt to Aung San's family bearable. This demanded a high degree of self-discipline and inner strength. Suu Kyi's mother possessed both, as also demonstrated through her determination to become a nurse.

It is reported that Khin Kyi was informed of her son's death through a telephone call at her work. She finished the day's tasks before returning to her residence and attending to the two other children. In the same vein it is reported that she did not cry at her husband's wake because she did not want to indulge his opponents with a sense of triumph.[8] Aung San Suu Kyi describes her mother as very disciplined, very strict, and a perfectionist. She saw this as a disadvantage in her childhood but later as something that helped her in life.[9] She held her mother to be more courageous than her father and believed him to have been heavily influenced by her.[10]

After Aung San's murder, his widow replaced him in parliament after winning a by-election with no opposing candidate. It was the seat Aung San had won after the April 1947 constituent assembly elections. She gave this up when Prime Minister Nu offered her a high-ranking and well-compensated post within the state's social welfare system. Going forward, she supported U Nu and accompanied him on state trips. By doing so she marked him as her husband's legitimate successor.

Khin Kyi, second from right, and U Nu, fourth from left, dancing with Chin people during a visit to the Chin Hills in 1950. (Government of Burma publication, 1951)

After the AFPFL's split in 1958, she joined U Nu's faction, the Clean AFPFL, and participated actively in his election campaign. As part of that she covered—like her husband during the 1947 election campaign—numerous neighborhoods in Yangon and other places.[11] After U Nu's election victory in 1960, she was sent by him as Burma's ambassador to India.[12] Until her voluntary retirement in 1967, she remained a single, working mother.

What Khin Kyi exemplified and conveyed to her daughter can be described as follows: In the private sphere, one had to practice self-discipline for protecting oneself from the vicissitudes of life. In the

Portraits of Aung San Suu Kyi and her mother from the 1950s. (Photo: U Kwalt)

public sphere, one had to give selfless service to the nation in Aung San's footsteps. Everything points to her being a committed Buddhist and also passing her faith on to her daughter. Then again, she had a pastor from the Baptist church called to her sickbed before her death, and he is thought to have given her Communion.[13] The influence of U Pho Hnyin, Khin Kyi's baptized father, is thus visible with the mother as with the daughter.

Aung San Suu Kyi appears to have internalized her mother's stance towards misfortune even in her childhood. She later spoke about the death of her brother in comparison to her reaction to the death of her father:

I felt my brother's death much more. I was very close to him . . . probably closer to him than to anybody else. We shared the same room and played together all the time. His death was a tremendous loss for me. At that time I felt enormous grief. I suppose you could call it a "trauma," but it was not something I couldn't cope with. Of course I was very upset by the fact that I would never see him again. That, I think, is how a child sees death, I won't play with him again. I'll never be able to be with him again. But at the same time, looking back, there must have been a tremendous sense of security surrounding me. I was able to cope—I didn't suffer from depression or great emotional upheaval.[14]

In this matter-of-fact, sober Buddhist description, Aung San Suu Kyi is very much her mother's daughter. That is also true in many other regards. The picture she has of her father is first and foremost the picture that was passed on to her by her mother. And this picture can only be an idealized one.[15] She grew up knowing that her father had been loved by the people and had sacrificed his life for the people.[16] She also knew that he was the founder of the Burmese army. As a child, Aung San Suu Kyi had imagined following in his footsteps and becoming a general in order to lead the country as he had done.[17]

Khin Kyi's close ties with U Nu—which came coupled with a rejection of Ne Win—are likely to have had an effect on her daughter. After the March 2, 1962 coup, Ne Win had U Nu and many other politicians put into "protective custody." U Nu was a devout traditional Buddhist and had made religion and its moral prescriptions the foundation of his politics. In contrast, Ne Win's attitude towards Buddhism was more distant.[18] He had the reputation of not being stirred by morals.[19] By participating in Nu's election campaign, Khin Kyi supported the program of the Clean AFPFL, including the promise to make Buddhism the state religion.[20] One of the reasons later used to justify the coup would be that this promise of the prime minister's was an affront to the non-Buddhist minorities, putting the country's unity in peril. Like her mother, Aung San Suu Kyi sided herself with a "clean" politics in her 1988 speech, and by doing so distanced herself from Ne Win and his military.

Only the daughter accompanied her mother to New Delhi in 1960. By then, the older brother, Aung San Oo, had already been sent to boarding school in England. Aung San's fame had spread beyond Burma's national borders and he was as omnipresent in the schools that his daughter attended as in the ambassadorial residence in New Delhi, where she lived. She lived with her mother until 1964. Aung San Suu Kyi then departed for England to study at Oxford. She left behind motherly care and supervision and started shaping her own life. She would continue to remain confronted with her father and the politics of Burma.

The Big World and a Man Named Michael Aris

The move from New Delhi to London took place with the help of a high-ranking British diplomat, Paul Gore-Booth, and his wife, Patricia. Gore-Booth's first diplomatic post had been Rangoon from 1953 to 1956. He had known Suu Kyi's mother at that time, and he described her as "a quiet lady of few words but great depth and strength of character."[21] The diplomat held U Nu—who had shown him Bagan and other historical places in the country—in high regard. He describes him as a "devout Buddhist" who often made a solemn impression but at the same time "had a unique smile compounded of saintliness and gaiety."[22] The couple again visited Burma in 1959 after the transfer of power from U Nu to the caretaker government under Ne Win and in 1962 shortly before the military coup, which would put an end to the period of parliamentary democracy in Burma for decades. In his memoirs published in 1974, Gore-Booth laments the downfall of the country under Ne Win's government. He also regrets the change in the population, which, under a Big Brother regime, "became dull and rather priggish, totally contrary to the national character."[23]

In 1960, the British government made him high commissioner in India. The title is given to senior diplomats in Commonwealth countries. In New Delhi, the diplomat and his wife again met Aung San's widow and her daughter. They generously made their Chelsea apartment available to Aung San Suu Kyi as a second home for the time that she did not spend at her Oxford college. Moreover, the couple introduced the young student to London's social circles.

The arrival of the daughter of a Burmese independence hero in 1960s Great Britain would have been a reminder of both victory against the Japanese in the Second World War and the loss of the empire in the postwar period. Now the Beatles and the Rolling Stones were taking over the world. Hippies, miniskirts, free love, and marijuana did not stop at the venerable gates of the University of Oxford. However, the protests against the war in Vietnam and capitalism only reached the university in 1968. That was a year after Aung San Suu Kyi had already left the university with a bachelor's degree.

Aung San's daughter was one of the few women from Asia studying at Oxford. She did this at St. Hugh's College, which only women attended until its hundredth anniversary in 1986. She had the reputation of being withdrawn and holding firm moral convictions. But her social life appeared to revolve around the Gore-Booths. It was through the Gore-Booths' twin sons that she met her husband-to-be, Michael Aris, who incidentally also had a twin brother.

When the two met, Michael Aris was preparing for his exams in history and Suu Kyi for her finals in philosophy, politics and economics (PPE). It was already clear for him that he would dedicate his life to Tibetology and research into Buddhism of the Himalayan region. Aung San Suu Kyi had not yet decided but already felt a sense of duty towards Burma. This made the relationship with a British man difficult. In large parts of Burmese society at the time, it was taboo to marry someone from the former colonial power. Aung San Suu Kyi's mother also took a long time accepting the son-in-law from England.

Judging only by her grades, Aung San Suu Kyi was no brilliant student. She completed her BA in PPE in 1967 with mediocre marks. After her exams, she worked for some time as a research assistant for Hugh Tinker, a professor at the School of Oriental and African Studies, a constituent college of the University of London. Tinker had spent a year teaching at Rangoon University in the 1950s.

In 1969 she moved to New York to study further with Frank Trager, another professor with a relationship to Burma. She lived with Ma Than E, an old family friend who was in her early sixties at the time. Ma Than E helped Suu Kyi find a position at the United Nations. Aung San Suu Kyi worked in a department tasked with clearing expenditures made by UN organizations. During this time, her well-known compatriot U Thant—

who was also a close friend of U Nu's—was completing his second term as United Nations secretary-general.

Michael Aris, a year younger than Aung San Suu Kyi, had completed his studies at the same time as her in 1967 and gone on to work as a tutor to the children of the royal family of Bhutan. Aris and Suu Kyi wrote letters to each other, got engaged in 1970 in New York, and got married on January 1, 1972, in London, with a Buddhist ceremony following the town hall wedding. Neither Suu Kyi's mother nor her brother took part in the wedding, but the Gore-Booths did. The diplomat set his hopes for Burma in the children of Khin Kyi and Aung San:

Our home in London has always been and I have no doubt always will be a home for Aung San's family. It remains our hope that his daughter Suu Kyi, who was married from our house, and his son Aung San U, both exceptional young people, will in their time be able to do some service to their country whose government in this time has done so little for them.[24]

They were prophetic words, but only in relation to the daughter. The son never directly engaged with Burmese politics.

An echo of the hopes expressed by the British diplomat can be found in the many letters that Aung San Suu Kyi wrote to Michael Aris before their marriage. In them she prepares him for the eventuality that she may have to return to Burma one day:

I only ask one thing, that should my people need me, you would help me to do my duty to them. Would you mind very much should such a situation ever arise? How probable it is, I do not know, but the possibility is there. Sometimes I am beset by fears that circumstances and national considerations might tear us apart just when we are so happy in each other that separation would be a torment. And yet such fears are so futile and inconsequential: If we love and cherish each other as much as we can while we can, I am sure love and compassion will triumph in the end.[25]

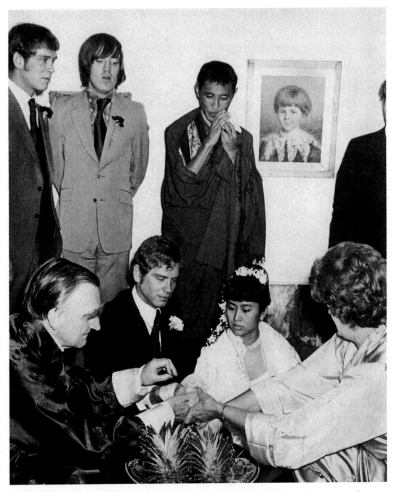

Wedding of Aung San Suu Kyi and Michael Aris on January 1, 1972. Next to the bride and groom the Gore-Booths; behind them a monk; top left Michael Aris's twin brother. (Photo: Getty)

These, too, were prophetic words. The marriage to Michael Aris would always have to come second. Should the people of Burma call her, she would answer that call in line with the imperative of selfless fulfilment of duty that her mother had instilled in her. Khin Kyi had originally not been in favor of her daughter's union with a foreigner, but she did later come to accept him. Could it be that this was not entirely based on his personable nature, but also because she was aware of his promise to never stand in the way of Suu Kyi's true calling? The promise Aung San Suu Kyi sought from her husband-to-be did not, however, mean that she possessed some perceptible great interest in politics. It is reported that she would have preferred to study literature over PPE.[26]

It took sixteen years, but the time for Michael Aris to deliver on his promise did eventually come on August 26, 1988. Before that point, Aung San Suu Kyi had lived with him, first for a year in Bhutan, then in London, and later in Oxford. Their son Alexander was born in 1973, and Kim, another son, followed in 1977. Michael Aris advanced his academic career as a Tibetologist during this time.

Aung San Suu Kyi's Writings

"Auntie" Than E recalls some incidents where Aung San Suu Kyi's life continued to be affected by Burmese politics. Once, at a party during her time in New York, for example, Aung San Suu Kyi was questioned by a member of the Burmese military because of her diplomatic passport, which she still used. Her mother had already left the diplomatic service by that point. The dispute remained without consequence, but the episode was seen as an indication that the military government under Ne Win wanted to find fault with the national hero's family.[27] No clear proof of this exists, but it is typical for personal animosities or sympathies to have high significance in Burma's political culture.

In the early 1980s, Aung San Suu Kyi started working on projects that went beyond her activities as a housewife and a mother, and required some political thinking. She wrote short books and turned towards the literary field, which had always drawn her fascination. The first publication appeared in 1984. It was a short biography of Aung San's life, following her university research.[28] Three books for young readers on Burma, Bhutan, and Nepal followed a year later.[29] Her first attempts to pursue further studies were thwarted when the School of Oriental and

African Studies (SOAS) rejected her PhD application because of her low BA grades. She had wanted to write a PhD focusing on her father's life.

However, SOAS subsequently accepted her as a student of Burmese literature. She studied there under the supervision of Anna Allott, a specialist in this field. While at SOAS, she came to know of a research scholarship at Kyoto University. She took this opportunity and moved to Japan with her younger son, Kim. She spent eight months between 1985 and 1986 in the country that her father, too, had known. Alexander, the older son, was at a boarding school during this time, and Michael Aris had accepted a position in the Indian city of Shimla for two years. Michael and Alexander visited their family in Japan over Christmas. After this research trip in Kyoto, Aung San Suu Kyi and Kim moved to India, where her husband had arranged a position for her that would allow her to continue with her studies. She thus continued her academic work in Shimla. Between Japan and India, she also spent three months in Rangoon with Kim, where they lived with her mother.

Two articles resulted from the study trips to Japan and India. The first, on literature and nationalism in Burma, appeared in 1987 in a compendium on cultural and social structures in Burma and Japan.[30] The second, comparing intellectual life in India and Burma, was published in 1990 by the institute in Shimla where Suu Kyi and her husband had been working.[31] At that point in time it was clear that Aung San Suu Kyi's academic career had been a temporary engagement—for two years already she had been deeply involved in Burma's politics.

The research that Michael Aris had conducted in Shimla was published in 1988.[32] It is interesting to compare his work with Aung San Suu Kyi's writings and also with her future political engagement. Aris reconstructs the lives of two Tibetan lamas. Tibet, like Bhutan, is a Buddhist country where religion and politics are inextricably interconnected. One of the biographies describes the sixth Dalai Lama's (1683–1706) short life. It also discusses his "secret life," which he supposedly continued to live after his official death and which continues to hold effect in the memory of his people. The other biography follows the life of a monk from the sixteenth century who shed light on forgotten treasures of Tibetan Buddhism through his writings.

Between the polar ends of Tibetan biographies embellished with magical elements on the one hand and Western rationalism on the other, Michael Aris attempts to bring out the universal human traits of his two protagonists. The sixth Dalai Lama distinguished himself through his unconstrained love for freedom. This led him to refuse the required ordinance of a monk and lead a very wordly life. This very peculiarity led to his later fame. After his official death, a second life full of miraculous deeds was attributed to him. Clear parallels can be drawn here to Aung San's "wild" life. Aung San, too, was a free spirit who did not mold himself to fit social expectations.

With this method, Aris points to the fact that what are often alien concepts to Western rationalists are in fact an intuitive part of Tibetans' reality and thus to be taken very seriously. Similarly, what is a natural truth for many inhabitants of multiethnic Myanmar to this day—such as numerology, astrology, and spirit worship—is sometimes difficult for Western observers to understand.

Aung San Suu Kyi's writings on her father and her country take a different approach. Her primary objective is not to illustrate the common humanity that binds East and West. Rather, she seeks to understand how her country's political culture can be adjusted to fit within a modern European framework. The publications she worked on during the four years preceding her decisive journey to Burma are useful; they provide an indication of her views on the history and political complications of the country in which she was born and which, as of 1988, she wanted to help overcome a deep crisis. Her analysis leads to the conclusion that Burma is at a standstill. She finds that the country has not yet had an opportunity to realize its potential. In her essay comparing intellectual life in India and Burma, she places the cause of this standstill in the country's colonial past.[33] Indian politicians were after a synthesis of East and West. Its leaders had been educated in the West and spoke English— the language of intellectuals. All of this was absent in Burma. There was no development of a political elite in her homeland who could connect tradition with modernity.

Nevertheless, she argues that although they were new to it themselves, Aung San and others of the younger generation of Burmese nationalists tried to open Burmese politics up to international thought. Their objective was to leave bigoted Burmese chauvinism behind. However, their efforts could not bear fruit. From this perspective, the Second World War presented a rather premature opportunity for the long-desired independence. As Aung San Suu Kyi concludes, Burma—in contrast to India—was set free in a state of political immaturity.

In her small 1984 study of Burma, Aung San Suu Kyi informs the reader factually about the country's history as well as its ethnic diversity and the special role of Buddhism for the majority of its inhabitants. Her verdict on the socialism of the Ne Win era (since 1962) is relatively mild. She points to the civil war and poor economic policies but projects an optimistic outlook for the future of the country, which lies "in the hands of its people." The people are understood as having much in common, so that one day Burma can rise to being a flourishing country thanks to its wealth of people and natural resources.

Aung San, she writes at the end of her father's biography, still remains "a source of inspiration" for people in the country. This is because of the virtues he possessed and that she highlighted in her speech of August 26, 1988: Aung San put the nation's interests before his own, and despite the power that was given to him remained a simple man who expected no privileged treatment. He had been the man that the people trusted, and thus unconditionally followed in the realization of his life's dream, to lead Burma into independence.[34]

The achievement of independence, Aung San's daughter quotes from his last speech before his death, is just the beginning of a long path. A blossoming nation can only be achieved if the Burmese—unlike in the past— "cultivate discipline, stamina and self-sacrifice."[35] The keywords that open the path to democracy in Suu Kyi's view are thus introduced. They will be the basis of her future speeches to her supporters in 1995 and 1996 (see chapter 6). Finally, she draws a parallel with the way Aung

San dealt with his own weaknesses. He was conscious of the fact that he had to work on his dreaded short-temperedness, because "what had been tolerated in a young student revolutionary would not be seemly in the leading statesman of the nation."[36]

Such references to Aung San's character and closeness to his people make up the core of the biographical sketch put together by his daughter. She includes a factual representation of his life in the context of the Burmese independence movement. She also does not spare the dark details, such as from the time of the bloody conflict between his independence army and the Karen in the region of her mother's birth.

The Need for a Second Struggle for Independence

The thoughts that Aung San Suu Kyi developed until 1988 on her country's history, politics, and culture came together—as mentioned earlier—in one key idea from her first big speech: the protests against the current socialist government had initiated Burma's second struggle for national independence.

The first independence struggle had been led by Aung San. His murder meant that he, his fellow freedom fighters, and the people could not bring an orderly and sophisticated political system to life. Civil strife, the collapse of Aung San's single-party AFPFL, and finally the takeover by the military followed in quick succession. The country was almost completely isolated from the world after that. The "Burmese chauvinism" that Aung San had tried to prevent took its course. In other words, after the first independence, the country was led off its original course because of Aung San's murder. Aung San Suu Kyi possessed a direct connection to her father's ideals, and a course correction was to follow from 1988.

Aung San Suu Kyi borrowed a set of terms from her father's last speech for her own debut speech. From these, the word "discipline"—which was used twelve times in total—stands out. The word "sacrifice" is used once, in connection with the students' efforts. The most frequently used word, "unity" or one of its derivations, is mentioned twenty times, yet only once in connection with the ethnic diversity of the country. The word is predominantly used in relation to the unity between the people and the army, which was under threat. In contrast to her earlier writings, a new and contemporary accent thus emerges: Aung San represented a unity between the people and the army. In the years of military rule under Ne Win, this unity was broken and must be repaired.

There is another novel element in her oration: "democracy." This word is used nine times in her speech and makes its presence continuously felt through the banners on stage. Democracy did not play a central role in her earlier texts and was only used in passing in connection with the period of parliamentary democracy that existed under U Nu in postindependence Burma. This means that the vague ideal of democracy, which drew her into Burmese politics, was initially just a word. Democracy was at best only vaguely connected to Aung San. Later, it was in diametric opposition to the single-party rule of Ne Win's Burma Socialist Programme Party (BSPP) and its attempts to transition into a multiparty system. The term would then go on to develop further in opposition to the military's ideas of what democracy entailed. At the time of Aung San Suu Kyi's first important speech, the word was an important but still empty shell. It worked easily as a uniting political armament, but both she and her audience had attached different meanings to the word. The word is rife with complexity to this day in Myanmar.

The complexity and ambiguity were in fact fully embraced by Aung San Suu Kyi from the very beginning. In this, she was channeling her mother's spirit, who at the time of her first big speech lay dying in the house on University Avenue. This spirit is apparent in the pledge that Aung San Suu Kyi took at her mother's funeral, cited at the beginning of this book. It was not primarily a political desire for democratic reform with which Aung San Suu Kyi stepped on to the stage of Burmese politics. Rather, it was what she owed her mother and had undertaken as her father's successor: to finally implement the will of the people of Burma.

Khin Kyi thus played an often-underestimated role in Aung San Suu Kyi's political activism. The painter Soe Moe, who had painted the larger than life portrait of Aung San for the August 1988 speech, understood this. After Khin Kyi's death, he painted a picture of her in traditional

Soe Moe painting Khin Kyi. (Photo: Soe Moe)

style. This was his way of illustrating the key person that Aung San Suu Kyi could thank for her iron will. This will allowed her to put all her energy into the cause that her mother had been waiting for since the end of colonial times. The last sentence of Aung San Suu Kyi's work on intellectual life in Burma and India reads, "[T]o this day, [Burma] still remains a society waiting for its true potential to be realised."[37] Aung San Suu Kyi was first and foremost her mother's daughter. It was through her that she learned to carry forward her father's legacy.

Aung San Suu Kyi's multifaceted youth and education in Myanmar, India, and Great Britain opened up many new horizons for her. She lived in political systems that her father and most of his young comrades only knew from books or short visits abroad. Her mother was a living example of dutifulness and raised her daughter accordingly. Aung San Suu Kyi knew that when the time came she would have to complete her father's legacy. In her youth, however, Aung San Suu Kyi was—unlike her father—no "political animal." She strived for an academic or literary career but never forgot what she owed to her country. This explains why, after twenty-eight years abroad, she dedicated herself to continuing in her father's path with all her energies and talents.

CHAPTER 4

The Struggle for the Right Path to Democracy

This national crisis could in fact be called the second struggle for national independence.

Ironically, it was Ne Win who first put democracy on Burma's political agenda in 1988. This happened a month before Aung San Suu Kyi's big speech would make the term a decisive yardstick for Burma's future development. In his farewell speech at the extraordinary party congress on July 23, Ne Win proposed a referendum on whether the one-party system should continue or whether a multiparty system should be introduced. Oddly enough, the party congress rejected the departing chief's proposition, exposing inklings of intraparty disagreement.[1]

Dr. Maung Maung, who took over Ne Win's post as the leader of the Burma Socialist Programme Party (BSPP) and the state, took up the idea again shortly after "the butcher" Sein Lwein failed to restore order through martial law. The new head of state gave an address to the people on August 24, 1988, which was broadcast through radio and television. He announced the lifting of martial law and called an extraordinary party congress, where the referendum proposed by Ne Win was to be considered anew. Dr. Maung Maung and other newly appointed leading functionaries said that they would resign should the conference again vote against the proposal. They thus signaled how important the proposal was to them.[2]

Dr. Maung Maung repeated his proposition in another speech on September 1. In this speech, he also responded to the demand made by Aung San Suu Kyi and others that the current regime step down immediately and be replaced by an interim government.[3] He questioned how such a change would work in practice by recalling the two interim governments that had existed from 1958 to 1960 and from 1962 to 1974. Ne Win had been the leader in both instances. For the first, he had been elected by the parliament, and for the second he became the leader of the Revolutionary Council that took over after the coup. The first interim government had been approved by parliament in accordance with the 1947 constitution. As for the second, Ne Win himself had declared that such a mode of transfer of power should not become the norm.

In order to play by the rules this time, Dr. Maung Maung advocated for the necessary transfer to happen in accordance with the constitution. Since the 1947 constitution enshrined a single-party system within it, a constitutional change was required before any multiparty system could be introduced. Under the legal framework, such a change to the constitution could only be implemented after holding a referendum.[4] At the BSPP party conference convened on September 10, 1988, however, the executive committee decided to clear the path for immediate elections and a multiparty system without holding a referendum. A day later, the parliament convened to promulgate the decision into law. An election commission was installed, and elections were scheduled to take place within three months.

On the same day, Aung San Suu Kyi announced that

the achievement of multi-party democracy is just one of our demands. The demand for forming an interim government is not yet met. In addition, there remains for them to hold a just and fair election. We cannot accept the election to be sponsored by an interim government which is formed by BSPP members and the present government. We only want the formation of an interim government which will be acceptable to the entire public.[5]

Three days later, a meeting took place between the election commission and representatives of the demonstrators. From the latter, the press only referred to Aung San Suu Kyi, Aung Gyi, and Tin Oo by name. The chairman of the commission was U Ba Htay, a former member of the British Indian Civil Service who had requested retirement shortly after Ne Win's coup in early 1963, and was well into his eighties at this point. He gave assurances as to the commission's nonpartisanship. The commission put in place by the parliament would ensure free and fair elections and also work with members of the sangha and the students. The activists, on the other hand, held the view that the commission did not enjoy the trust of the people. Besides, new parties could not mobilize sufficient funds in three months to be on equal footing with the incumbent state party. For that reason alone, the elections could not be free and fair. The student activists reiterated their demand that the government immediately step down and that an interim government be put in its place.[6]

The students had been pushing for an interim government to be appointed within forty-eight hours. But after the meeting, the three lead negotiators bid the students—who, through their protests, had made the negotiations possible in the first place—to have patience and be disciplined. Aung San Suu Kyi and both her fellow delegates found that the short, forty-eight-hour time frame was going to be problematic, if not dangerous. It would lead to the existence of parallel governments if the old government did not step down.[7] Bloody confrontations could follow, leading even to civil war.

The problem illustrated here is one that has continuously accompanied the country's politics in various forms. It is in fact a key question for any country's political organization: the political system and the transfer of power.[8] This period in Burma was really about creating a new system given that the public had lost all faith in the prevailing one. Ne Win—and Dr. Maung Maung after him—had advocated for a process of transition within the framework of the existing constitution. On the other hand, the students and prominent leaders of the protest movement were of the view that the transition could not be driven by the old regime, not even under the oversight of a man who had been educated under the British and had not been a member of the BSPP.

Aung San Suu Kyi and her team's bids for a measured approach were to no avail. The protest leaders had entirely run out of patience. More and more new public-interest organizations sprang up in a new wave of activism. In the short period between August 31, 1988, and the military coup of September 18, 1988, alone, newspapers reported the formation of thirty-five new associations. Among them were five teachers' organizations and five student unions, various professional and common interest unions, and some ethnic organizations. The demand for setting up an interim government was also supported by Aung Than—Aung San's older brother and "name giver"—in a letter to the "big four" (U Nu, Aung Gyi, Tin Oo, and Aung San Suu Kyi).[9]

All the newly formed organizations had a similar hierarchical structure. There was a nominal "patron" at the apex; then there was a president or chairperson, a secretary, and eventually their deputies as well as members of an executive committee. What the various groups also shared was their demand for democracy—whatever that may have meant in detail—and the prompt introduction of an interim government. Some of these groups announced a strike.

The emergence of these new organizations led to an accelerated dissolution of public institutions, which to this point had been centrally organized. The state crumbled. The more the government tried to meet the demands of the demonstrators, the faster it disintegrated. Numerous towns and neighborhoods saw the formation of local committees that tried to maintain public order. Elsewhere it was anarchy that prevailed.

This new dynamic can be traced back to the breakdown of communication between the actors involved and the lack of an entity to mediate between the parties. The mistrust towards the old regime created a rift that could not be bridged. In this, Aung San Suu Kyi's public appearance, the confidence placed in her, and her demand for a completely new beginning primarily worked as catalysts to further strengthen public opinion against the regime. Besides, with the slogan of democracy she provided a common battle cry to the demonstrators. This was something new. On August 8, 1988, the day that the students called for demonstrations around the country, the slogan had still been

Employees of the state newspaper New Light of Myanmar *(Myanmar Alin) holding the flag of socialist Burma upside down. (Photo: Htein Win)*

an older one, one that had been used in earlier years: *doh ayei!* (our cause!). The term "democracy" started being used regularly only after Aung San Suu Kyi's speech, which turned the term into a motto for the opposition movement, making it a title phrase for a yet-to-be-developed political program.

On September 17, Aung San Suu Kyi expressed her conviction that "the fight for genuine democracy has reached the final stage and the people's aspirations will soon be fulfilled."[10] Although the statement reveals a sense of impending victory, Aung San Suu Kyi found herself in a dilemma. On the one hand she shared the demonstrators' enthusiasm. On the other hand, as mentioned earlier, she recognized the need for patience and moving slowly. If Aung San Suu Kyi had been right in her convictions, it would follow that the government would very soon give in to the pressure exerted by the demonstrators and step back.

Yet no such thing happened. On September 18, 1988, just one day after her optimistic statement, the conflict was resolved. The military stepped in and Burma saw its second coup. After Ne Win, the military had remained under the leadership of his commander-in-chief and minister of defense, Saw Maung. It was thus still controlled by the country's political class. It was the military that had shot at demonstrators under martial law imposed by Sein Lwin. It retreated after Dr. Maung Maung lifted martial law, but now it seized political power. The Tatmadaw (the Burmese name for the military) remained the only functioning state institution in the late summer of 1988. It rigorously set forth on its prerogative to—once again—save Burma from chaos.

Split Opposition

The stepping in of the armed forces can partly be explained by the division that existed within the opposition. Although the antiregime movement collectively embraced democracy, there were highly varied conceptions of what a concrete path towards a new order could look like. Discipline and unity were a hope but not a reality. Various politicians sensed opportunity in this crisis. Some were purely after power, and others—like Aung San Suu Kyi—were genuinely committed to carrying the national hero's legacy forward.

The most prominent example of the former sort is U Nu, who now saw the chance to make a comeback. He had governed Burma from 1948 to 1958 and stepped down after the AFPFL split and—with parliamentary approval—handed over power to the supreme commander of the armed forces, General Ne Win. Ne Win had assigned himself the task of preparing for the next elections.[11] The elections were held in February 1960.[12] U Nu won these with a clear margin at the lead of his wing of the AFPFL, to which he had added the prefix "clean." This prefix carried a religious connotation in line with Nu's promise to make Buddhism the state religion after an election victory. This pledge certainly was a factor accounting for his victory, but it was also one of the reasons relied upon by the army under Ne Win to stage the March 2, 1962, coup. The constitutional change required to make Buddhism the state religion had also contributed to the largely Christian Kachin ethnic group in the north of the country taking up arms against the central government.

Many other politicians along with Nu were arrested after Ne Win's 1962 coup. U Nu was released in 1966 and, three years later, left the country with the government's permission to go on a pilgrimage to India. He used his stay abroad to assemble other Burmans in exile. As the leader of his newly formed movement, he tried to topple the Ne Win regime by means of armed force from Thailand. The attempt failed miserably. U Nu then returned to Burma in 1980 after the government granted a general amnesty.

Three days after Aung San Suu Kyi's August 1988 speech, U Nu ended his retirement from politics and founded the League for Democracy and Peace, of which he became the patron. The seventy-two-year-old Mahn Win Maung, an ethnic Karen and former president of Burma (1957–1962), took over the chairmanship. As of September 1, the league had published a series of declarations in the style of official bulletins of a ruling party.[13] And on September 9, at nine o'clock in the morning,[14] U Nu proclaimed himself to be the rightful prime minister of the country. A few days later, a newspaper reported his future plans:

> U Nu said he was still prime minister of Burma under the 1947 Constitution. . . . He had no ministers under him, and if the leaders of democratic forces U Aung Gyi, U Tin Oo, Bo Yan Naing,[15] and Daw Aung San Su Kyi (who is "friendly like a daughter"), would join with him he will create 20 ministerships, including representatives of students, workers, peasants, and boycott leaders. If the majority accepted, elections would be held January 1, 1989. If the BSPP disturbed the election, he would seek assistance of UN peace keeping forces. He would ask donors for the Ky 5 million needed for holding the general election.[16]

Prior to this message, Tin Oo had already announced that he had ended his cooperation with U Nu's league together with a few other original members.[17] The league soon saw itself forced to fight off rumors that it had already been dissolved. It in fact continued to exist until the 1990 elections, at which it remained without success.

U Nu (left) next to Aung San Suu Kyi and Tin Oo at a public event in September 1988. (Photo: Getty)

A few days after U Nu's prime ministerial proclamation, a daughter of his former adversary Kyaw Nyein set up the AFPFL anew. The league had been dissolved in 1964 by Ne Win's Revolutionary Council. She demanded that the government release the seized assets of the party. She called upon Aung San Suu Kyi to take over the leadership of the party that had been cofounded by Aung San and was now being revived. Aung San Suu Kyi, on her part, just as she had done following U Nu's statement, issued no response to this invitation.[18] Like her father before her, she had always been in a political league of her own.

These examples highlight how uncoordinated the appearance of new groups was after the fall of the single party. All had but one objective: the dissolution of the old regime and the creation of a new one, under their own leadership if possible. Reflecting on these events, Dr. Maung Maung remarked sarcastically, "Myanmar did not appear to be denuded of 'leaders' in August–September 1988. We had so many we could have exported them if there had been markets."[19]

Aung San Suu Kyi versus Khin Nyunt, Aung San versus Ne Win

By its own account, the military had taken over in order to guide democracy on the right path after the chaos of the uprising and to further prepare the elections initiated by the last BSPP government. Parties started forming as of September 20. Among them, founded on September 27, 1988, was the National League for Democracy (NLD). It was thus the military junta that made possible a multiparty system, which included Aung San Suu Kyi's party. The irony mentioned at the beginning of this chapter thus continued after the military coup. Aung Gyi, whose house the party was founded in, became party chairman, Tin Oo his deputy, and Aung San Suu Kyi the general secretary and thus the main person responsible for the day-to-day running of the party. Around the same time, the head of the secret service, General Khin Nyunt, was named first secretary of the State Law and Order Restoration Council (SLORC).[20] The general secretary of the NLD and the first secretary of the junta were to be the key actors opposing each other in the country's political arena between 1988 and 2004.

Khin Nyunt was seen as the puppet who implemented orders issued behind the scenes by Ne Win. Aung San Suu Kyi, in contrast, was seen as much more. She represented her father's legacy against a military that had in fact been founded by him. But today's Tatmadaw was not what the military had been in Aung San's time. In the eyes of the public, it had been subjected for decades to the leadership of his former fellow fighter Ne Win.

The confrontation that started in 1988 now played itself out on different levels. The preparations for the elections were the primary concern. A law on the registration of parties was passed on September 28, and the official party registration process started on September 30. By February 28, 1989, there were 235 parties that had registered throughout the country. The wave of party formation can partly be explained by the fact that parties received access to petrol rations and the right to a telephone. The most important parties besides the NLD were the successor party of the BSPP, namely the National Unity Party (NUP); U Nu's League for Democracy and Peace; and the Union Nationalities Democracy Party under the leadership of Aung Gyi, who in the meantime had left the NLD. As a result, from the four most influential heads of the opposition movement, only two continued to work together in the same organization: Tin Oo, who replaced Aung Gyi as the NLD's chairman, and Aung San Suu Kyi, who remained party secretary.

The parties had to submit their objectives and agendas at registration. They were—as an American observer noted—in all "largely general, lengthy, repetitive, and non-controversial."[21] Some "groups" like the NLD and the NUP (the proxy party replacing the BSPP) were exempted from this judgment by the compiler of the issues of the *Working People's Daily*. The official newspaper published this extract of the NLD's program:

> Aims:
> (a) to bring about a true and genuine democratic government which is in accordance with the aspirations of entire people [*sic*] and which would guarantee the fundamental human rights;
> (b) to bring about a systematic democratic struggle based on the united strength of the people under the leadership [of] this League for realising the aim (a);
> (c) to lay a foundation so that Burma would be a stable and developed Union where democratic political system flourish according to the aspirations of the people for generations to come;
> (d) to co-operate with peaceful democratic forces of the world so that peaceful democracy would flourish.
> Future Programmes:
> (a) to organize in such a way that all democratic forces would attain unity;
> (b) to support and protect the democratic rights of the public;

(c) to create situations in which free and fair general elections could be held to form a true democratic government according to the wishes of the entire people.[22]

This program boils down to one word—the word that was inaugurated on a banner at Aung San Suu Kyi's speech on August 26: democracy. This one-point program resonated through the numerous other parties, many of which had adopted the D-word in their party name. This shows just how unified the people were in this regard. Just like the AFPFL had won the 1947 elections under Aung San's leadership, the NLD presented itself as a single party with the aim to defeat its one opponent. During Aung San's time, the united front had stood up against the Japanese and the British colonial powers. Now, it was targeted against the country's own military.

The military's dual role as both organizer of multiparty elections and as unelected ruler created a predicament for the NLD. The new party saw itself pushed into taking part in a democratic election process in which it could not trust the organizers. The SLORC had organized democratic elections that took place under the framework of martial law and thus could not really be said to be democratic. A curfew was in place, and gatherings of more than five people were forbidden. On the other side, the military, too, faced a problem. Its main opponent was none other than the daughter of the founder of the army. She thus had to be treated with respect. At the same time, it saw its task as curtailing her influence. After all, the military also held itself to be the true representative of the people's interests and the warden of Aung San's legacy.[23]

The groundwork for a confrontation was hence set in place. Each side blamed the other. Aung San Suu Kyi turned to the international community and called upon them to recognize the "massacre" of unarmed demonstrators by the army.[24] In turn, the military blamed Aung San Suu Kyi for undermining the unity of the armed forces.[25] Blame was also attributed to her supporters for bringing about chaotic situations similar to the ones before the coup.

The accusations also always carried a personal undertone and became shriller with time. The situation lent itself to plenty of opportunities for each side—by design or by default—to participate in the name-calling. Aung San Suu Kyi undertook various trips through the country beginning in October 1988. She visited members of the NLD and held speeches of which little of the content is known.[26] In doing this Aung San Suu Kyi ignored the government's decree of September 1988, which banned the gathering of more than five persons. Such breaches were generally tolerated by the government. Nevertheless, a number of confrontations with the police and the military took place during her travels. The courage she demonstrated on such occasions increased her popularity in the country. It would also be later highlighted by her foreign admirers.

One particular incident drew special notice. It happened in Danubyu, a town in Irrawaddy Division, famous because it was here that General Maha Bandoola was killed in 1825 in the first Anglo-Burmese war; after the death of the leader, the Burmese army's resistance had fallen. In April 1989, this historic place witnessed another incident involving the Burmese army. There was a confrontation between Aung San Suu Kyi and an officer of the Tatmadaw, who was escorting her travel party. At the height of the incident, she unflinchingly stepped towards soldiers who had been ordered by the officer to shoot should she continue on the path. She fearlessly set forward one step after the other. No shots were fired. The orders were revoked shortly thereafter by a superior officer.[27]

Another cause for confrontation and media commotion was the June 1989 law that set out how the country and various geographical terms should be referred to in English. Instead of Burma, the country was to be called Myanmar in the future. In this context, one of Suu Kyi's supporters is said to have allowed himself a joke at the expense of the government, saying that it would refer to the Buddha as "Muddha" in the future. This was regarded as blasphemy by the authorities. Aung San Suu Kyi herself was later accused of calling the Buddha a "very normal person."[28]

In an interview at the beginning of July, conducted shortly before she was confined to house arrest, Suu Kyi lamented that she was being defamed on account of being married to a foreigner. "[They say] things like I have four husbands, three husbands, two husbands. That I am a communist—although in some circles they say I am CIA. They even have been trying to get prominent monks to say I have been insulting the Buddha!"[29]

Caricature denigrating Aung San Suu Kyi. (From the Working People's Daily)

Suu Kyi held Ne Win personally responsible as the mastermind behind the SLORC's actions. In doing this she was in fact representing a generally held opinion. As early as October 1988, shortly after the founding of the NLD, she had responded to an interview question about her relationship to Ne Win as follows: "Officially, he's nowhere in the picture [but] the general feeling is that if there's something sinister going on, he must be behind it."[30] In an interview from mid-1989, she called the junta "poor SLORC." When asked for an explanation she clarified, "Yes, poor SLORC. Any organisation totally under the thumb of a dictator can be described as poor. They have to act under his orders. I don't think there will be free and fair elections as long as U Ne Win is at the helm of power."[31] As the situation intensified, she challenged the armed forces to choose between her father and Ne Win.

In numerous speeches in the run-up to the eventually discredited May 1990 elections, she accused Ne Win of being personally responsible for the dismal developments in the country. She again and again painted a stark picture of her father's comrade-in-arms:

> It is almost 42 years since my father passed away. He (Aung San) was not only a national leader but he was the father of the Tatmadaw (Armed Forces). Are they proceeding according to my father's wishes? My father was very worried that the arms held by the Tatmadaw might be misused— and exhorted them not to do so just because they were holding them. But they have now followed the wrong path. It is U Ne Win who put them on the wrong road. Is it Aung San's army or Ne Win's army? My father's way is for the country, for democracy. . . . The armed forces have only one father. We cannot accept a second. . . . There must be honour in following his exhortations. There can be unity in doing so—and progress. Do not be diverted. Follow the right path.[32]

With such characterizations, she too played a part in creating an atmosphere of absolute disdain and discrediting of the political opponent. In 1989, a few days before the national holiday in memory of her father's murder (known in Burma as Martyrs' Day), she referred to the military as "fascist" and accused it of using the holiday to lure people into a trap that was a killing field.[33] With the term "killing field," Aung San Suu Kyi was making a reference to the mass killings by the Khmer Rouge in Cambodia, where hundreds of thousands had fallen victim.[34]

After all the accusing and disparaging from both sides, the events preceding Martyrs' Day on July 19, 1989, presented the last straw. Aung San Suu Kyi had announced a competing event to celebrate the day. She was thus demonstrating that she denied the current government the right to represent the country and its people on this central day commemorating the national hero. She then canceled her event on short notice, possibly for fear of violence by the armed forces. However, not all of her supporters came to know about the cancellation. The SLORC responded to this latest provocation with the first house arrest of Aung San Suu Kyi (and Tin Oo), which came into force on July 20, 1989. This was also the result of a vituperating contest on the legacy of Aung San, defended bitterly by both sides. Aung San Suu Kyi's contributions to this fight in no way match up with the attitude of the gentle and all-forgiving personality that emerged to the public at the end of the first house arrest in 1995.

Furthermore, her comments created a significant and long-lasting picture of the Burmese military command as a misguided and power-hungry clique. International media subsequently largely accepted and took over this image. Overall, Ne Win and the military had previously not exclusively been perceived as unscrupulous power seekers, as Robert Taylor shows in his political biography of Ne Win.[35] The rhetoric of these first months played an important role in shaping the strongly antagonistic image of Burmese politics.

First Steps to International Fame

The military coup of September 18, 1988, led to the creation of two understandings of reality that to this day cannot be reconciled with each other. Two separate accounts continue to exist in relation to the events of that time.

From the military perspective shared by Dr. Maung Maung in his memoirs, the stepping in of the Tatmadaw was a necessary—although by no means a desired—response to the nationwide chaos.[36] As the name State Law and Order Restoration Council suggests, the military regime saw itself as the instrument necessary to bring a derailed political situation back on track. Its first announcement on the day of the coup promised multiparty elections once law and order as well as communication channels had been restored in the country, and once the people's economic situation had improved. The army duly continued with the preliminary preparations for multiparty elections that the dissolved government had already started.[37]

The other interpretation of the situation was that the old regime had resurfaced with a new face. This is the view expressed by Bertil Lintner, among others. Lintner's book on the 1988 unrest, *Outrage*, has significantly shaped perceptions of that time. "The old regime had reasserted its power under a different name—and it appeared to show no genuine willingness to yield to the demands of the Burmese public at large, or even to take note of the almost total international condemnation."[38]

The two opposing accounts expose the abyss that existed between the people and the government. This seemingly insurmountable gap became visible to the public eye in 1988 and deepened even further following the September 18 coup. Martial law was put back into place after the coup, and the military put a violent end to any demonstrations, again resulting in a number of deaths. For the second time in Burma's history, the military took on a dual role. It was both the government and, in its own view, the agent for democratic change. To draw an analogy with football, one could say that the military took on the role of both center-forward and referee.

It was around this time that the internal Burmese conflict caught the eye of the world. The Western world, alarmed by reports of the military's intervention—Lintner speaks of "senseless massacres and summary executions"—spontaneously sided with the people's opposition led by Aung San Suu Kyi.[39] The internationalization received another boost when a number of students fled the country after the coup. They tried to fight the regime from abroad, in part with weapons but later especially with the help of the media. Traditionally, the Burmese-language broadcasts of the BBC and Voice of America had been regarded as the only reliable news sources by the politically interested public of the country. The state media was not even trusted when it—and this did happen—in fact accurately reported on events. This is how two separate conceptions of the road to democracy came to exist. One was represented by the institution of the military, the other by the person of Aung San Suu Kyi.

The perception of the conflict in the international media and the global political arena became an essential component of Burma's internal politics. At the very beginning, Aung San Suu Kyi did not actually play an important role from the international perspective. Until the 1988 coup, she had been seen as one of the many actors opposing the government and was not held in especially high estimation given her lack of political experience. As late as January 1989, just after her mother's funeral aroused another demonstration of sympathy for her, the *New York Times* referred to Aung San Suu Kyi as an "accidental politician."[40] She only really became internationally famous when she was put under house arrest in the run up to the 1990 elections. And domestically, she now came to be known in her own right—as Aung San Suu Kyi—rather than just the daughter of a national hero who had stood beneath the shining pagoda in August 1988.

Like her father before her, Aung San Suu Kyi could credit her own rise to prominence in large part to the actions of those whom she opposed. Aung San had become known throughout the country after he was suspended from university. In a similar vein, his daughter was ennobled as a freedom fighter by virtue of her house arrest. Reporting on her captivity, global media not only brought Aung San Suu Kyi to international fame; it also had a hand in shaping her image within the country. She soon came to be seen as the central figure against the government both within and beyond Burma's borders.

Monarchical versus Constitutional Democracy

The personalization of politics—Aung San Suu Kyi as the legitimate heir of her father's legacy versus Ne Win and his military "puppets"—that followed the September 18, 1988, coup does two things: one, it falls in line with a long tradition of vilification of political opponents in Burma; and two, it reveals much about the political expectations of the Burmese population. Instead of institutions, it is individuals that are the focus of attention. Party manifestos are of subordinate importance. This was already the case during Aung San's time. His political agenda rested solely on the authority of his commanding personality.

In an essay written prior to her house arrest, Aung San Suu Kyi elaborates on the democratic aspirations of her country against the contention that democracy is "un-Burmese."[41] For this she draws upon a Buddhist text describing the ancient election of the earth's first ruler, the Maha Sammata or the "Great Elect." At the beginning of the story, society is at risk of descending into chaos. In order to avert this danger, the people unanimously elect a just ruler. They give him a part of their harvest in return for his government based on law and order.[42] This, according to Aung San Suu Kyi, is "the Buddhist version of government by social contract."[43] This contract is democratic—despite there being only one potential candidate for rule—because the teachings of Buddhism bind the ruler to the principle of not acting against the will of the people. She summarizes, "The people of Burma view democracy not merely as a form of government but as an integrated social and ideological system based on respect for the individual."[44]

She uses Buddhist moral virtues to evaluate the current military leadership and Ne Win, its behind-the-scenes puppet master. This exercise leads her to construe an absolute polarity between on the one hand a good collective "us" under Aung San's spiritual leadership and on the other hand an evil collective "them" under Ne Win's influence.

Such a political system may be described as a "monarchical democracy." The contract between the typically undisciplined populace and the good ruler is an agreement between "those down there" and "the one up there." The hierarchy is not set by power structures. Rather, it is the possession of special qualities that allows one to be ruler. After all, the Great Elect was "the handsomest, the best-looking, most pleasant and capable."[45]

In light of this Buddhist story, the gathering of August 26, 1988, as well as the later elections of 1990, 2012, and 2015, amounted to the people's confirmation of Aung San Suu Kyi's leadership qualities. No opposition—as understood within a framework of a parliamentary system—can exist in such a conception of democracy.

The major shortcoming of such a system, of course, is that everything grinds to a halt when the chosen ruler dies. Indeed, in its long history of kings, Burma has often experienced this darker side of the model. The clearest example comes from the time shortly before independence. Aung San had been confirmed as the elect during the constituent assembly vote in April 1947. The country began its descent into the chaos of civil war and party politics after his murder.

Min Ko Naing in the 88 Generation offices in 2013. In the background, an image of a peacock, a national Burmese symbol since royal times. (Photo: Rodion Ebbighausen)

The behavior of one of the most prominent student leaders of 1988 sheds more light on this unique understanding of democracy. In reality this leader was called Paw Oo Tun, but he eventually took Min Ko Naing as a nom de guerre. Min Ko Naing means "he who topples kings" or "kingmaker." The adopted name worked as a sort of collective pseudonym that functioned to point to the people's chosen leaders. The students signed off their fliers and other texts with Min Ko Naing. In an interview out of a hiding place in Burma in October 1988, Paw Oo Tun said, "I'll always be with the people. I'll never die. Physically I might be dead, but many more Min Ko Naings would appear to take my place.

As you know, Min Ko Naing can only conquer a bad king. If the ruler is good, we carry him on our shoulders."[46]

This conception of a "monarchical" democracy stood at odds with the one espoused by the military leadership that succeeded Ne Win. But here, too, the myth of the Great Elect played a role. The Great Elect's charge had after all been to restore law and order for a good life (so the name of the junta, State Law and Order Restoration Council, carries a strong Buddhist connotation). The order-restoring function of the Elect, who reins in the anarchistic inclinations of the populace, is of central import. The military was the only institution in the country with the capacity to achieve this. It thus fulfilled in part the role of the Great Elect, but in a collective form with its own collective identity. However, Ne Win, who had stood at the helm of the Tatmadaw, lacked other important individual attributes of the Elect. The leader had never been a charismatic ruler and there were many stories about his moral faults. He had been married four times and been a fond participant in horse betting in his youth (but he later closed the racetrack in Rangoon). He also had a house in London, the capital of the former colonial power.

After 1962, Ne Win and his followers had tried to restructure Burma. The structure borrowed the socialist elements of the 1947 framework drafted by Aung San himself but did not include a multiparty system. In some ways this was an attempt to replace the Great Elect with a single party that would translate the will of the people into political action. The attempt finally crumbled. The system failed to provide the people with the personal and economic freedoms that had been hoped for. Ne Win stayed in power as the central representative of the new system until 1988.[47] General Saw Maung, who took over after the 1988 coup, himself admitted that he lacked all the qualities required of a political leader.

As mentioned, the coup led by the Tatmadaw in September 1988 set the restoration of law and order—the primary objective of the Great Elect—as its foremost task. It subsequently wanted to put a political structure in place that it would later call a "disciplined democracy."

The "discipline," something that Aung San Suu Kyi also stressed, had to, however, be encoded within a constitution. Simply embodying the moral qualities of the country's leaders would not suffice. This emphasis, at least formally, on the constitution over the politician (rather than vice versa) was present as of the beginning of Ne Win's political career after the end of World War II. Keeping in line with the 1947 constitution, Ne Win resigned from his post as deputy prime minister in U Nu's first government in 1949 after six months. When he was elected prime minister in 1958 after U Nu's stepping down, he announced that he would resign again after half a year because his government had not been able to organize elections during this period of time. This time, parliament approved changes to the respective constitutional article in order to allow Ne Win's government to continue. Free and fair elections were finally held in April 1960.

Poster highlighting the importance of the constitution adopted in 2008.
(Photo: Hans-Bernd Zöllner)

In 1988, the military rulers saw Aung San Suu Kyi and her supporters as obstructions in this path of law and order, and as a result imposed restrictions upon them. This led to a deepening gap between the two envisaged and opposed models of democracy. Aung San Suu Kyi's house arrest and her supporters' imprisonment were naturally seen as arbitrary by the public, even though the government took great pains to ground these punishments in the existing laws of the country.[48] The military argued that Aung San Suu Kyi's popularity could be politically exploited because of the public's "hero worship mentality."[49] But the military maybe underestimated the influence of a political ruler who had been chosen by the people (and whose rule was formally endorsed by the elections held in 1990).

What was the right path for democracy in Burma? The disagreement on the answer to this question is what has drawn out into a decades-long, fundamental battle in which the international community became involved in a central way.

CHAPTER 5

Birth of a Global Icon

I have always thought of myself as a politician, and not as an icon.
I always object to that name. It is static. It just hangs on a wall,
whereas I have always worked very hard.

On the afternoon of July 10, 1995, Aung San Suu Kyi received a visit from Kyaw Win, the second-in-command of the military secret service.[1] He was there to deliver a message from General Than Shwe;[2] Her house arrest was ended as of now. It was—as she would later confirm in an interview—exactly the day on which she should have been released by the SLORC according to the outcome of her legal case. Upon further questioning she clarified that the length of her arrest had been the result of a bending of the law, but that the government had behaved correctly within its own conception of the law. In a statement on the following day, she explained how the "friendly and heartfelt message" included, besides the news of her release, three other points:[3] "First, the authorities would be happy to help me in matters of personal welfare. Second if I wish, the authorities would continue to take care of security arrangements in the house, and thirdly, he [Than Shwe] would like me to help towards achieving peace and democracy in the country." She added, "First of all, I would like to say that I appreciate deeply both the tone and content of the message. I've always believed that the future stability and happiness of our nation depends entirely on the readiness of all parties to work for reconciliation."

These words are in true contrast to the statements Aung San Suu Kyi made before being placed under house arrest. The tone is conciliatory.

It corresponds to the polite words used by the head of the military junta in delivering his message of her release. She concluded the statement—which was crafted in the style of a government notice—with the words, "I, on my part, bear no resentment towards anybody for anything that happened to me during the past six years."[4] Here, Aung San Suu Kyi expresses a personal conviction that she would later set out in a different form in an interview with Alan Clement: nothing that others do can cause one suffering.

One starts to sense a formative change in the backdrop. In fact, Aung San Suu Kyi did engage intensively with Buddhism during the years of her house arrest. This is something she would go on to explain in various interviews. Meditation played an important role in this pursuit, as is apparent from the daily routine she logged with Bill Richardson, the American congressman who visited her in 1994:

> I get up at 4:30 a.m., meditate, listen to the radio, do exercises, spiritual reading, bathe, read, and do household chores. After lunch I meditate, read, and listen to music. I listen to the news at fixed times. I also listen to music. I keep myself on a rigid routine. I go to sleep at 9:25 p.m., after the *Democratic Voice of Burma* stops broadcasting.[5]

Her life resembled that of one in a monastery. Monks also wake up before sunrise and start the day with meditation and personal care. As she mentioned in another interview, it was important for her to be both physically and spiritually clean before turning towards the events of the outside world. This spiritual stance included controlling one's own emotions, such as any feelings of hostility, as these only lead to self-caused suffering.

Firm Principles

The new tone of the first announcement and subsequent interviews should not be seen as a "softening" of her political stance. In no way did it mean that her position on the state of her country had changed during the years of house arrest. Her attitude was friendly but firm. This can be seen from her first comments on the subject of reconciliation after the end of the house arrest. She drew inspiration from South Africa, where bitter enemies of the past were able to collaborate. Her country also—so she explained—faced the choice between "dialogue or utter devastation."[6] But certain principles were nonnegotiable. For example, she continued to call for her supporters who were still in custody to be released.

In relation to the latter, she reshaped an earlier demand. Previously, the demand was accompanied with a strong action of protest; she had gone on a hunger strike one day after the imposition of her house arrest. She did this not for herself but for her imprisoned supporters. She demanded that the terms of their custody match her own privileged house arrest. She refused food and drank only water and fruit juices. Both her sons were visiting her at this time and her husband, alarmed by the news, flew to Yangon some days later. He found his wife in a state of physical decline. With the help of the British Embassy, he eventually succeeded in mediating between the military and Aung San Suu Kyi. The military agreed to treat the imprisoned members of the NLD fairly. She stopped her hunger strike after twelve days.

Aung San Suu Kyi had remained uncompromising in other ways during the entire duration of her house arrest. She refused to accept food from the government and insisted on sustaining herself. That meant that household items and furniture, including for example the bathtub, were sold via the security guard in exchange for some cash with which the house help could buy food. The financial situation changed in 1991 when Michael Aris published a book that marked the occasion of Aung San Suu Kyi winning the Nobel Peace Prize. The royalties from the book were paid into an account in Yangon and could be used by her.

Her refusal to be dependent in any way on the government was reaffirmed once more after her release. It came to be known that the household items had not been sold at all. Instead, they were being held in storage by the military. She repaid the money that she had innocently received for these items from her wardens and rejected having them reinstalled in her home in 1995.

This act of protest stemmed from Aung San Suu Kyi's unshakeable opposition to the regime. At the same time, on a personal level, the dealings between her and the soldiers who guarded the house were friendly. She also had a good relationship with the officer appointed as her intermediary. One of the soldiers tasked with guarding the house said to an American journalist who was allowed to interview him, "There was a great dignity about her and the way she responded to everything that happened and I can say that her biggest concern was always about her friends who were in prison."[7]

54/56 University Avenue in 2009 while Aung San Suu Kyi was detained in Insein prison. (Photo: Reuters)

J.S. Bach Goes Silent

Aung San Suu Kyi was connected to the outside world in multiple ways during the six years of her house arrest. Besides her Burmese contacts (including her doctor from time to time), her husband and children as well as others would occasionally visit her.[8] Michael Aris had permission to send her packages. This is how she was supplied with books, magazines, and other items. Aung San Suu Kyi was thus always well informed as to what was happening in the world. Radio was her most important medium after the telephone lines were cut by her guards. The news from, for example, the BBC or the Democratic Voice of Burma, which she listened to, was partly broadcast in Burmese in order to give the population access to "objective" information. The radio connected her to her government-critical compatriots, who, like her, held a deep distrust of the state media. The books she received from England included works on Nelson Mandela. His example showed—according to her announcement after her release—that good will overcame even greater antagonism than that represented between the conflicting parties in Burma. The information she received from the outside world supplied her with ever more arguments to fundamentally oppose the military government's politics.

The house arrest thus gave Aung San Suu Kyi time to broaden her political thinking. In addition, the intensive engagement with Buddhism helped her become personally stronger. These two components are key. They are what eventually made it possible for her to become a national and international icon.

While Aung San Suu Kyi was following what was going on in the world from within the walls of her house, the world—on the reverse side— observed her. People wanted to know what was happening, both to her personally and to the movement she represented. The keen observation of Aung San Suu Kyi within the country was not limited to whatever snippets foreign news broadcasters could provide. It was much more local than that. For example, her neighbors noticed one day that she had not played the piano for a long time. The news spread rapidly through Yangon and raised fears that something had happened to her. In fact, it was just a few broken strings that prevented her from playing pieces by Johann Sebastian Bach.[9]

During that same time, the Burmese public came to know some details about Aung San Suu Kyi's channel to the outside world. The packages sent from England were delivered through the British Embassy and first opened by Burmese officials. One day, images of a Jane Fonda aerobics video and a tube of lipstick appeared in the state newspaper. This was supposed to let the public see for themselves that the detainee was living a foreign-financed luxury life.[10] The government thus played its part in maintaining antagonism, at the same time keeping Aung San Suu Kyi present in the public consciousness.

The 1990 Elections

The 1990 elections took place on May 27. Events both before and after this day played a decisive role in making Aung San Suu Kyi the democratically legitimized leader of the country. There had previously been an ambivalent attitude on all sides in relation to these elections.

The 1988 demonstrators had rejected the BSPP-organized elections. The rejection only strengthened when the military junta usurped power. Just nineteen days before she was put under house arrest, Aung San Suu Kyi had been certain that the elections would not be free and fair. At the same time, she had the NLD registered and committed herself to campaign trips. She had thus accepted the process to a certain extent. Campaign trips have been a fixed component of the political system since Aung San's trips of 1947. This can be explained by the fact that at the time the country's mass media was notably less widespread than in other countries of the region. (Note that Myanmar is now catching up in leaps and bounds.) Aung San Suu Kyi also traveled to various parts of the country in 2002, 2003, 2012, and 2015. Everywhere she sought out crowds to convince them of her cause.[11] The documents available reveal Aung San Suu Kyi and the NLD's two-pronged approach; a united population with a sacrificial will combined with international pressure would bring the junta to its knees.

Two weeks after standing up to the officer who had threatened to shoot at her, she held a speech in Myitkyina, the capital of Kachin State. The main subject of the speech was sacrifice in the service of national unity.[12] For this, Aung San Suu Kyi recalled how her mother, by working together with nurses of different ethnicities, had set a real-life example for national unity. In order to achieve this unity today, the people had to summon a sense of selflessness themselves.

> I think the BSPP gained control of the government because the citizens failed to carry out the duties of citizenship. If we want a stable democracy in the future, every single one of us must bear this responsibility conscientiously. We must be willing to sacrifice. We must understand that there is great merit in sacrificing for others and that by doing so we live the full life.[13]

With the backdrop of her own courageous approach as demonstrated a few days earlier, Aung San Suu Kyi called for her listeners to do as she did. Not a word was said about the upcoming elections. The fundamental issue for her was adopting the correct democratic attitude. She was aware of the fact that this would involve a long process, so she focused on the youth. In a speech on National Day on December 3, 1988, she said,

> I should like the students and young people to continue their work while keeping in mind that we can win. We still have . . . great work yet to do and not merely for months. We are going to have to work and struggle for years. Even if there are elections and the forces of democracy win, the movement is not yet finished. . . . The youth of today will have possibly fifty years of struggle ahead of them.[14]

What Aung San Suu Kyi is demanding is a profound change in consciousness from the generation that chose her as their leader on August 26, 1988. She sent similar appeals to international organizations as of September 1988.[15] She continuously called for compliance with human rights as the basis of a democratic government in which the will of the majority would be respected.[16] To some extent, Aung San Suu Kyi was trying to launch a colossal education and development program in which the elections formed just one milestone. In order to achieve this particular milestone, Aung San Suu Kyi had to play by the junta's rules in some ways (which she also did by participating in the elections) but at the same time embody a fundamental critique of the system for the sake of the higher and further goal. The parallels to today are manifold.

The SLORC, too, found itself in a conundrum. In its first postcoup declaration, the junta had announced that elections would be held. However, elections were only to be the fourth step, after the restoration of law and order, the securing of communication channels in the country, and an improvement of economic conditions. The first two self-assigned tasks had been completed at least superficially, but there was no sign of any great flourishing of the economy six months after the coup. In an interview at the beginning of 1989, Saw Maung, the junta's chairman, clarified that the elections would take place before the introduction of any long-term investment plans.[17] Furthermore, Aung San Suu Kyi's first appearances had made it clear that the number of people opposed to the junta increased in correlation with support for her. It could therefore be expected that elections would lead to a win for Aung San Suu Kyi, even if the party leader herself could no longer participate in the process as of July 1989.

The SLORC's behavior in the run-up to the elections was thus unsurprisingly inconsistent.[18] The junta's leader, Saw Maung, said early on that the military had no intention of running the government for longer than was necessary. In early 1989, when a journalist asked him what he would do after the elections, he responded, "I'll retire (laughs). Those who are still young enough will carry on."[19] A few months later at one of the regular press conferences, the junta's press contact said,

> We cannot transfer power as soon as the elections are held. The government would be formed according to a constitution. If the state power is hurriedly transferred, it would lead to a shaky and weak government. This can be worked out by any person with intelligence. Stability can be achieved only by systematically forming a government based on a constitution.[20]

Such wording was in line with the concept of constitutional government to which the Tatmadaw adhered. Aung San Suu Kyi was aware of the uncertainty of the situation. In her last interview before she went into house arrest, she said that she was working on the basis that the first thing to do after the elections would be to work out a constitution. This would have to happen prior to the transfer of government power. The problem was that no one knew just how a constitution could be formally and concretely adopted.[21]

The elections also represented a stepping stone for the junta. They were to be a transition to a new state regime, where law and order reigned supreme. This, too, required a new constitution, since the one from 1974 had been put out of force after the coup.

There were very different perceptions as to what this new constitution would look like, but it boiled down to this: one of the first tasks of the new parliament would have to be to pass a resolution to prepare a constitution.[22] In all, the political actors after the coup were navigating a realm that lacked a constitutional framework. In this vacuum, there were no rules to guide the expression of political disagreements.

Still, elections were held and were—to the surprise of both domestic and international observers—free and fair. The NLD won just under 60

NLD election aides on election day (May 27, 1990) in front of campaign banners showing Tin Oo and Aung San Suu Kyi. (Photo: Getty/Sandro Tucci)

percent of the vote and, thanks to the first-past-the-post election system inherited from the British, more than 82 percent of seats in parliament.[23] This was a clear rejection of the military and a confirmation of the popularity of Aung San Suu Kyi, whose portrait the party had used for campaigning all around the country.

The NLD demanded a parliamentary assembly and expected to subsequently take over the political responsibility for the country. Yet the parliament never convened. Just like the mass demonstrations of August and September 1988, the events following the 1990 elections appear to be the result of a massive failure in communication where, in hindsight, each side would blame the other.[24] In 1988, the representatives of the socialist regime and the leaders of the opposition had failed to reach a settlement. Now, the military leadership and the winning party could not even agree on simple facts, let alone the modalities of further engagement.

Both sides lacked direction, albeit in different ways. With Aung San Suu Kyi and Tin Oo under house arrest since July 1989, the NLD had been left without a leader in the run-up to the elections. The SLORC, on the other hand, had Khin Nyunt—someone with an ability to think. However, this first secretary was just a pawn of Saw Maung's. Saw Maung was not at the head of the junta because of his political aptitude; rather, it was because he had happened to be the commander-in-chief of the armed forces just before Ne Win's unexpected resignation. Under Ne Win's successor, he became the defense minister and after the coup, because of the hierarchy of military ranks, automatically took the position of chairman of the junta. Taking over the offices connected with this position, namely as head of state, prime minister, and foreign minister, was hopelessly beyond his capacities.[25] In short, competent leaders who could manage the transition were unavailable on both sides.

There were other peculiarities to the elections. Both sides could simultaneously feel like the winners and the losers. The NLD, under Aung San Suu Kyi's indirect leadership, had clearly won the elections. The government for its part had managed to hold free and fair elections.

Yet the military was seen as the loser both nationally and internationally, and the NLD's victory led to an impasse.

After the elections, the SLORC pushed ahead with the previously announced preparation of a constitution, in which the military government would only take on the role of a jury. On July 27, 1990, the junta announced that until a constitution was put in place, it regarded itself to be the only legitimate government of the country. This extended to the legislative, executive, and judicial branches. It thus distanced itself from its original assurance of taking over governmental power only temporarily.

Two days later, the NLD's elected representatives met and demanded that the newly elected parliament be convened in November at the latest. In August, monks in Mandalay started protesting against the government. Alms were no longer accepted from members of the military and their families. This was a serious act. It amounted to the military's expulsion from the Buddhist community. The monks drew a moral-religious line. This put the military in the same category as the heathen British, against whom the monks had protested during colonial times. The protests were smothered after a while through arrests.

An alternate government emerged as a result of the unbridgeable rift that appeared after the elections. Some elected representatives of the NLD and friendly parties fled to the Thai border after several meetings within the country. They founded a government-in-exile in Manerplaw, which had been the headquarters for anti–central government fighters of the Karen National Union since 1975. They did this under the leadership of a cousin of Aung San Suu Kyi.[26] Thus, this Thai border came to mark the third symbolic seat of power, with the other two being the official seat of government and Aung San Suu Kyi's house. Besides the Karen, other ethnic rebel groups had their headquarters in Manerplaw. Now dissidents of the Burmese majority, including many students, joined them. The great shortcoming of the large new coalition was that it was only held together by its opposition to the military junta.

In any case, a compromise between elected parliamentarians and the organizers of the elections was out of the question. Thus began the next stage of internal political conflict. The Western world contributed to this by seeing Aung San Suu Kyi in a one-sided way as a victim of the confrontation, when it was in fact a confrontation that she was very much entangled in.

From Electoral Victory to the Nobel Prize

The Aris family accepting the Nobel Peace Prize on December 10, 1991, in Oslo. (From left to right: Alexander, Kim, Michael). (Photo: Picture Alliance)

Aung San Suu Kyi was awarded numerous prizes after 1990. In many cases the prize givers were more honored by her acceptance of it than she by the award. The wave of honors and recognitions began shortly after the 1990 elections. The crown, of course, was the Nobel Peace Prize in 1991, received just three years after the start of her political engagement. Oxford's St. Hugh's College, which had refused to let her pursue a further academic career because of her low BA grades, now named her an honorary fellow. In September of the same year, she was awarded a Norwegian prize named after Thoralf Rafto, a human rights activist who spoke up for the rights of Eastern European dissidents. In December, the European Parliament announced that the Sakharov Prize would be awarded to Aung San Suu Kyi in July 1991. This prize is named after Andrei Sakharov, the Russian physicist and dissident who won the Nobel Peace Prize in 1975. The prize was first awarded in 1988 to none other than Nelson Mandela. Aung San Suu Kyi was the winner in the award's third year.[27]

Both prizes that Aung San Suu Kyi was awarded in 1991 can be understood as being part of a global political shift. In the beginning of 1986, Mikhail Gorbachev led the perestroika, which culminated in the end of the cold war and the fall of the Soviet Union and the Eastern Bloc. The dissolution of the Communist Party of Burma and the end of state socialism in the country can be seen as byproducts of this development. A new era was on the horizon. The global victory parade of human rights and democracy seemed irreversible. In his famous essay published in 1990, Francis Fukuyama proclaimed the end of history.[28]

This is the context within which the prizes extended to Aung San Suu Kyi by the various committees in Bergen, Strasbourg, and Oslo should be placed. They were an investment in the future. The prize committees' hope was that their recognitions would contribute to Burma—like the rest of the world—moving towards a future where human rights were respected, democracy prevailed, and various ethnic groups formed friendly relations with one another.[29]

However, these good intentions had an unintended and counterproductive side effect. In their reasoning behind the award, the committees took on statements made by Aung San Suu Kyi during her first speech, the one delivered under the pagoda in August 1988. These statements were now also published in a book by Michael Aris. The book and the Peace Prize worked to strengthen the diametric opposition between the "democratic" forces on the one hand and the "brutal" regime on the other.

The timing of the prize is important. Just like Aung San Suu Kyi's presence in Burma in April 1988 because of her mother's illness turned out to be fateful, there was something fateful about Aung San Suu Kyi's

Nobel Prize nomination. The first initiative towards this came from a friend of the couple, John Finnis, an Australian lawyer studying in Oxford. Later the proposal was supported by Vaclav Havel, who had formerly fought against the communist regime in Czechoslovakia and was now, since 1989, the president of his country. During a visit to Prague in September 2013, Aung San Suu Kyi said that he forewent his own nomination for her.[30] The committee predominantly relied on information coming from those close to the future prizewinner. This was unsurprising as little was known of Burma in the West until 1988.

Her eldest son, Alexander, speaking on her behalf on December 10, 1991, in Oslo added some liberal comments on the Burmese economy to his praise of his mother's struggle for democracy and human rights. He expressed the conviction that through the "sheer economic unworkability of totalitarianism this present regime will be swept away" after mismanaging the country for thirty years and that "the Burmese government is undoubtedly reaping as it has sown."[31] This remark did not account for the fact that the SLORC had acknowledged the economic failure of the "Burmese Way to Socialism" and tried to implement some kind of market-oriented economy that welcomed foreign investment. This invitation was, however, rejected by the Western powers, and subsequent sanctions were supported by Aung San Suu Kyi.

The awarding of the Nobel Peace Prize in October hardened the SLORC's attitude towards Aung San Suu Kyi and her supporters, reflected in the libelous reports that followed in state-controlled media. Ironically, this led to a further elevation of Aung San Suu Kyi's role. Those in power in the country accused Suu Kyi of being a puppet of the West. Western media that broadcast through radio in Myanmar was accused of wanting to destabilize the country. Multiple cartoons in the state newspapers continuously reiterated this message. One of them depicted Alfred Nobel appearing to a patriotic Burmese citizen in a dream saying, "The Nobel Prize given to your nation is no peace prize, it is the dynamite that I invented."

The Oslo prize marked the beginning of a development characterized and criticized by Bertil Lintner—one of the fiercest opponents of the

Newspaper cartoon on the Nobel Peace Prize. (From the Working People's Daily)

military regime—as a deification of Aung San Suu Kyi.[32] A cult started to develop around her without any encouragement from her. She later distanced herself from it, albeit without actively opposing it. During the time of her house arrest, she was not only the junta's captive but also a captive of her admirers.

Aung San Suu Kyi could only personally accept the Nobel Peace Prize on June 16, 2012, after a delay of twenty-one years. The speech she gave on this occasion provides some indication of why she behaved the way she did in the early 1990s.[33] She started with an anecdote from her time in Oxford, when she told her son Alexander that she may one day win the Nobel Prize for Literature. Both had then laughed at this "welcome but unlikely" prospect. Now it was her audience that laughed at this point.[34] When she received the message about her winning the Nobel Peace Prize, she was not surprised. Her husband had already informed her of the nomination. She described her immediate reaction to the message: "It did not seem quite real because in a sense I did not feel myself to be quite real at that time."[35]

She was referring to the time of house arrest when, in her own words, she felt as if she were living in an unreal, parallel world. Through the various news broadcasts that she listened to on the radio, the prize slowly and gradually brought her back to reality and the human community. More importantly, the prize had drawn the world's attention to the fight for democracy and human rights in Burma. She and those who had been fighting for this ideal in her country had not been forgotten. For to be forgotten, she held, is similar to dying.

With these words, Aung San Suu Kyi identified her own fate with that of her people "forgotten" by global society. The Nobel Prize reassured her of herself and her mission, with which she had captivated her audience during her first appearance in August 1988. With her several gifts—intelligence, diligence, wit, and, of course, charisma—she dedicated herself to the great cause. She had become part of a global movement. There was a connection between the people of Burma, who were just making the long journey towards a genuine democracy, and the international community, which was just celebrating the third wave of democracy.[36] Aung San Suu Kyi, like Gandhi, Martin Luther King Jr., and Nelson Mandela, became a symbol of this connection between global and local movements, which—ideally—are mutually reinforcing. This happened without regard for the fact that her Western admirers had no conception of what "democracy" could actually mean in a Southeast Asian country.[37]

Encounters without Consequences

The encouragement that Aung San Suu Kyi received through the great prize from Oslo during her house arrest led, as previously mentioned, to an aggravation of the tension between her and the SLORC. This in turn brought intermediaries to the scene.

In July 1995, during the latter period of her house arrest, Aung San Suu Kyi met with a number of foreign visitors as well as the leaders of the military. These meetings raised hopes in Myanmar as well as outside. People imagined that despite their fundamental differences, the junta and Suu Kyi could come to an understanding. Disappointment quickly followed; all three meetings led to no results. Not even rudimentary progress was made to resolve the conflict between the two sides.

The American congressman Bill Richardson visited Myanmar for one and a half days in February 1994. He had met Khin Nyunt in the preceding year, who had promised to let Richardson meet Suu Kyi. This was one of the parliamentarian's many private missions. As someone who spoke with dictators, Richardson described himself as "undersecretary for thugs" in his autobiography. He spoke twice with Khin Nyunt and Aung San Suu Kyi as well as with prominent prisoners in Insein Prison. During his first visit to University Avenue, he delivered to the lady of the house a personal letter from President Bill Clinton.[38]

Richardson gave a press conference in Bangkok after his visit to Myanmar. He described his trip as "a very productive visit," praised Aung San Suu Kyi as someone who stood for the best ideals of democracy, and called Khin Nyunt "a pragmatic individual" who was sincerely committed to resolving the country's problems. He was convinced that "the Burmese should settle the Burmese issue. And not outsiders."[39] He hoped that his mediation would contribute to both sides speaking directly with each other. He had wanted to allow for a "predialogue" to take place in order to build each side's trust in the other. The transcript was published in its full length a day later in the Burmese state media. A leading member of the SLORC highlighted the phrase that it was not foreigners but the Burmese who had to solve their own problems—a familiar topic in Burmese politics, especially under Ne Win.

The minutes of the discussion between Richardson, his two escorts, and Aung San Suu Kyi were published a good two months later.[40] From this publication one can gather that Aung San Suu Kyi rejected any cult surrounding her person and insisted that there be a dialogue between the SLORC and the NLD. Democracy had to be founded on solid principles and not on individuals, as was generally the case in the political systems of Asia. A liberal democracy based on a Western model was needed and not a "Burmese path to democracy" mirroring the failure of the Burmese Way to Socialism. She called for a dialogue on equal footing with the SLORC and was of the opinion that intermediaries were not needed in Burma, because the conflict here was not—like in other parts of the world—a conflict between different peoples. She called on the United States to put further pressure on the government. The SLORC, according to her, was unpredictable and one could currently not trust it. She explained that the junta's actions were "led by fear" and some of its members had not behaved like "officers and gentlemen."

In August 1994, a few months after Richardson's first visit, Rewata Dhamma traveled to Myanmar.[41] He was a Burma-born Buddhist monk now living in England who had previously met Aung San Suu Kyi in India and London. His conversations with her, Khin Nyunt, and the head of the junta, Than Shwe, were part of a mission that he had planned together with a UN diplomat in 1993. High hopes were placed in this visit. A monk would be well placed to mediate between Buddhists. Nothing is known of the content of his conversations. In the end, the initiative came to nothing.[42]

The greatest hope was placed in the meetings that took place between Aung San Suu Kyi and the leaders of the junta in September and October of 1994. The state media of Myanmar also reported on these. She met with Than Shwe and Khin Nyunt on September 20. Another meeting took place with Khin Nyunt and other government officials on October 29. No announcements were made in relation to the content of the meetings, except that they were amicable. The public drew connections

"Family dinner" 1994. Next to Aung San Suu Kyi: Khin Nyunt (left) and Than Shwe (right). (Photo: Ministry of Information)

between the meetings and Rewata Dhamma's visit from the preceding month, and saw a possible beginning of a substantive dialogue between the two sides.

However, January 23, 1995, brought an end to all speculation about Aung San Suu Kyi's possible involvement in any initiatives to negotiate with the leaders of the junta. On this day, after visiting his wife, Michael Aris delivered a statement written by her to a press conference in Bangkok. The statement was about the two meetings with the leaders of the junta. Aung San Suu Kyi had participated in discussions with SLORC leaders as a measure of good will; however, she insisted,

> There have not been and there will not be any secret deals with regard either to my release or to any other issue. I adhere to the principle of accountability and consider myself at all times bound by the democratic duty to act in consultation with colleagues and to be guided by the aspirations of those engaged in the movement to establish a truly democratic political system in Burma. I remain dedicated to an active participation in this movement.[43]

With this she once again clearly stated that her attitude towards the government had seen no fundamental change in the six years of house arrest. She again insisted on a substantive dialogue between the opposition forces and the government—a request that had also been sanctioned by a UN general assembly resolution in December 1994.

The different meetings that took place in 1994 are evidence of her well-known openness to speaking with everyone. However, in line with her principles, speaking to the SLORC could only really happen under the auspices of her party's support and ultimately the will of the majority of the Burmese population. Both sides thus had differing ideas as to what the preconditions for a dialogue would be. The junta saw the dialogue as a negotiation between family members, who could discuss their differences in opinion without any external pressure. Aung San Suu Kyi, however, insisted that the international standards formulated by the United Nations be the foundation for any discussion.

The heightened international attention and the involuntary badge of "democracy icon" that came with it were in fact a double-edged sword. The Nobel Prize and visits by Richardson and others showed that Aung San Suu Kyi's sphere of influence had grown. She could now exert pressure on the junta through international intermediaries. However, as illustrated by the Bangkok declaration, her raised stature ran the risk of losing contact with the party base and her supporters. Last but not least, the internationalization of the conflict made it increasingly difficult to negotiate with the SLORC, who insisted upon an internal, domestic resolution. The antagonism within the country intensified.

CHAPTER 6

The People's Voice

We will succeed when we are united on our sense of responsibility
and sacrifice.

The news of Aung San Suu Kyi being released from house arrest spread like wildfire in Yangon in early July of 1995. A hectic bustle of activity started in front of the house on University Avenue. Than Shwe's message of her release meant not only that Aung San Suu Kyi would now be free to leave her house but also that she could once again receive visitors— and without any special permit from the government. In the last five years, besides the house help Maria, Aung San Suu Kyi's doctor, the soldiers who guarded her house, and her military intermediary, no one was allowed access to her unless they held a special permit from the government.

Her first visitors were the so-called uncles, or the older men who together with Aung San Suu Kyi formed the leadership of the NLD.[1] They were her colleagues in the business of politics. As she stated in the Bangkok announcement delivered by her husband in January, these men were the ones whose backing she sought before making decisions. Tin Oo had stopped serving as party chairman since 1991, when the election commission had disqualified him like Aung San Suu Kyi. Aung Shwe, also former military, had stepped into his place. Kyi Maung was more politically active. He had also originally made a career in the military and like Tin Oo had spent some time in jail under Ne Win. He had been the NLD spokesman before the 1990 elections.

The party leadership saw its primary task as being the reorganization of the NLD, a party weakened through the government's repressive measures. This reorganization was completed in October, at least to the extent of filling key positions. Aung Shwe remained chairman, Tin Oo and Kyi Maung became his deputies, and Aung San Suu Kyi once again took the post of general secretary.[2]

At the same time, Aung San Suu Kyi had to deal with an onrush of foreign visitors. She gave various press conferences and patiently answered questions, regardless of whether they were banal questions about her private life or questions about her political stance and her role as an opposition leader. Here is a selection:[3]

Q: Have you had contact with your husband?

A: No! Not at all. I don't have a telephone in the house.

Q: Did you expect your release this time?

A: Well, to tell the truth, I thought I would be released around the first week of August. I thought that the authorities would wait for people to give up hope that I haven't been released and then suddenly release me. But obviously, I was wrong and I am very grateful to say that they have observed the law strictly this time.

Q: Could you work with Gen Khin Nyunt and Gen Than Shwe?

A: Oh, I can work with anybody. Why not?

Q: The election in 1990, the main subject was the dialogue with the government.

A: I'm sorry. Oh, the election of 1990. The most important thing about the election of 1990 is: it expressed the will of the people, very clearly. And that should be one of the main subjects of the dialogue with the government. The will of the people. Because, true democracy means respecting the will of the people, identifying it and respecting it.

Q: When do you think the democracy will come?

A: I am not a fortune teller, you know. I never encourage people to go to fortune tellers. And this is not the sort of thing that I ever encourage.

Q: The government controls the information. So, how do you inform people about your ideas?

A: Through people like you!

Q: Do you think that the SLORC government would change and start a dialogue with you?

A: I hope that they will change to do whatever they see to be the will of the people. I hope that they will study the will of the people. I hope that they will listen to the voice of the people and act accordingly. I am sure that they also desire what is good for the nation.

Q: Are you optimistic about the future of Burma?

A: Yes, I am cautiously optimistic about the future of the country. Because I believe in the people. I believe in the people. I think they have some way to go. I think we all have to change. I think we all need to improve ourselves. But I think basically there is a lot of good in Burma.

Q: Would you mind telling me your body weight?

A: 106 pounds.

Q: What changes have to be made?

A: I think that we have to change the way people think. It is only by changing the way that people think that we can progress towards peace. I think that the change is coming. I think that many people are beginning to realise now that material development is not everything. The last century has been one of material development, great material development, but I think that people are now starting to realise that material development did not bring with it more happiness as it were.

Aung San Suu Kyi demonstrated a continuous willingness to provide information both domestically and when speaking with international media. This confirmed that she really believed in what she had told the American politician Bill Richardson, namely that international perceptions and the resulting political pressure on the government would have a positive influence on the development of her country.[4]

Different Forms of Dialogue

Within the sphere of domestic politics, Aung San Suu Kyi's main concern remained unchanged. She was going to push for a dialogue between the government and the NLD as well as other "democratic forces" within the country. As an example, she again referred to South Africa, where a successful dialogue had taken place despite international isolation.

Already a year and a half before the end of Aung San Suu Kyi's house arrest the government had started its own particular brand of political exchange. It had put a national convention in place that was tasked with working out a new constitution, since the parliament elected in 1990—which could have taken on this task—never convened. The assembly comprised representatives of all groups within the country in accordance with a formula prescribed by the junta. The parties were represented too, but not in a way proportionate to the election outcome of 1990.[5] The assembly had to work in accordance with six principles. The last of these stated that the armed forces were to play a "leading role" in the politics of the nation in the future.

In its second sitting in September 1993, the assembly adopted a further 104 basic principles. These principles formed the foundation for further work on the constitution and were individually discussed and deliberated upon by the assembly until its conclusion in September 2007. With respect to the role of the military, it was decided that 25 percent of the members of parliamentary bodies would be named from the high command of the armed forces. In addition, key ministries, such as defense, interior, and the ministry of border affairs, would be filled by the military. This arrangement remains valid today.

This method employed by the junta to "explore" the people's will was unacceptable to Aung San Suu Kyi. She had made this clear during her conversation with Bill Richardson and his fellow visitors. Before answering her guests' first question on the political state of the country, she asked how the visitors saw the national convention. After obtaining her visitors' skeptical answers, Aung San Suu Kyi summarized her opinion with the sentence, "It is very much a façade."[6]

Aung San Suu Kyi saw herself as a figurehead for the 1990-elected NLD and thus as a legitimate representative of the people's will, if only for a transitory period. Her responses show that she perceived of herself as the "voice of the people." She found the focus on individual persons to be damaging as there were already so many who wanted to be in charge. "I don't want the focus to be on individuals—there can't be all chiefs and no Indians."[7]

The pressure on the NLD had increased with the entrance of the Union Solidarity and Development Association (USDA). This was a mass organization set up by the government in 1993. It counted twenty-four million members by 2007. It was, at least on paper, real competition to Aung San Suu Kyi's party. The NLD had also largely lacked orientation in the years without its charismatic leader. The democratic movement thus found itself on the defensive during the summer of 1995. Aung San Suu Kyi had to find new ways of connecting with the people, acknowledging their will, and delivering her own message.

The first chance for this came immediately after her release. It was in fact the international media that had conveyed the news of her release to her supporters. The state media only came to publish this important information when reporting on the Martyrs' Day celebrations, which are held each year to commemorate Aung San. The report included a photo of her at the Martyrs' Mausoleum. Aung San Suu Kyi took part in the memorial activities for the first time in seven years. In 1988, she had stood in for her ill mother. In the following year, she had refused to participate in the activities planned by the government and had announced a competing NLD event instead. This in turn had led to her house arrest. Now, in 1995, the events had come full circle.

Ten days before the festivities, hundreds of supporters—informed by the international press—gathered in front of the gates of 54 University Avenue. Everyone wanted to see the revered daughter of the great father for themselves. The numbers became larger and larger in the following days. Each time, Aung San Suu Kyi spoke briefly—standing on a chair or a table—to the people beyond the gate and the wall that surrounded her house. She reassured those beyond of what her husband Michael Aris had already told the press in Bangkok: she had made no secret deals with the junta. She also pleaded for patience and warned against inflated hopes.[8]

As was the case at the pagoda in August 1988, it was primarily the fact that she was *there* (again) that electrified people. "I am so happy, I just

Aung San Suu Kyi, accompanied by Lt. Gen. Than Tun, her military relations officer, at the ceremony on Martyrs' Day, July 19, 1995. (Photo: Getty)

Aung San Suu Kyi on July 20, 1995, at the gate of her house. (Photo: Reuters)

want to see her," one visitor told a reporter.[9] Another stated that there was now hope for the country. But there were also fears that she could now be in danger, given that she was free again and could pursue her mission.

It was no longer just the magic of her name that drew the masses as it had done in August 1988. Now it was the magic of her person, who with her willingness for sacrifice had proven that she was serious about her efforts for her people. Just like seven years earlier, calls of "long live Aung San Suu Kyi!" decorated the air. She was no longer just the daughter following in the footsteps of a famous father. She had proven that she was fully worthy of his legacy.

Foreign political observers present in the country commented on Aung San Suu Kyi's release with guarded optimism, echoing her own assessment. The governments of numerous countries and a range of organizations that supported the opposition movement in Myanmar expressed their support. They revealed their hope that the release may herald a process of reconciliation. However, they also remained skeptical and questioned whether the measure was not just a tactical move by the government to placate the international community.

For Aung San Suu Kyi, nothing was more important than finally being able to have contact with her supporters. In one of the first press conferences she said,

> I always feel very at home with the people. When I meet them, [it is] just like meeting friends and family. They were very informal. . . . They treat me very much as a friend, as family, as elder sister, their younger [sister] or aunt or their daughter. . . . I like the fact that they are not afraid to talk to me. And they are not afraid to disagree with me. But when I [reason with] them, then, they [accept] it. I feel very proud of my people when I meet them like that. So, they are so [kind], and they don't look to me like somebody great and big but just as somebody who belongs to them. And that is [a] very nice feeling.[10]

After six years, Aung San Suu Kyi was once again reunited with the people for whom she was targeting her efforts. But the statement above is more than just an emotional expression of relief. The quote illustrates an important political conviction: society is like a family, where members can ideally freely express their opinions and resolve problems through mutual dialogue. By promoting open critique that can be expressed free of fear or persecution, Aung San Suu Kyi is also distancing herself from the preceding government under Ne Win and the military government, where free speech was not approved of. The cited passage is a further refinement of Aung San Suu Kyi's 1989 thesis that democracy for the people in Myanmar is an "integrated social system." She thus keeps within the Burmese tradition of the government playing more than an administrative role in the country. Following the great leaders of the past, the government must also set out a moral order in service of the people, based on Buddhist teachings. The big sister Aung San Suu Kyi was on her way to becoming the mother of the nation.

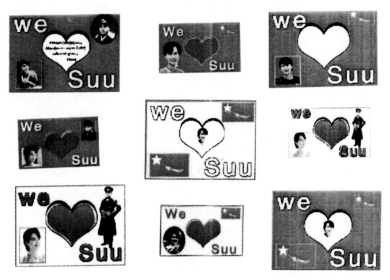

Stickers sold in Yangon in 2012. (Photo: Hans-Bernd Zöllner)

Talks over the Gate

The family-like relationship became especially clear in the speeches that Aung San Suu Kyi gave to her supporters in 1995 and 1996. At first these were spontaneous communications after her release. The talks quickly became "unofficially institutionalized." The authorities never gave their formal permission but tolerated the proceedings on both sides of 54 University Avenue, in front of the compound gate. The audience that gathered in front of her house, filling both sides of the busy road, was addressed from behind the gate. Policemen were present to prevent accidents. Vendors sold drinks and snacks. It was a weekly weekend event, a mixture of regular pilgrimage, political demonstration, public lecture, and festival. Some of these speeches were recorded, and the audio and video recordings circulated through Yangon.[11] Of these, twenty-five transcripts landed in Japan, where they were published.[12] These speeches provide an insight into the political family that had gathered around Aung San Suu Kyi.[13] The tradition started at the end of August or the beginning of September 1995. Only Aung San Suu Kyi spoke on Saturdays. On Sundays, Tin Oo and Kyi Maung, the two deputy chairmen of the NLD, also spoke. The speeches by the two "uncles" have not been passed down in the records.

There are some noteworthy aspects to the speeches. Aung San Suu Kyi answered questions that had been put into her mailbox. The speeches were thus more like dialogues or were, in a sense, directed by the people. This method was a very practical way of demonstrating how power in a democracy rested with the people. Those with political responsibility had to remain accountable. This arrangement also showed that the people trusted Aung San Suu Kyi and at the same time hoped to learn something from her.

During the weekly address, Aung San Suu Kyi always appeared as part of a team, which also included younger people besides the old coleaders of the party. Two young party members stood silent on both sides of the speakers; others guarded the gate. This symbolically illustrated how the future of the NLD, as of the whole country, depended on the youth. The party urgently needed to nurture its next generation. Not only was the party leadership composed of older people, also the party base lacked qualified young members. This challenge still exists today.[14]

The number of participants was limited due to external restrictions. The listeners stood on both sides of the street while traffic passed through. It is estimated that up to five thousand visitors participated in the weekly event. Whether all of them could hear what was being said through the loudspeakers set up over the gates is unknown.

The dialogues between the people and Suu Kyi were of course asymmetrical. The questions were generally short, the answers much longer. The speaker would sometimes add her own elaborations, which were often unconnected to a question. Follow-up questions were—because of the nature of the setup—only possible through interruptions and in exceptional cases.

The setup was improvised and provisional. It came about as a result of a compromise; the military junta wanted to prevent another breach of peace and order and at the same time keep its promise of letting Aung San Suu Kyi's release take place without any conditions. Aung San Suu Kyi once herself pointed to the curious character of the weekly event; here the participants had the freedom to ask their questions anonymously, but they could not otherwise freely express themselves due to a lack of legal and political protections normally granted within a democracy.[15] Both she and her audience were, as she later put it elsewhere, still "prisoners in [their] own country."[16] It was but a small playing field for freedom that the authorities granted on University Avenue during the weekends.

At the beginning of the first recorded address, Aung San Suu Kyi briefly clarifies the house rules. The weekly event was to give people an opportunity to put their concerns into words—complaints, factual questions, goals, and hopes. Aggressive questioning would not receive a response.

The questions put to the speaker provide an insight into the way of thinking of the Burmese population in the mid-1990s and—importantly—into the expectations of the voters who had chosen Aung San Suu Kyi and her party in 1990.

A selection of the questions and answers from the first available set of notes, from Saturday, September 23, 1995, shows what a large spectrum of queries was put to Aung San Suu Kyi:[17]

Q: Is it possible for Burma to become a modern state, or the capital Rangoon to become a city of high standard of living? (applause)
A: Only when our people's basic needs for food, shelter, clothing, and for health care, education and public transport are met, we can call our nation a modern nation, in our opinion (applause).
Q: Can you explain the concept of democracy by the father of our nation, Aung San.
A: He said "A genuine democratic system is not just a government of the people, by the people and for the people theoretically. A democratic government has to be able to provide equal opportunities for the people economically."
Q: Are Shwe Pyi Thar, the author of *A Person Like Maung Ba Than*, and MS, the author of *It's Time for Pragmatic Analysis in Burma*, professional [propagandists]? [Both had published in state media previously.]
A: I don't know . . . I do not read such writings and I do not even know their names. . . . I would like to urge the people to read valuable literature when you have time.
Q: If there are foreign dignitaries inspecting Than Hlyin–Rangoon bridge, the bridge is usually closed at least four hours before their visit. Cooking is not allowed at our homes. Shops are shut down. How do we survive the Visit Myanmar Year 1996?
A: They ordered not to cook, right? Then we should go fasting in the year 1996. . . . We just want to change the system that does not care for the people. We do not want power. We want democracy.
Q: What should one make of the government's claim that foreign radio channels spread lies?

Monument commemorating the completion of the Yangon-Thanlyin Bridge on July 31, 1993. (Photo: Hans-Bernd Zöllner)

A: The main problem of our country is that there is no free press.

Q: What radio station broadcasts 'a skyful of lies?' (applause) [the phrase "a skyful of lies" was a stereotype in common use by the state media to characterize foreign media outlets and foreign news]

A: It depends. When a radio station attacks you, you call it "a skyful of lies." If the same station says what you like, it is airing the truth. We do not want to use the term "skyful of lies" since it is a pejorative. Our politics are not meant to slight anybody. Our criticism is aimed only at policy and ideological levels. . . . The lack of freedom of expression and freedom of press often lead to unreliable information.

Q: Many trees are being planted to commemorate the diamond jubilee of Rangoon University. I would like to request that the Student Union building[18] which was built to commemorate the golden jubilee of the Rangoon University be rebuilt for the diamond jubilee.

A: Are we the right people to answer this question? Of course, I do want to help. But I do not have any authority to do that. Time will come, I believe, when we can rebuild the union. (applause) Students, do not despair. Time will come.

Bo Aung Gyaw's tomb in October 2017 near the entrance of Yangon University's gate. The wreaths were laid down some months before by the NLD. (Photo: Hans-Bernd Zöllner)

Q: These days we often hear talks about nationalism. Wouldn't you like to build a grand mausoleum for Bo Aung Kyaw [A student who died in anticolonial protests in 1938]. His tomb has been covered with grass and weeds. (applause)

A: These days nationalism is being used for ad hominem attacks. This makes nationalism sound cheap. . . . If Bo Aung Kyaw's tomb is weedy, why doesn't the student who asked the question go weed it? (laughter)

Aung San Suu Kyi with Tin Oo (left) and Kyi Maung (right) and young party members on Sunday, March 10, 1996. (Photo: Hans-Bernd Zöllner)

Q: How does building hotels, as if one were attempting to drown in a dry creek, benefit people?

A: This implies that hotel business does not affect the employment rate. This is why I think hotel business is good only for hotel-related people, not for the general population. (applause)

Q: Girl students from the ninth grade . . . they ask if an organization can be set up without defining objectives, basic principles, responsibilities and duties of members such as chairperson and general secretary.[19]

A: If you join an organization because of rewards, the organization must be a hollow shell without any essence. (applause)

Q: These days road accidents can cost drivers severe punishment as if accidents were murders or robberies. Is it fair?

A: To be honest I don't know what punishment should be handed down for a driver who has caused an accident since I'm not a law expert. Please ask law experts such legalistic questions. I don't want to pretend to know things that I don't really know.

Q: What about democracy and Burmese culture.

A: In our Buddhist culture, one of the ten royal codes of ethics is 'thou shall not oppose your people.' It's a democratic concept.

As the transcripts show, the speaker's words were again and again punctuated with applause and laughter. The listeners are inclined to agree with everything she says. The audience trusts her and the affirmation is reflected in the ritualistic nature of the event; at the beginning and at the end, the listeners wished her good health and a long life three times.

Foreign visitors were fascinated by this atmosphere, even though language constraints kept them from understanding the content of the messages. A young Canadian writer commented, "It doesn't matter that I don't understand. . . . The small woman who stands on a table and smiles at the crowd when she speaks . . . this woman is the myth incarnate, the beautiful warm-hearted heroine, the daughter of her father. . . . We Westerners are not her real audience."[20] Amitav Ghosh, the Indian author of the novel *The Glass Palace*—which ends with a chapter on Aung San Suu Kyi's entry into politics—writes after a visit to one of her weekend speeches, "In listening to her, and thinking of what she had been through and achieved, we could not but marvel at the extent of her sacrifice, the greatness of her commitment."[21] In due course, the weekly speeches also became a foreign tourist attraction. As a result, in mid-1996, Aung San Suu Kyi started the practice of giving a short summary in English at the end of her talk.[22]

Many Questions

Before answering the questions put to her, Aung San Suu Kyi usually hinted at the author of the question. She only rarely stated actual names; generally it was pseudonyms or self-descriptions that conveyed the questioner's stance or background. Many of them "love democracy"; one was identified as someone who "hates lies." Of the roughly two hundred questions answered in the twenty-five speeches, fewer than half mentioned the professions of the individuals who asked the question. The largest group was comprised of students or "young people," followed by twelve men who identified themselves as monks. These two groups were also the ones that voiced the majority opinion and had protested against the government since the beginning of the nationalist movement in the 1920s. Only four of the questioners were identified as coming from the countryside, which is where the majority of the Burmese population lives to this day.

"Democracy" appears more frequently than any other keyword among the large breadth of subjects covered. It is followed by questions about the education system and the economy. Personal questions to Aung San Suu Kyi appear less often and are only answered by her briefly and somewhat reluctantly. The questions are almost always connected to actual events, mostly on news and articles in the state media, as well as measures introduced by the government. The questions and answers cited above in relation to the mass organization USDA confirm the widely held view that people joined the organization only because it allowed them to have certain privileges.

Then there were general knowledge questions, for example, on the history of the Association of Southeast Asian Nations (ASEAN) or whether buses in other countries were also so jam-packed. Finally, there were requests for clarification on some fundamental points: Would federalism lead to the secession of certain parts of the country? What is true peace? What are the criteria for economic advancement? What is more important—economic progress or democracy?

Aung San Suu Kyi was seen not only as an expert on abstract political problems but also as an authority on all sorts of day-to-day problems. Inhabitants of one area wanted to be able to buy cheap rice. People complained about their land being taken away from them so that others could build houses or factories on it. One father had trouble explaining the importance of completing one's studies to his son. Aung San Suu Kyi had to help with all of this.

Aung San Suu Kyi's supporters supplied her with information on the reality of life in the country in this way. She had spent a long time away from the country and had been confined to house arrest since 1989. In all, she had been cut her off from Burmese life. She could not have had such experiences herself. Besides, as she had noted in one of her speeches, she did not read the state newspapers and only became aware of what they reported through her questioning audience and the subsequent research she conducted together with her team.

The conversation that took place on weekends between the people gathered on both sides of the gate of 54 University Avenue had a multilayered significance. It was about establishing an emotional relationship between the people and Aung San Suu Kyi. For the people who went, it was like a pilgrimage to the Nobel Peace Prize winner's home. It was about an exchange of information and lastly, about reinforcing a common rejection of the ruling military government. The majority of questions had an undertone that was highly critical of the regime. This is unsurprising. A large number of questions were really about supporting Aung San Suu Kyi. They reaffirmed the united opposition and furnished it with further arguments.

The communication between Aung San Suu Kyi and her supporters thus sometimes had the air of an exchange within a closed, self-validating system. The feeling of community came about through the delineation of the "other"—the members and propagandists of the government—who operated within another closed system. Paradoxically, the weekend exchange had the effect of contradicting Aung San Suu Kyi's aim to resolve the country's problems through dialogue. After all, a dialogue always requires two parties, and it only bears fruit when both parties represent different points of view.

The second difficulty with the configuration of the weekend meetings—with the questioners on one side and the responder on the other—was the great distance between "the people" and Aung San Suu Kyi with respect to knowledge, education, political awareness, and especially the expectations for the political future of the country. Some of those asking questions behaved as if they lacked agency, and blamed the government for this. They expected groundbreaking change from Aung San Suu Kyi. The pertinent question then is what they themselves were prepared to do to bring an end to this state of dependence. The seeming unwillingness of people to *themselves* take responsibility is striking. Instead, they wanted to replace the "bad" ruler (the military) with a "good" one (Aung San Suu Kyi).

A Comprehensive Answer

Aung San Suu Kyi's answers show that she was fully aware of this issue. A number of her responses put the authors of the questions in their rightful place in a friendly but firm way. She asks her listeners to work within the options available to them and take matters in their own hands. Her answers have a clear pedagogical tone. They are aimed at closing the gap between her and the audience, and encourage the audience to free themselves from their self-imposed state of dependence: "As I said earlier, please be self-reliant and use your own initiative to right the wrongs. Please try."[23]

In essence, Aung San Suu Kyi has one underlying answer to all questions: Empower yourselves and get ready for embarking on the path to democracy. Only a collective effort will lead to the resolution of the many difficult tasks that the country is confronted with—from the concerns relating to the price of rice to the adherence to human rights. She conveys this message by connecting the concept of Western democracy to the teachings of the Buddha, as the following quote illustrates:

> A unilateral I-can-do-it-alone attitude is not democratic. It lacks the fairness of the *dhamma*. (applause) Please note that none of us can do anything alone. . . . We must not blame others for our failures. It's not at all appropriate to scapegoat others for our problems. If we do things together, we will succeed. In twenty to thirty years [*sic*] time, as I said, when a democratic system is entrenched, we will be able to leave behind our worries for democracy.[24]

She is revisiting the theme of self-reliance here—passed down from her mother—and sets out the long time frame necessary to reach the goal. The idea of collective action comes directly out of the dhamma. It requires that there be unity of democratic forces. She urges her listeners to engage in dialogue with the respective responsible authorities at the local level. She reminds her listeners that patience is needed because the government cannot be forced into such a dialogue; it can only be persuaded. Again and again she pleads with her audience to have patience. A dialogue with the government with any chance of success could only take place within this framework.

Aung San Suu Kyi suggests that Burmese governments of the past did not share this desire for unity, prescribed by the dhamma. Perhaps more importantly, they lacked the key attributes of selflessness and self-sacrifice.[25] Burma now had to learn from its mistakes of the past. Independence was achieved through Aung San and his fellow fighters' selfless acts, but deep rifts existed in the movement both before and afterwards. Her father did not live long enough to achieve his aim of uniting the country. The spirit of selflessness and self-sacrifice was needed once again now in order to realize the country's potential. Aung San Suu Kyi uses both terms frequently. She offers herself as a role model for her supporters in each respect. Selfless willingness to sacrifice requires courage. One must be willing to stand up for a higher purpose and, if necessary, pay a high personal price for that purpose. This is after all what happened to many members of the NLD. They ended up in prison for their political convictions.

In Aung San Suu Kyi's understanding, democracy has a spiritual basis, namely, the freedom from fear. This concept plays a key role in her politics, as illustrated by the fact that the word "fear" is mentioned almost a hundred times in the twenty-five speeches across the gate that have been recorded and published. It therefore makes sense that the book her husband published when she was awarded the Nobel Peace Prize was titled *Freedom from Fear*. "It is not power that corrupts but fear," starts Aung San Suu Kyi's famous essay from the collection of writings.[26] The essay argues that the 1988 protests did not erupt due to economic reasons; rather, they were aimed against a culture of corruption that had emerged out of fear. What she conveyed to her audience across the gate of her house was the more developed version of this earlier intellectual agenda. She was trying to apply the fundamental concepts of *Freedom from Fear* to political realities.

A Democratic Dilemma

The military also used the terms "democracy" and "dialogue" but in a very different way to the NLD. The tradition of mutual misunderstanding that had started in 1988 thus continued. Although both sides used the very same words, they managed to speak past each other. The central theme of unity—which was referred to regularly by both Aung San Suu Kyi and the military—was no exception in this regard. The military junta stressed the integrity of the nation as unity, which was under threat from politicians' agendas and the rebels fighting for autonomy. Aung San Suu Kyi on the other hand emphasized the unity of the will of the people, which had come to the fore in the 1988 demonstrations and was subsequently expressly confirmed during the 1990 elections.

In reality, the 1990 election result did reveal an all-encompassing unity. Just like the past forced election victories of the BSPP, NLD's victory was total. This had happened previously, at the 1947 elections for the constituent assembly under the leadership of Aung San Suu Kyi's father. Each of these three elections took place under very different conditions, but they all suffered from the same single problem: there was no strong parliamentary opposition of note in any of the three.[27]

Aung San Suu Kyi recognized the problem and reflected upon it in detail in one of her speeches. A remarkable thought process is apparent here, one that has been entirely overlooked in the discussions on Myanmar's path towards democracy. It is hence cited below at some length:

> One party system cannot be democratic because just one party will always be in power whether the people like it or not. If there is more than one party, people can remove the party they don't like in an election. A party that does not please voters will have to leave the government. So parties have to be careful to abide by people's wish in order to remain in power

[*sic*]. That's why my priority is the NLD. As we all know our party has to operate under so many restrictions and, as a political party, we cannot do all the things that a political party should do.

We're trying to improve the situation, not just for our party, but for all. . . . In the 1990 elections, the NLD won more than 400 seats . . . this means that other parties are extremely weak. *It's not good that only the NLD is strong. We need to empower the opposition. We need to encourage opposition parties. If the NLD is growing too strong, we have to take time and efforts to encourage other parties.* (applause) If the NLD is too strong, the NLD members can get complacent and less diligent. In a democracy, all political parties have to be strong. Now we have relations with other parties. We would like to be on good terms with them, as we want them to have popular support too.[28]

The upshot is highly unusual: the party that wins an overwhelming majority of votes itself has to see about having a strong opposition in place. It has to keep in mind both unity and pluralism. Without this, the dominance of one party leads to complacency and corruption, as was the case during the time of the BSPP.

This idea demonstrates an altogether different understanding of democracy compared to the Western conception. Constitutions of Western democracies are based on the understanding that opinions differ within the population. These differing views are handled through constitutional principles in a way that preserves the sanctity of the state. In Aung San Suu Kyi's argument, the basic starting point is different. She starts with an understanding of an organic unity of the people. Thus, she has to ensure that plurality is also accounted for and that an abuse of power is avoided. She tries to push back against the country's tradition, in which the entire populace gathers under the wings of one good leader. The unity described in the teachings of the Buddha, or the dhamma, where everything is interconnected, persists in the background. These teachings rank higher than any worldly constitution. This is reflected in Aung San Suu Kyi's often-cited comment that in the event of her party's victory in the 2015 elections, she would stand "above the president"[29] (see chapter 11). She had always tried to encourage pluralism in Burmese society. But with elections looming, she relies on the traditional unifying all-for-one approach in order to obtain the best possible election outcome for her party.

The Buddhist foundations of Aung San Suu Kyi's political ideas also color her stance on the constitution. A constitution must reflect the will of the entire people: "If a constitution is not inscribed in the hearts of the people, it's no more than a piece of paper. . . . A country's constitution must be respected by both her people and the international community. Asking a few select people to come up with a constitution won't do."[30]

Democracy is a matter of the heart for Aung San Suu Kyi, and she would like to convince her supporters to embrace this democracy. A truly democratic constitution must, however, also meet international norms. This is problematic when the will of the people—compounded by the first-past-the-post voting system inherited from Great Britain—practically leads to a one-party system. This system in turn rests on the trust placed in a popular political leader as well as the rejection of his or her opponents.

In her speeches, Aung San Suu Kyi tries to convey an idea of democracy as a synthesis of "integrated" (Buddhist) and "formal" (Western) modes of political organization. The difficulty with such an ambitious attempt is visible in the failures of the first two stages of Burma's political system after independence. From 1948 to 1962, the country was ruled under a constitution modeled after a Western parliamentary democracy. The model, however, did not work because of prevailing sectarianism within both the ruling AFPFL and the monkhood, which had traditionally legitimated political rule.[31] Nu's promise to make Buddhism the state religion after an election victory in 1960 illustrates that the constitution was not the main basis of uniting the country. Nu as well as other politicians in Burma viewed political conflicts as "winner-takes-all battles,"[32] rather than as opportunities for power sharing. Ne Win tried to establish a political system that eliminated conflict. He tried to install a mechanism aimed at integrating the whole society, not through the Buddhist religion but through a secular party based on a particular

"Burmese" conception of socialism. This did not work either, because, as Ne Win admitted in his farewell speech in July 1988, it was unsatisfactory to the people.

With this backdrop, Aung San Suu Kyi could only offer a distant political vision. Her kind of political state was only achievable after the completion of a prerequisite "revolution of the spirit." The new democracy envisaged by her demanded a long initial process of learning. Her talks over the gate can be seen as the beginning of a process to educate the people and at the same time learn from them. It was a utopian project proposed by a highly revered person who had not held political office. Her responses to her followers' questions did not outline a political program. Rather, she started setting out ways to develop such a program together. Her aim was to create a society in which unity and diversity would be harmonized. She recognized the lack of and need for a loyal opposition. This would be years in the making and she knew that a long way lay ahead before her vision could be realized.

CHAPTER 7

Revolution of the Spirit

I'm not telling people that they can flee the fear. It is important,
however, that they don't allow fear to control their lives. You have
to maintain control.

On the occasion of his wife receiving the Nobel Peace Prize, Michael Aris
introduced a book to the world, *Freedom from Fear*. The book was titled
after the speech that Aung San Suu Kyi had written for the reception
of the Sakharov Prize, awarded to her by the European Parliament. As
she could not be personally present to receive the prize, the speech was
published in various newspapers in July 1991.[1] It was in this speech that
Aung San Suu Kyi introduced the idea of the "revolution of the spirit" as
a fundamental condition for political change.

The premise of the revolution that she aspired towards was based on
a Buddhist understanding of fear. She explained that fear is the most
difficult form of corruption of the spirit, as it distorts the perception of
what is right and what is wrong. Such fear not only corrupts the single
mind but can corrupt society as a whole. The corruption referred to here
was not only of the sort tied to material gains. The way Aung San Suu
Kyi saw it, the 1988 Uprising was not just because of the poor standard
of living that the people had to endure, it was also the humiliation of a
way of life disfigured by corruption and fear. The students were protesting
not just against the death of their comrades but against the denial of
their right to life by a totalitarian regime, which deprived the present of
meaningfulness and held out no hope for the future.[2]

In *Freedom from Fear*, one can detect how Aung San Suu Kyi bases her political program on Buddhist foundations. These Buddhist foundations are in turn composed of various spiritual and moral elements. What, then, are the fundamental principles of Aung San Suu Kyi's "political Buddhism"?

Aung San Suu Kyi and Religion until 1988

A visitor to Aung San's childhood home—now a museum—will find a traditional Buddhist domestic altar on the first floor. The altar has been in the house since Aung San Suu Kyi's childhood. As in millions of other Buddhist homes, the altar would have received daily offerings of fresh flowers and fruit in front of an image of the Buddha. Candles would be lit in the evening, with the family and employees of the house getting together for some quiet meditation. This is one of the many rituals in the country with which Buddhists express their commitment to the teachings of the Enlightened One. They seek refuge in him and his teachings, the dhamma, through the community of monks, the sangha. It is not without cause that it is often said that "being Burmese means being Buddhist."

Khin Kyi, who kept to Christianity in her youth and her old age, had taken on Buddhist traditions and passed them on to her children. The soldier who escorted her in 1945 through the Irrawaddy Delta later explained that she had started believing in Buddhism after an impending threat of fighter jets disappeared once he recited a Buddhist prayer. It was faith that led Khin Kyi to embrace Buddhist traditions, and one can safely conclude that it was also faith that led Aung San Suu Kyi to continue honoring these traditional rituals. Examples include the wedding ceremony with Michael Aris as well as the traditional *shin byu* ceremony for both her sons, which they underwent during one of their visits to Burma. During this ceremony, youth are introduced to monastic life for a short period of time. In this period, they follow the path of the Buddha. First the youth are dressed as princes; then they receive their monastic robes at a monastery and become novices. The parents bow to these novices to demonstrate that the sons are now sons of the Buddha and not of their biological parents. Aung San Suu Kyi's connection to Buddhism after her long-term return to Myanmar also found expression in her regular giving of alms to the monks. She would do this, for example, on the nineteenth of every month in memory of the day that her father died. She took over this tradition from her mother.

Shin byu *ceremony for Aung San Suu Kyi's sons in 1980s Rangoon. (Photo: Getty)*

Although in theory the spiritual world (*lokuttara*) and the "worldly" world (*loka*) are totally different, in practice both realms are closely interconnected. The symbol of this connection is the alms bowl. In return for a material gift, the layperson receives a small portion of the monk's spiritual "merit," needed to progress on their path towards achieving *nibbana*. It follows that the monks have an interest in good government that enables laypeople to make donations. In times of political and economic chaos, the existence of the sangha is endangered, along with the "spiritual promotion" of laypeople. That is why the first task of the Maha Sammata (the proto-ruler or "Great Elect") is to ensure law and order.

Given this close connection between Buddhism and politics, it was inevitable that the simple but important act of giving to the monks, a tradition rooted deeply in folk Buddhism, would become politicized. Aung San Suu Kyi found the junta blaming her party for driving a wedge between the sangha and the government.[3] Other members of the NLD leadership also took part in the monthly almsgiving.[4] They similarly took part in the *kathina* ceremony, where monks traditionally receive new robes at the end of the Buddhist fasting period.[5] After the imposition of house arrest, Aung San Suu Kyi was no longer permitted to commemorate the day of her father's or mother's death in this manner. Her aunt did so on her behalf. Eventually, Aung San Suu Kyi also gave up petitioning the government for permission, as any such permission to remember her father could be used as propaganda by her captors. They would have classified it as an act of generosity by the junta rather than the heartfelt traditional practice of a daughter.

The overlap between the religious and political spheres has existed in the country since colonial times. Under the royal government of the past, the king as head of state and protector of the Buddhist religion resolved any conflicts in cooperation with the sangha leadership. During the anticolonial struggle, the commemoration of those who had sacrificed their lives for the betterment of the country played an important role. The first memorial for a martyr of the independence struggle, the monk U Wisara, was erected in 1943 near the Shwedagon Pagoda. It was at this same spot that Aung San Suu Kyi would hold her first big speech years later. It was also here that Aung San, her father, acting then as minister of defence during Japanese occupation of the time, spoke at the unveiling of the memorial:

That is why it is important that we now also breed this martyr spirit. As the national independence we have attained is not yet permanent, as we have not yet won this war, we are unable as yet to enjoy the taste [of] national independence, of *loki nibbana*. I want us to, even if we are the last ones remaining, from today to develop this martyr spirit.[6]

Whether Aung San Suu Kyi came across these words while researching her father's biography is unknown. It is, however, clear that Aung San's message behind these words remained—despite his early death—ever present in his family. After all, like U Wisara and many others, he too had given his life for the country's independence. The Buddhism of Aung San Suu Kyi's childhood thus had political undertones from the very beginning.

Aung San Suu Kyi experienced religion in another important way. Her mother had a Christian father, who held the post of deacon within the Baptist community of Maungmya and is buried at the community's cemetery. There are rumors that Khin Kyi was even baptized. When she was ill in 1988, she called for a priest from the Baptist Judson Church and received holy Communion from him several times. This church, named after the first American missionary in the country, is the most reputable Protestant church in all of Myanmar. Aung San Suu Kyi continued to respect Khin Kyi's Christian past after her death by also holding an annual Christian memorial service for her mother on Aung San's death anniversary.[7] After Aung San's death, Khin Kyi's father, Pho Hnyin, lived in the house in which the Buddhist altar was honored every evening. Aung San Suu Kyi thus grew up in a multireligious environment. She would later go to Christian schools—first the Catholic St. Francis Convent in the vicinity of her home, followed by the renowned Methodist High School near the central station.[8] In India, she first studied at the Catholic Jesus and Mary Convent and then went to the prestigious Lady Shri Ram College for women, from where she went to Oxford. In this way, Aung San Suu Kyi was met with many different religious traditions during her childhood and school years. This was reflected both in the different denominations of the schools as well as in her fellow students, who came from a variety of different religious backgrounds. It was in the Indian schools—if not before then—that she was introduced to Gandhi's concept of nonviolent resistance, which had spiritual roots that bound the traditions of many religions together.

In Bhutan, where Aung San Suu Kyi and her husband lived for a year, she came to know another form of Buddhism. As in her home country,

Buddhism played a crucial role in shaping the social and political life of the Himalayan kingdom. In her brief study of Bhutan, she emphasized the close connections between the state and religion even after the end of the lamas' reign. She also highlighted the unity of the country despite the existing ethnic differences. Of course, there were biases here, like everywhere else in the world, against inhabitants of farther parts of the country. Yet she sensed the "deep feeling of unity" as much stronger. She found the primary explanation for this, besides the uniformity of living standards, in the single religion. She held this to be true although the country to this day has a large Nepalese minority that practices Hinduism.

Aung San Suu Kyi's drawing of the female bodhisattva Tara.
(Courtesy of Aung San Suu Kyi)

In contrast to her study of Bhutan, no reference is made to Buddhism in her essays on literature and intellectual life in colonial Burma. The word does not even feature in the index of *Freedom from Fear*, first published in 1991. Buddhism remained unmentioned in her August 1988 speech and in all known accounts leading up to her house arrest.[9] A direct link between Buddhism and political action thus seems to have been made in the first six years of Aung San Suu Kyi's house arrest. It was this time that led her to an understanding of a "revolution of the spirit." Two factors were key to Aung San Suu Kyi's turn towards Buddhism: reading books and practicing meditation.

U Pandita

For Christmas in the year 1989, Aung San Suu Kyi received, among other presents, a book from her husband. The phrase "freedom from fear" appeared in this book, titled *In This Very Life*. It was written by the Burmese monk and meditation teacher U Pandita. U Pandita (1921–2016), was a student of the famous Mahasi Sayadaw.[10] After the latter's death, he took over the leadership of the meditation center founded by his teacher. He eventually opened his own meditation center in an upscale part of Rangoon in 1991. The center, named Panditarama after himself, now has branches in different countries. Both he and his teacher Mahasi Sayadaw taught the *vipassana* (true insight) form of meditation aiming at achieving ultimate wisdom (Pali: *paññā*).

Sign at the entrance of the Panditarama. Sīla (virtue) as the starting point of spiritual liberation is surrounded by five other terms emphasized by U Pandita: saddhā (trust), vīriya (effort), sati (mindfulness), samādhi (concentration), and paññā (wisdom). (Photo: Hans-Bernd Zöllner)

After her release from house arrest, Aung San Suu Kyi, together with other members of the NLD, honored the meditation center by handing out monastic robes at the beginning of the fasting period and by listening to one of U Pandita's talks.[11] She also spent some days at the Panditarama in 2010 for a retreat.

Aung San Suu Kyi would later describe how she had already attempted practicing meditation with another student of Mahasi Sayadaw's during one of her short visits to her home country. Yet these attempts were as futile as her first attempts to practice without guidance after she was put under house arrest.[12] Tin Oo, one of her closest confidants from the NLD, had practiced meditation while he was in prison during the Ne Win era. It was he who recommended *vipassana* to Aung San Suu Kyi.

Vipassana is one of many forms of Buddhist meditation. It is held to be particularly enlightened as it does not include any traditional elements of folk Buddhism and does not promise the practitioner supernatural capabilities. The core mode of concentration and meditation is the breath. The precepts for practicing this meditation date back to the teachings of the Buddha. *Vipassana* was rediscovered in Burma at the end of the nineteenth century and has spread through the country since then. After the Second World War, this type of meditation became something of a key spiritual export of the country. U Pandita, for example, gave lectures on the topic in the United States. The book that Aung San Suu Kyi received as a present went back to one such lecture series from 1984. The monk explained *vipassana* as follows:

> *Vipassana* meditation can be seen as a process of developing certain positive mental factors until they are powerful enough to dominate the state of the mind quite continuously. . . . This final product, intuitive wisdom . . . , is the force in the mind which cuts through into the deepest truth about reality, and thus liberates us from ignorance and its results: suffering, delusion, and all the forms of unhappiness.[13]

According to this teaching of meditation, fear is a manifestation of an unhappy consciousness with cowardice as its consequence. The antidote is courage, which can only grow out of a profound understanding of the very limited nature of our physical, corporeal existence. A willingness to give one's life to escape this suffering is a normal consequence of such courage.

U Pandita's book is aimed at readers who wish to learn the art of meditation. It has no political dimensions. The word "power" is never used in a political context and the term "politics" appears only twice. The first reference made by U Pandita is to meditation training, when politics, food, and business are not to be discussed. He refers to talking about these topics as "animal speech." His second reference relates to leaders in the worldly matters of economics, politics, and education, who must work hard to reach the top. The same labor is required in the pursuit of meditation.

U Pandita. (Photo: Hans-Bernd Zöllner)

In contrast to his teachings, Aung San Suu Kyi brings the concepts of individual and political liberation together. This especially makes sense in the Burmese context, given that the words for individual release and political independence have the same linguistic root. She calls for her supporters to join her in a mass meditation movement of sorts, where fear is confronted through one's own political actions. The immensity of such a task is known to her.

> I don't know how to eliminate fear from people's mindset. Soon after my release, an Uncle, who is not an NLD member, came to me. He told me that his fear disappeared after listening to my speeches. Yet whenever he was threatened by the authorities, his fear got the better of him again. (laughter) (applause) What can we do? Shall we encourage one another? Shall we fear the authorities in turn? (laughter) Instead of fearing the authorities all at the same time, we should take turns to fear them. If you're married, for example, you can have a deal with your spouse to fear the authorities in turn on every other day. (laughter) If you're a group of five, you can assign fear to each person for each day. Don't fear. (Daw Suu laughing) We have to find ways to eliminate fear. We cannot live in fear.[14]

The arduous task of using freedom from fear, as preached and taught by U Pandita, as the foundation of a political mass movement becomes clear here.[15] This message must have formed the personal basis of Aung San Suu Kyi's fearlessness in the struggle for democracy. Yet her frame of mind could not easily be transferred en masse to her supporters. *Vipassana* was aimed at the deliverance of the individual, even when practiced by many in an organized way. Aung San Suu Kyi was undoubtedly a role model for her followers. However, the fascination she evoked in them was rooted in the people's own local Buddhist way of life. This is demonstrated through the example of the second Buddhist monk venerated by her.

Thamanya Sayadaw

Aung San Suu Kyi's second mentor was Thamanya Sayadaw, a monk who lived in Kayin State and whose work had a strong social component. Aung San Suu Kyi must have held him in high regard, as she visited him some months after being released from house arrest—her first and only trip which went beyond the reaches of Yangon. She traveled to the esteemed Thamanya Sayadaw's monastery again when she was released from her second house arrest in 2002. This trip was the beginning of her many journeys across the entire country.

Aung San Suu Kyi spoke about her first trip in her speeches at University Avenue and in *Letters from Burma*.[16] The latter first appeared in a Japanese newspaper and was subsequently published as a book. Four notes on this first journey make up the beginning of *Letters from Burma*. The letters are short weekly reports describing life in the country, in which the writer elucidates on her and her fellow revolutionaries' political activities. In the travel descriptions in her letters as well as in her speeches, Aung San Suu Kyi begins at a tangible and practical starting point: the road from Yangon to Thamanya Hill.

Thamanya Hill and adjacent village (2016). (Photo: Hans-Bernd Zöllner)

Aung San Suu Kyi describes the joys and sorrows of traveling in poetic and humorous prose. She finds joy in nature, sorrow in the old Mitsubishi Pajero and the poor roads. That changes as she nears her destination.

The roads were so bumpy that the car was going 'clank, clank, clank' all the time. I felt I was floating in the car. I came to understand the expression, 'nose in the air', during that bumpy ride. (Applause) The roads improved as we approached Thamanya Hill. I saw some monks and nuns happily working for the maintenance of a road leading to the hill. They looked pleased. More pleased than the people here. (Laughter) They've been well provided for by the Abbott. Even in the scorching sun, their skin looked great and the spirit looked high. They understand that the road is for their own good. It was gratifying to see how they had built the road in unison, in good spirit. (Applause) So, if we are building a road, be it democratic or asphalt, if people understand that it's for their own good, they'll also understand that gravel and asphalt, meant for the road, should go to the road construction, not to anyone's pocket. (Applause) We should have such a strong conviction.[17]

In her speech, road construction becomes a parable for the building of any path "be it democratic or asphalt." It can only succeed if all are united in the pursuit of the common good. Aung San Suu Kyi goes on to speak about the widespread corruption in the country and summons her listeners to take matters into their own hands and to be more selfless and less fearful. Her appeal ends with the following request: "Please believe in yourself. I'd like to end here by urging you to collectively contribute to building a system that will provide you with self-confidence."[18]

A popular and dichotomous image of Burma is painted here. On the one hand there is the state, incapable of constructing decent roads because the funds assigned for such activities are being pocketed by corrupt supporters of the system. On the other hand, there is a functioning community in which people happily and voluntarily work towards the common good under the guidance of a well-meaning and competent abbot. The workings of the community on Thamanya Hill are stylized as a good counterimage to the failing country. What can only be achieved through forced labor in a dysfunctional state is a voluntary service to the community under the auspicious leadership of a Buddhist benefactor.[19]

The dichotomy of the image becomes clearer when one recalls how the adoration for Thamanya Sayadaw came into existence. Thamanya

Sayadaw, as he came to be known, was born in 1912 in what is today Kayin State.[20] He came from a family of Pa-O, one of the ethnic Karen groups. He became a novice at the age of thirteen and a monk at twenty. He then lived in various monasteries in Burma and spent some time in Mae Sot, Thailand. In 1941, at the request of one of his teachers, he took the post of abbot at a new monastery in the Karen region. He stayed there for more than three decades, until the late 1970s, when he started practicing a specific form of ascetic meditation in the forest-monk tradition. In contrast to monks that live in monasteries, monks of the forest tradition inspire particular reverence in recognition of the hardships of a reclusive life.

On March 2, 1980, Thamanya Sayadaw climbed a hill together with a companion in order to meditate there. In 1981 he vowed to continue the meditation for three years without interruption. His school of meditation was not *vipassana* but *samatha*. The *samatha* method allows the attainment of peace and absorption, which are ephemeral and different to the insight to be gained through *vipassana*.

The monk quickly became renowned. His tale was woven together with the local myths and legends of different ethnic groups. Many Karen, Mon, and other people thus came to believe in a long historical connection between the monk and the hill upon which he had settled. People ascribed supernatural powers to Thamanya Sayadaw. Many of his followers started wearing amulets with his image. The news spread and inspired people to visit him. In January 1984, a road was constructed by his devotees. This connected the village at the foot of the hill with Hpa-an, the capital of Kayin State, and Myawaddy, a town at the Thai border.

The construction of the road was largely carried out by the Indian (by descent) population of the country. They refused money and gave their labor as a gift (*dāna*) to the revered monk. Through this work they participated in and benefited from his holiness. In return, the monk allowed for a production of the Ramayana, the second-most-important Indian epic, to be staged on that spot.

The new road came with a number of consequences. It allowed devotees of the monk to reach him without great effort and leave their contributions. The road also symbolized the connection of his virtues to the worldly sphere. The monk practiced *mettā* (loving kindness and empathy towards others), a Buddhist quality that—in emulation of her father—also lies close to Aung San Suu Kyi's heart. In one of her speeches to her supporters she says, "*Mettā* should empower the people, so that they can stand on their own feet, and develop their own capacity."[21] In the end, Thamanya Hill became home to a multicultural and multireligious center. Thamanya Sayadaw, as he was now known, attracted people from different ethnic and religious backgrounds. Shortly after his three-year-long vow, his fame spread through the country and for a long time he was held to be one of the most honored monks in all of Myanmar.

This fame led to a rush of pilgrims who also made it necessary to expand the infrastructure around the hill. As of 1984, the monk had arranged for all visitors to eat vegetarian meals.[22] In order to achieve this he needed donations and labor. The donations came from the pilgrims. Slowly, a workforce, too, took root, leading to the emergence of a small town with some five thousand households. The inhabitants had been drawn to this place by the monk's charisma, but also because here they found a safe and peaceful place within a region struck by strife. A civil war involving a number of different groups continued in that part of the country. The vegetarian diet was linked to a strict interpretation of one of the five Buddhist precepts, namely that believers are to avoid killing or harming living beings. Hence the spot became a sanctuary where human beings and animals could equally enjoy the peace preached by the Buddha. The monk's impact on his followers was thus more external or communal than internal or individual. This stands in contrast with those who sought to integrate U Pandita's teachings in their day-to-day life.

Thamanya Hill's position as a place of refuge developed over the last decade of the twentieth century. The land encompassing a three-mile radius around the spot where the monk carried out his meditation was officially recognized as religious land. With this new status, it fell into the same category as monasteries, churches, mosques, or other places of worship. No taxes were payable here, and the administrative responsibilities fell to the religious leader and his followers. Like many other religious centers around the country, Thamanya Hill became a state within a state. The economic core of this "state" was pilgrimage tourism, widespread in the country to this day.[23]

The monk and his establishment's growing fame unavoidably took on a political dimension. This is also illustrated in Aung San Suu Kyi's travel diary. Thamanya Sayadaw had received a high title from the government as early as 1991. He did not come to Yangon for the award ceremony but accepted it in his own realm. The public interpreted this as him not wishing to extend legitimacy to the military junta. It was also suggested that Aung San Suu Kyi received a far friendlier reception from him than Khin Nyunt, the first secretary of the junta who had also paid him a visit. Something similar happened again in 2002, when the monk traveled to Yangon for health reasons. It was then believed that he permitted Khin Nyunt to pay his hospital expenses but visited Aung San Suu Kyi's house after his release. Among the many rumors that circulated in Myanmar, it was also believed that the monk's special powers allowed him to visit Aung San Suu Kyi's house even though it was so closely guarded. Meanwhile he declined an invitation from Khin Nyunt.[24]

The revered monk passed away in 2003, not long after Aung San Suu Kyi had visited him for a second time. After his death, four monks could not reach an agreement as to his succession. Pilgrims and donations dwindled. In 2005, the place lost its special legal status and fell, once again, under state administration. In 2008, the revered monk's body was stolen by armed men along with the abbot's rosary of pure gold.

Two Paths to the Buddha's Teachings

The two Burmese monks who influenced Aung San Suu Kyi represented two different but interconnected approaches taken by the monk community to pass on the Buddha's teachings to laypeople. In Thamanya Sayadaw's case, the social dimension of the Buddha's teachings is key. Through proximity to the heightened spirituality of a "religious

Memorial hall for the Thamanya Sayadaw (2016).
(Photo: Hans-Bernd Zöllner)

virtuoso"—as Max Weber would say—laypersons may advance in the cycle of rebirth. Alongside a spiritual sanctuary, the master creates another, worldly refuge, one that provides individuals with protection and livelihood. This was an important element for Aung San Suu Kyi. With her dedication to this monk, she could demonstrate that Buddhism could also have positive social impacts. In other words, a politics rooted in Buddhism could materially improve living conditions for the people.

At the same time, commitment to the ways of Thamanya Sayadaw has two shortcomings: First, the desirable social consequences are linked to the person who introduces them. What is lacking is continuity, as there are no hard and fast rules as to the succession of an empowered Buddhist persona. The second shortcoming lies in the fact that it was primarily the monk's "moral capital" that led to the social impact.

Aung San Suu Kyi's description of the good and the bad roads in her country can be read as a metaphor for the leaders in the country, polarizing them as either good or bad. The image of Aung San Suu Kyi, the politician, as "good" because she is virtuous, versus her military opponents as "bad" because of their immoral acts, is strengthened and reinforced through religion. The people had already interpreted Thamanya Sayadaw's rumored unwillingness to engage more closely with the government as his denial of extending legitimacy to its leadership. Consequently, Aung San Suu Kyi's association with the monk limited the possibility of an open dialogue with the military—a dialogue that she had, however, been demanding.

A politics based on individuals such as the monk of Kayin State runs the risk of becoming a politics of episodic succession. In this, single enlightened or knowledgeable leaders—be they monks or laypeople—bring a movement to life for a relatively short period of time. It is a movement that is shaped on selfless ideals and one that benefits a large, but manageable, group of people. Hidden in the background of such a politics is a critical question: can the workings of an "ideal republic" such as the one constructed by Thamanya Sayadaw or other socially engaged monks be transferred to the scale of an entire state? With respect to worldly rulers, modern Burma's own history provides the best example of the pitfalls of a politics where the well-being of the nation is attached to a single person. Aung San was the great hope of independent Burma—a hope that was crushed with his death.

In contrast to Thamanya Sayadaw, U Pandita taught a form of meditation that was to be internalized by laypersons. The meditation center of Mahasi Sayadaw that U Pandita led for a number of years was established in 1947 at the behest of U Nu, Burma's first prime minister. Since then, hundreds of thousands were educated in the art of practicing *vipassana* meditation and, through that, finding enlightenment. After the training, they would return to their home states.[25] As at the center founded by Aung San Suu Kyi's teacher himself, such establishments would be run by lay committees. In this way, laypersons could—within limits—influence the activities of the monks who came to teach there.

This meditation movement was thus largely sustained by laypeople and, since its beginnings in the mid-twentieth century, spread and institutionalized further. This movement certainly had political implications but not to the extent that they could be seen as training spots for the spreading of democratic ideals. The centers did expand during the different phases of military rule, but always under the watchful—and sometimes strained—supervision of the authorities. The important distinction in Theravada Buddhism between *loka*, the visible world inhabited by laypeople under some given form of political leadership, and the *lokuttara*, the supramundane, may have shifted in postcolonial Burma but remains essentially unchanged. The three cornerstones of the supraworldly Buddhism—Buddha, dhamma, and sangha—are not up for democratization in the Western sense, as that would lead to a loss of their unitary nature.

It follows that Aung San Suu Kyi's attempts to bring in social reforms through a "revolution of the spirit" had little prospect of success. U Pandita, like Thamanya Sayadaw, was one of many monks who drew crowds around them. It would have been unrealistic to expect his teachings on the inner insight of individuals to be adopted by the majority of the country's Buddhist population, let alone those who practiced other religions. At their core, U Pandita's teachings were wholly unpolitical. The social dimension of his teachings was restricted to the "revolution of the spirit" of *individual* persons. This connection to the Buddhist principle that each must find his or her own path to salvation—like the Buddha himself—meant that such teachings could not be used for state-building. Like many other teachers of meditation, U Pandita's focus was on the individual emancipation of his disciples.

The Western Perception

In the West, where the above-mentioned aspects of Aung San Suu Kyi's worldview were and remain little known, there was initially only admiration for her. There were important reasons for this. Her personal courage after her release in July 1995 shone through as she continued to stand behind her ideals despite all difficulty. She also maintained astounding composure when speaking about her years of arrest. In the first press conferences, she was not once asked about the role of Buddhism in her personal and political life. In contrast, seven questions were directed at the theme of democracy. It was only after the publication of her *Letters from Burma* and her interviews with Alan Clements in 1997 that Buddhism was discovered to be one of the central tenets of her thinking.

In a *New York Times* review of Alan Clements's book—one of the first books written about Aung San Suu Kyi—the reviewer summons up the contrast as "light versus darkness, truth versus deception, spirituality versus greed."[26] The Buddhist ideals that she lived by distinguished her honest democracy from the one represented by her opponents. Yet there was no critical examination of the relationship between Buddhist virtues and democratic state-building. No questions were asked as to the extent to which Buddhist ideals could contribute to the largely mundane institutions and legal systems that were the daily business of a democracy.

There are no surprises here. In all aspects, Myanmar was an unknown country. Only a handful of experts had considered the connections between religion and politics in the country's history, and they were never consulted by the media. As a result, Aung San Suu Kyi's image as a dedicated Buddhist and good politician was reinforced in the West. The cliché of a gentle and peaceful Buddhism—as an alternative to the aggressive, Western materialism—that could pave a way out of vacuously expanding globalization was propagated. It suited this position that Aung San Suu Kyi was a woman in a world of uniformed men.

The little-understood core principles of Aung San Suu Kyi's "revolution of the spirit" as the foundation for a politics informed by Buddhism worked as a projection screen for the unfulfilled yearning in some Westerners for a connection between spirituality and politics in their own societies. Such perceptions, far from the political reality within Myanmar, led to a long-held belief within the international community that Myanmar had two governments. One was morally legitimate while the other relied on the brute force of the gun. No attention was paid to the fact that the "alternative government" that Aung San Suu Kyi represented, much like that small kingdom of Thamanya Sayadaw, or the free and independent Burma charted by Aung San, could be nothing more than another historical episode, one that would dissipate into thin air with the passing of the carrier of hope.

The differences and contradictions between Buddhist ideas and Western politics are often overlooked. Democracy, after all, is a collective project that rests on institutions rather than personal spirituality and role models. The West projected on Aung San Suu Kyi an unachievable connection between spirituality and politics.

CHAPTER 8

One Country, Two Governments

I am not attacking or opposing the SLORC groundlessly. If the
SLORC is doing the right thing, I will support their right activities.
If not, I will oppose them.

Aung San Suu Kyi's house at 54 University Avenue remains one of Myanmar's political centers—even though it has lost some importance since the NLD took office in 2016. At times it has even served as a kind of alternative seat of power of the shadow government under Aung San Suu Kyi's leadership. The importance of this place has grown over time and in phases.

Until the beginning of 1988, the property on the shores of Inya Lake was just one of the many noble addresses of the city. Khin Kyi, Aung San's widow and the former Burmese ambassador to India, lived a withdrawn life here. When Suu Kyi's ill mother was hospitalized, her daughter moved into the house in April of the same year to take care of her from there. Students, activists, and politicians started coming to the house regularly from then on, and the home increasingly buzzed with life.

After Khin Khyi's death at the end of December 1988, the house—for the first time—became a place of pilgrimage. A book of condolences was laid out and many came to sign it. Among them were leaders of the military junta, who used the opportunity to have a short conversation with Aung San Suu Kyi. The government sanctioned a memorial ceremony for her mother. The ceremony took place with the active support of government officials at a revered location at the foot of the Shwedagon Pagoda. Monuments for the remains of Supayalat, the last queen of Burma, the national poet Thakin Kodaw Hmaing, and U Thant, the long-serving secretary-general of the United Nations, all already stood here. A fourth memorial was now erected commemorating Khin Kyi. Not far off was the Martyrs' Mausoleum for the martyrs of July 19, 1947, which of course included Khin Kyi's husband.

Khin Kyi's tomb (second from left). The tombs are for, from left to right, Thakin Kodaw Hmaing, Khin Kyi, Supayalat, and U Thant. (Photo: Hans-Bernd Zöllner)

More than a hundred thousand people lined up to form the long funeral procession from the house on University Avenue to the Shwedagon Pagoda. The large gathering was in honor of the deceased but also to a great extent in support of her daughter. Aung San Suu Kyi had made a powerful appearance on Burma's political stage just four months previously. The beginning of the long line marked the house that was slowly becoming the center for the opposition's struggle against the military regime.

Ironically, the junta itself played a role in transforming the house on University Avenue from a civilian home to a political center. On July 20, 1989, it placed Aung San Suu Kyi and the NLD's chairman Tin Oo under house arrest. Half a year later, Tin Oo was sentenced to three years in prison. He served his prison sentence in the infamous Insein Prison like so many other members of the opposition. With such unequal treatment, both Aung San Suu Kyi and her home were attributed special status.

The military junta's decision was in line with the precepts of the country's absolute rulers of the past. Those rulers had shown clemency to rebels with unique accomplishments. Rather than being imprisoned, such rebels were banished to a remote corner of the kingdom in the hope that this would cast them into oblivion.

The military's excuse was that Aung San Suu Kyi's public appearances posed a threat to security and order. In order to frustrate her efforts, it used existing laws to restrict her freedom of movement. This was not just done out of respect for Aung San or because of some Buddhist conception of clemency. Rather, the point was to stop Aung San Suu Kyi from continuing to engage in political acts.

If such was the tactical thinking behind the junta's decision, it was—at least as far as the West was concerned—a complete miscalculation. In reality, instead of a gradual casting off of Aung San Suu Kyi's memory into oblivion, the military's attempts helped in amplifying her image. And image is an essential source of power. This is especially true in a Buddhist country where rule is legitimized by reputation.

Thamanya Sayadaw's story offers a way of understanding the growing importance of Aung San Suu Kyi's house. The monk's work as spiritual regent of a small republic had started with an oath to meditate on an unknown hill for three years. The hill is now named after him. Later, he came to be widely known as a miracle worker. He was believed to have magical powers. His ability to provide vegetarian food to all pilgrims confirmed this perception (see chapter 7).

Aung San Suu Kyi, too, had taken an oath when her mother passed away, albeit one of a different nature to that of the monk's. She was forced into the life of a hermit by the junta. However, she took this coercive measure and transformed it into a voluntary act. By embracing a Buddhist way of life in her prison home, she transformed her place of incarceration into a monastic sanctuary. During the period of her house arrest, Yangon brimmed with stories of her having supernatural powers. People reported having seen her lifted into the air and flying around the Shwedagon Pagoda.[1]

When it came to be known that she had used the time of her house arrest to learn a popular form of mediation, it became all the more clear that Aung San Suu Kyi was not just a worldly but also a spiritual leader. Like Thamanya Hill but in its own unique way, her house, too, had become a place of pilgrimage.

Aung San Suu Kyi's University Avenue prison became a symbol for the suppression of an entire people. But the house also stood for something else; people still held the hope that this little place of banishment in the middle of Yangon would be the doorway to the country's liberation. Their hope was strengthened by the developments in South Africa, where Nelson Mandela had been released in February 1990. The address of 54 University Avenue—like Mandela's prison on Robben Island—became a magical place, a symbol of self-sacrificing dedication to the well-being of others and of hope for the success of a people's struggle.

Magical Centers of Power

In Theravada Buddhism, the location of the seat of political power is of unique significance. The last palace of a Burman king, built as late as the mid-1900s, was—like the famous Angkor Wat in Cambodia—a portrayal of the cosmic universe.[2] One of the king's tasks was to create harmony between the cosmos at large and the smaller universe of the earthly world that fell under his protection. The idea is visible in the practice of the annual Royal Ploughing Ceremony in Thailand, which traditionally takes place every spring under the oversight of the king or one of his family members. The king represents and guarantees cosmic order on Earth. The religious ritual carried out by him augurs a good rice harvest and thus the well-being of the state and its inhabitants.

Until 2005, independent Burma's seat of government was located at the Secretariat—built by the "heathen" British—where Aung San was murdered in 1947. The calamitous history associated with this place was one of the reasons why the military junta decided to move the capital to a new location in 2005. The new capital was named Naypyidaw—or "royal city."³ In this move, the junta was in fact following in the footsteps of the kings, who also marked a new political era by either moving the capital or building it anew.⁴ The seat of power had thus traveled over the centuries from Bagan to Ava (or Innwa), from Ava to Amarapura, from Amarapura to Mandalay, from Mandalay to Rangoon, and now from Rangoon (or Yangon) to Naypyidaw. It was not only power but also physical architecture that moved from an old capital to a new one.

Parade with commander-in-chief of the armed forces Min Aung Hlaing on Armed Forces Day 2013. (Photo: Myanmar Times)

Both in the past and the present, the seat of government has functioned to make the reign visible in all its might. In Naypyidaw, the government constructed a replica of the Shwedagon Pagoda, but one that was a meter shorter than the original. Statues of the founders of the three Burmese royal dynasties were erected on the military's central marching ground. The army that Aung San had established now thrust itself forward as the founder of a fourth Burmese dynasty. The national hero himself was relegated to the background. After all, any mention of him would remind the population of his daughter. Banknotes with his image were pulled out of circulation for the same reason.

The sites of power, however, are always just manifestations of rule. They say nothing about the legitimacy of the prevailing rulers. In the Theravada Buddhist system—following the model of the Maha Sammata or the Great Elect set out in Buddhist scriptures—rule depends on the moral qualities of a ruler. A ruler can, however, be toppled at any time by a morally superior rival. The latter may wait for an appropriate opportunity within the palace walls or in an alternative center of power. In the Buddhist teachings on virtuous leaders, there are no clear provisions on how a change in leadership is to take place. In theory, the most competent and virtuous contender to the throne should take over governance after the death of a king. In practice, the king picked a suitable successor, or the decision was made by the royal family and advisors of the court. This method, often tainted by the intrigues of the court, is a key reason for the instability of Buddhist kingdoms. In 1878, as the last king of Burma, Thibaw, rose to the throne, around eighty members of the royal family were killed out of fear of competition. This blatant cruelty provided the British with an official reason—masking economic self-interest—to engage in the last Anglo-Burmese war, which led to the end of royal Burma.

More than a hundred years later, Aung San Suu Kyi was chosen by the students as the new morally superior, future ruler of the country. Her legitimacy came with her bloodline, her own charisma, and the approval of the people. The people's choice had resounded clearly during her first speech and was formidably confirmed with the 1990 elections.

Her presence within the house on University Avenue turned it into an alternative center of power and, under the banner of democracy, also into a center for a new order.

Outside, the barriers strung with barbed wire announced that a troublemaker lived here. They marked the military's control and ring-fenced the political sphere. At the same time, the barricades added their own flavor to the house's status as an alternative seat of government. After all, all official seats of government were protected by barricades and barbed wire. The officials' security measures contributed to Aung San Suu Kyi remaining a continuously present and publicly visible thorn in the junta's side. The NLD headquarters on Shwegondine Road only played a subordinate role in comparison.[5]

Barricades blocking the road into University Avenue on the day of Aung San Suu Kyi's release on November 13, 2010. (Photo: Myanmar Times*)*

The antipode lay on the other side of Inya Lake, on Ady Road (later renamed to May Kha Road). This is where Ne Win lived. His house, like Aung San Suu Kyi's, was heavily secured and not publicly accessible. But everyone knew where it was located and who lived in it—the wicked mind who continued to use his power after stepping down in 1988 to prevent the rightful rule of Aung San Suu Kyi.

Ne Win was eighty-four years old in July 1995, when Aung San Suu Kyi was released. He had stopped making public appearances and also lived a reclusive life, albeit in the company of his large family. However, Ne Win was not seen to be cut off from politics at all. General Khin Nyunt, the first secretary of the junta who had been appointed head of the secret service by the "old man," was held to be the agent of Ne Win's sinister plans. Khin Nyunt came to be known as the "prince of darkness." Only General Than Shwe stood above him.

All three men lacked everything that Aung San Suu Kyi possessed in abundance: legitimacy, credibility, and a morally unquestionable home from where power could be exercised. In the public eye both inside and outside the country, the rulers from within Ne Win's orbit were seen as wrongful intruders.

Between them, each of the two protagonists in the fight for leadership of the country possessed one of two central traits of the Great Elect. On the one hand, the military ensured law and order at least superficially and attempted to advance the economic development of the country. However, in the eyes of the public, both nationally and worldwide, it lacked the necessary moral qualities. Under these conditions, even honest efforts to advance the well-being of the country would have received no recognition. Aung San Suu Kyi, on the other hand, held the moral legitimacy without being able to transform this into political deeds.

The Secretariat in Yangon, or Naypyidaw after 2005, and the house on University Avenue were the two centers of power that largely neutralized each other in the years to come. The military junta tried to secure the stability and unity of the country from within government buildings. Aung San Suu Kyi's house symbolized a future democratic Burma under her leadership at the helm of the NLD.

Madeleine Albright Draws the Battle Lines

There is a surreal quality to the eight years spanning from 1995 to 2003, during which Aung San Suu Kyi was allowed a semifreedom before the imposition of yet another house arrest. This time was marked by the struggle for ascendency of two diametrically different but equally strong opponents. Each side sensed or knew that there would be no solution to the country's conflict without the cooperation of the political opponent. Yet each side insisted that any conciliation happen in accordance with its own terms.[6] Aung San Suu Kyi, her party, and large sections of the international community unyieldingly held on to the demand that the outcome of the 1990 election be translated into some form of political reality. The junta on its part insisted that a new beginning would only be possible if law, order, and the unity of the country were not at risk. And given that the junta saw itself as the sole keeper of law, order, and unity, it could not agree to give up governmental responsibility.

The polarity of such staunch positions resulted in a stalemate. Despite the obvious standstill, the parties could not even agree to the fact that the situation was a stalemate. Each insisted on playing by its own rules—a move that was politically real and deadly serious.

After the turbulence caused by the 1990 elections, the SLORC had convened a National Convention to work on a new constitution. The NLD, deprived of its leaders because of imprisonment (either at home or in jail), had initially succumbed to this framework and participated in the consultations. The NLD thus ended up—at least provisionally—adding its own legitimacy to the convention's decisions and the writing in of the role of the military in the future politics of the country.

The party changed its strategy after Aung San Suu Kyi's release. On November 22, 1995, six days before the next gathering of the convention, Aung San Suu Kyi said at a press conference that it was "not acceptable to the people."[7] A week later, the eighty-six representatives of the NLD boycotted the National Convention. They were barred from the convention a few days later. The episode once again demonstrated how the party relied on its leader.

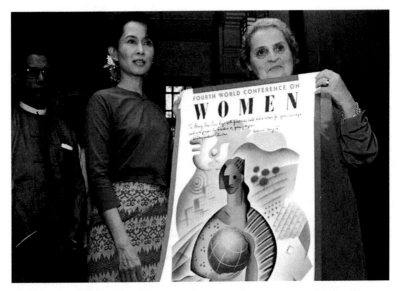

Aung San Suu Kyi and Madeleine Albright in September 1995. (Photo: Getty)

Just prior to this boycott, it had become patently obvious that the disagreements between the two opposing parties within the country had moved beyond internal politics and taken on an international dimension. Madeleine Albright, the US ambassador to the United Nations and later secretary of state, became the first prominent politician to visit Aung San Suu Kyi after her release in September 1995.[8] Albright had just attended the Fourth World Conference on Women in Beijing, where Aung San Suu Kyi had addressed the delegates through a videotaped recording. Albright was continuing a tradition. American politicians had been visiting Myanmar for some years now, starting with Stephen Solarz in August 1988 and followed by Bill Richardson in February 1994.

Albright met with General Khin Nyunt and then Aung San Suu Kyi, thus covering both seats of government. She set out her view on the country's state of affairs in a later press release in Bangkok.[9] She stated that she had delivered a "tough message" to Khin Nyunt, demanding steps towards "true democracy" as a prerequisite to ending Burma's political isolation. She had rejected Khin Nyunt's claim that the National

Convention was the appropriate vehicle for political dialogue and demanded a conversation with the leader of the democratic opposition. She wholly supported Aung San Suu Kyi's position. In her arguments against Khin Nyunt, Madeleine Albright explicitly drew on concepts from Aung San Suu Kyi's writings. She cited her phrase "freedom from fear" and concluded her announcement by noting that the SLORC could have no doubt as to the US position after her visit. "The choice is theirs," read the last sentence of the press release. Aung San Suu Kyi welcomed the American politician's lucid words.

Acts followed words. In her role as UN ambassador and later as Secretary of State under Bill Clinton, Madeleine Albright would play a decisive role in shaping US sanction policies against Myanmar. In this way, the demands of the Burmese opposition leader were accepted to a great extent and translated into political practice. Although she was domestically barred from an official political role, Aung San Suu Kyi managed to affect change at home through international action. She had been forced, over the years, to find a way to play beyond the margins. The United States saw Myanmar's government as illegitimate. The unambiguous stance was highlighted by the US not using "Myanmar," the name decreed by the junta. Between September 1990 and July 2012, the US was also not represented in the country by an ambassador but by a chargé d'affaires.

The chairman of the National Convention connected the boycott by the NLD delegates with the American diplomat's visit. He stated that Aung San Suu Kyi "after a tête-à-tête between the two . . . adopted a harsher attitude towards the National Convention."[10] He specifically referred to Albright's press release. On the other side, after the end of the party's participation in the convention, the NLD's chairman Aung Shwe sent a series of letters to the leaders of the junta. In them, he repeated the party's claim that it continued to be the legitimate representative of the people on the basis of the 1990 elections.[11]

Establishing a Shadow Parliament

The NLD's ejection from the National Convention marked the beginning of another long period of contestation between the two opposing parties. Again, the international dimension continued to play a central role. The NLD, especially, took the battle outside the playing field. The situation intensified day by day.

At the end of March 1996, after one month of meetings, the National Convention was adjourned. It only reconvened in 2004. In May 1996, an NLD party congress took place at Aung San Suu Kyi's house. The SLORC prevented numerous delegates from participating. The NLD congress tasked the party's central committee with the drafting of a new constitution for the country.

The state media responded to this by launching a smear campaign against Aung San Suu Kyi. A series of slanderous articles about her were published until the beginning of October. She was accused of having given up the good manners of Myanmar and was described as being power hungry and greedy for money.

One day after the launch of the smear campaign, Myanmar was granted observer status at ASEAN despite hefty protests from the United States and the European Union.[12] Three months later, in October, the US imposed its first sanctions against Myanmar under the aegis of Madeleine Albright. The European Union formulated a "common position" shortly thereafter, which also included sanctions.

As the international confrontation became more heated, state officials imposed restrictions on Aung San Suu Kyi's freedoms as well as those of members and supporters of the NLD. In her *Letters from Burma*, Suu Kyi describes how the situation escalated in an "absurd" manner as of September 1996.[13] An attempt to travel to Mandalay in March was thwarted because the train carriage in which she had booked a seat was supposedly unfit for service. Security forces again and again blocked the road to her house at the end of September once an NLD congress had been announced to mark the party's eighth anniversary. Party members were arrested for short periods of time. The talks over the gate of the house on University Avenue could also no longer take place. As a result, Aung San Suu Kyi and her colleagues tried to meet with their supporters at other locations. While driving to one such meeting, stones were thrown at the convoy, causing light injury to Tin Oo. History repeated itself in December when universities were closed due to student unrest.

The situation calmed down to an extent in the course of 1997. The junta renamed itself in November from SLORC to SPDC, or the State Peace and Development Council. The government was reshuffled. NLD party congresses could again take place at University Avenue. A resolution was passed at one of these in May 1998 calling once again for the convening of the parliament elected in 1990. At the congress, where there was a "carnival atmosphere" according to observers, Aung San Suu Kyi said, "We are determined not to accept the holding of another election without materialising [*sic*] the results of the 1990 elections." She closed her speech with the words "See you again at parliament."[14]

One month later, the NLD party chairman issued an ultimatum to the government asking for the parliament to be convened within two months. The government responded with an ordinance requiring the elected parliamentarians to report to the officials. They were required to sign a form in which they agreed to have their freedom of movement restricted. In doing this, the government relied on a measure stemming from colonial times that was supposed to keep political agitators in check. A refusal to sign could result in imprisonment.[15]

Aung San Suu Kyi reacted to the ordinance by trying to visit some of her supporters outside of Yangon. She undertook four such attempts in July and August. Each time her car was stopped at a roadblock. Aung San Suu Kyi refused to turn around. In the longest of these "standoffs," as they came to be known in the international media, she held out for eleven days in her car. In all four cases she eventually returned to Yangon, either voluntarily or in response to mild force employed by the officials.[16] Both the government as well as the NLD issued statements on their position in connection with these events. Such announcements—like others issued by the NLD—were made in the style of official government notices.

Suu Kyi's car during a standoff on July 29, 1998. (Photo: Getty)

Preparatory meeting of the committee on August 29, 1998. Left to right: Sai Nyunt Lwin (Shan), Aye Tha Aung (Arakan), Naing Tun Sein (Mon), Phu Chian Siang Thang (Chin), U Lwin (NLD), Saw Mra Aung (Arakan), Aung San Suu Kyi (NLD), Aung Shwe (NLD; only hands and feet visible). (Photo: Phu Chian Siang Thang)

On September 16, 1998, two days before the tenth anniversary of the 1988 military coup, the NLD announced the establishment of a committee that would represent the unconvened parliament of 1990. The committee's functions resembled those of a politburo within a communist system. It initially comprised ten individuals, mostly representatives of the NLD as well as some representatives of ethnic groups.

This institution drew its legitimacy by having the support of 251 of the parliamentarians elected in 1990. As a consequence, it was to have the authority to deal with matters normally dealt with by an elected parliament. In the first sitting it was decided that "all laws, rules, procedural laws, orders, and notifications made on and after September 18, 1988, without confirmation of the people's parliament have no legal authority."[17] The committee held its sessions in Aung San Suu Kyi's house, thus affirming the house as an alternative seat of parliament from where laws and decisions were passed at regular intervals.

The opposition committee's establishment was also the burning of all bridges between the two sides. Aung San Suu Kyi and the military no longer spoke to each other at all. In the period that followed, any disagreement and debate was almost always voiced through the media.

An especially tragic episode that took place during this period was Michael Aris's death in March 1999. When it became apparent that he was terminally ill with cancer, the government denied him a visa on the grounds that his illness could not receive adequate medical attention in Myanmar. It did offer to let Aung San Suu Kyi leave and return to the country. She rejected the offer, not trusting the promise of being allowed to return. Her husband died without them having had the chance of seeing each other once more.

Aung San Suu Kyi and Tin Oo tried to leave Yangon once again in August 2000 in order to visit fellow party members outside the city. The attempt was foiled by the officials after ten days. The pair tried again in September. This time there were apparently no seats available in the train to Mandalay. Aung San Suu Kyi was placed under ambiguously defined restrictions after this until May 2002, even though she was not under any formal house arrest.[18]

A moderator from nearby

In April 2000, United Nations secretary-general Kofi Annan named a Malaysian diplomat, Razali Ismail, his special envoy for Myanmar. This led to a gear shift in Myanmar, with some resulting dynamism between the two stiffened fronts. Razali's predecessor, the Peruvian national Alvaro de Soto, had been unable to bridge the gap between the two sides and left his post frustrated at the end of 1999. Writing to the secretary-general he had stated that both sides remained skeptical of any mediation attempts. Of Aung San Suu Kyi he said,

> Aung San Suu Kyi describes her confrontational approach as psychological warfare, in which every bullet counts. She is not willing to let the SPDC take credit for anything at all and is therefore unwilling to give her blessings to any engagement with the SPDC. She rejects with indignation any suggestion that the loser of any longer confrontation might be the people of Myanmar.[19]

Razali Ismail had one advantage over his predecessor. For ten years until 1998, he had been Malaysia's ambassador to the UN and was among the confidants of Malaysia's Prime Minister Mohamad Mahathir. Mahathir was a critic of Western hegemonic aspirations and had been instrumental in ensuring Myanmar's membership in ASEAN. The junta's perception of Mahathir as being well disposed to Myanmar worked in Razali's favor. This was already apparent during Razali's second visit to Myanmar in October 2000. He was received by none other than the head of the junta Than Shwe himself, an accomplishment achieved by neither his predecessor nor other international emissaries.

The new envoy set off on his mission with a busy travel itinerary. He was allowed to come to Myanmar every three months. Each time, he met with Khyin Nyunt and Than Shwe. Each visit also included two meetings with Aung San Suu Kyi. After his third visit at the beginning of January 2001, he could already report that there had been talks between the two sides. Details were not known but they were followed by a series of positive gestures from the government towards the opposition. The media attacks aimed at Aung San Suu Kyi stopped in January 2001, and some members of the party were released from prison. On the other side, the NLD and Aung San Suu Kyi avoided further provocations and signaled their desire for a dialogue, without, however, making any concessions.

Progress was made on an international front as well; the International Committee of the Red Cross was allowed to visit prisons, and the International Labour Organization entered into an agreement with Myanmar's government in March, which allowed it to open an office in the country. A path was thus carved out for at least investigating the continuous claims of civilian forced labor in the country.

These positive developments peaked in May 2002. Aung San Suu Kyi was again granted full freedom of movement, and she was now allowed to leave the city and move around the country. This widely celebrated outcome was the result of conversations between Aung San Suu Kyi and military representatives. It was the direct consequence of Razali's efforts. He described the ongoing reconciliation process as of the end of 2000 as "homegrown" and stressed that his work in Myanmar was that of a moderator, not a mediator.

Given that—as was the case with her 1995 release—there was no information available on the agreement between the two sides, the future lay entirely open. The contest between the two seats of government and their protagonists continued. The truce left some questions open: would there be a compromise? Or would one of the two sides ultimately hold the winning hand?

CHAPTER 9

A Victory Parade Cut Short

The greatest obstacle in the way of peace and progress is a lack
of trust: trust between the government and the people, between
different ethnic groups, between the military and civilian forces.
Trust is a precious commodity that is easily lost, but hard indeed
to take root.

Aung San Suu Kyi was declared unconditionally free on May 6, 2002. The lifting of restrictions received a mixed response. Her supporters, dressed in their best clothes, had gathered in front of the NLD headquarters on Shwegondine Road and cheered for her with as much fervor as during her first big speech in August 1988: "Long live Aung San Suu Kyi!" The spokesperson for the government proclaimed that a "new chapter for the people in Myanmar and the international community" had begun. He added that all citizens could participate freely in the political process and that the government was focused on the keeping of unity, peace, and stability.[1]

International observers remained largely skeptical. The release was to be welcomed, but it was also long overdue. Whether Aung San Suu Kyi and the Burmese people would really be free of government restrictions remained to be seen.[2] As so often before, the West equated Aung San Suu Kyi's destiny with that of the entire population.

Aung San Suu Kyi's own stance remained unchanged from her 1995 release: friendly but firm. She welcomed the government's move as symbolizing a new dawn and, agreeing with the government spokesperson, said that enough confidence-building had taken place and it was now time to start a serious political dialogue. In her conversations with diplomats she confirmed that her position on sanctions remained unchanged. She continued to hold that a strict sanctions regime was necessary to move the military to reason—even if a part of the population suffered as a consequence. Aung San Suu Kyi believed that the international sanctions were key in pressuring the government to release her. She also said that she was disappointed with the marginal number of political prisoners that had been released and stressed that she would continue to fight for a genuinely democratic system in the future. In this context, her release was no breakthrough event. Finally, she stated that she would visit her supporters throughout the country in order to strengthen the party and achieve its central aim of implementing democratic reform. Mobilizing the people so that the NLD could become a "people's party" that represented the interests of the whole population was the way to achieve this goal.

Her agenda for the next twelve months was thus set. The core idea was to travel through different parts of the country where NLD offices would either be reopened or inaugurated. She continued the tradition of political travels started by Aung San.

A Fine Balance

Back in the late 1980s, tense circumstances under martial law had led to Aung San Suu Kyi's first house arrest. Now it was again expected that the "stable limbo," as one observer described Myanmar's political situation in the years preceding 2002, would not last long.[3] The lifting of travel restrictions meant that Aung San Suu Kyi was now in a position to add political influence to the moral legitimacy she already possessed. Her sphere of influence ballooned from her doorstep on University Avenue to the farthest parts of the country. As an inevitable consequence, the power of the government and its mass organization, the USDA, had to decrease. All of this held potential for considerable conflict since both the NLD and the USDA aspired to represent the entire country.

The stable limbo could only be maintained if the government's loss of influence were to be compensated for in some manner. Perhaps this could have been achieved had Aung San Suu Kyi approached the government and its mass organization with an offer of finding ways of working together for the well-being of the country. It would have been entirely possible for the trust created by Razali between the opposing upper ranks of the NLD and the military government to seep through to the party base. There were, however, no signs of any such initiatives, which would have required Aung San Suu Kyi to share part of her moral capital with her former adversaries. Neither the UN special envoy nor the political rivals themselves expressed any intentions to this end. Further talks between the two sides were proposed, but no information was available on any concrete agreements or a timeframe that the parties had agreed to. How the new dawn proclaimed by all sides would transform into a bright midday sun remained unclear. Besides the declaration of Aung San Suu Kyi's "unconditional release," there was no evidence of a real plan setting out steps to be taken together.

International reactions to the release were one-sided, and the expectations for political dialogue were aimed solely at the government. One *New York Times* commentator saw Myanmar as being on a long path that would culminate not in a compromise but in the overarching triumph of the democracy icon. Still, the observer remained skeptical as to the future of Myanmar. It was unclear whether Aung San Suu Kyi would be able to resolve the country's manifold problems after a victory.[4] In May 2002, there was no sign of any form of cooperation between the two sides that could lead to a discernible improvement. The trips that Aung San Suu Kyi took shortly after her release were like journeys into the wide blue yonder.

With these travels, Aung San Suu Kyi was once again following her father's example. Aung San had undertaken an election tour in 1947, which his daughter described as "gruelling" in her father's biography. Aung San back then had traveled in an attempt to use his personal reputation to guarantee the AFPFL's victory and to demonstrate the unity of the Burmese people.[5] Aung San Suu Kyi, too, sought approval from the people of Myanmar in her travels of 2002 and 2003. But her call for solidarity with the population was not to unite against British colonial rule or communists or other dissidents. Her movement was a response to a military government disdained and feared by the people. In a way, she undertook a political pilgrimage through all parts of Burma in the footsteps of her father to purify and reclaim the country for the rightful owners. The rightful rulers were the people—and her task was more or less that of a midwife who brings the will of the people to life.

Aung San and Kachin women in November 1946; painting by Soe Moe based on an old photograph. (Photo: Hans-Bernd Zöllner)

A Foreshadowed Escalation

The trips began with visits to party offices in Yangon. Aung San Suu Kyi left the capital for the first time in June 2002 to travel to Thamanya Hill in Kayin State, just as she had done in 1995. As mentioned in chapter 7, the hill had become a spiritual and political center for Burma after its namesake monk had meditated there for three years. Now it was a symbolically powerful starting point for Aung San Suu Kyi's seven further trips. Starting here also provided Aung San Suu Kyi with spiritual blessings for her ensuing travels to different parts of the country. It was widely believed that Thamanya Sayadaw himself was among the junta's opponents. So Aung San Suu Kyi's visit here was quite contrary to being a conciliatory move to bridge the gap between her and the government.

The official aim of the trips was to establish party offices. This was done in a ritualistic way; a sign with the words "National League for Democracy" would be put up in each party office in Aung San Suu Kyi's presence. She would then give a speech.

The practice had the approval, or at least the tolerance, of government officials and required each visit to be registered with the local authorities. The local authorities were hence always aware of Aung San Suu Kyi's whereabouts. Her itinerary was no secret in any case. Her supporters and the population remained well informed, both through local NLD members and by international media, which reported on her travels regularly. U Lwin, the NLD spokesperson who acted as the main contact person between the NLD and government officials, issued regular notices for the international media.

The official rationale for the constant communication between the government and the NLD headquarters in Yangon was ensuring a smooth course of travel. The communication of the heroic freedom fighter's movements globally, and the availability of such global media in Myanmar, also gave the trips an additional layer of meaning. Her trips were seen as litmus tests to gauge whether the government would stand by its concessions on the freedom of speech, opinion, and assembly.

After the trip to Mandalay from June 22 to 30, 2002, observers agreed that the government had passed the first test. Many people had come together unhindered to see and listen to Aung San Suu Kyi in the old royal capital and other places along her route. However, some voiced regret that there were no meetings with the local military command in Mandalay. Instead, Suu Kyi was given a tour of the newly reconstructed palace for just one hour. One day later, at the government's invitation, she visited a dam project in the vicinity of the later capital Naypyidaw. Here she was received like a guest of honor.[6] The government had also shown her three other development projects a few days earlier, on her way to Mandalay. The junta saw Aung San Suu Kyi's visits to these development projects as hope "that her attitudes would surely become more flexible to lean towards cooperation with the government."[7] External observers

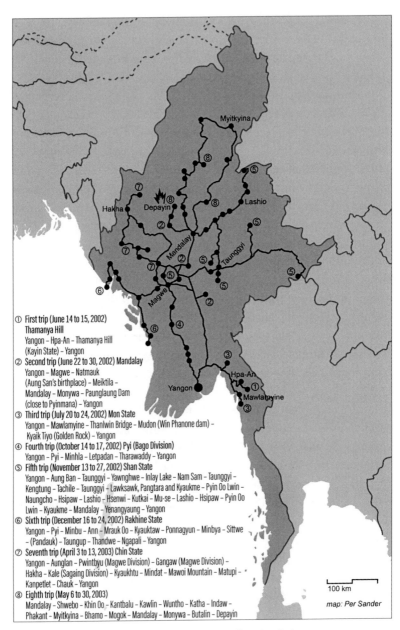

① First trip (June 14 to 15, 2002)
Thamanya Hill
Yangon – Hpa-An – Thamanya Hill
(Kayin State) – Yangon
② Second trip (June 22 to 30, 2002) Mandalay
Yangon – Magwe – Natmauk
(Aung San's birthplace) – Meiktila –
Mandalay – Monywa – Paunglaung Dam
(close to Pyinmana) – Yangon
③ Third trip (July 20 to 24, 2002) Mon State
Yangon – Mawlamyine – Thanlwin Bridge – Mudon (Win Phanone dam) –
Kyaik Tiyo (Golden Rock) – Yangon
④ Fourth trip (October 14 to 17, 2002) Pyi (Bago Division)
Yangon – Pyi – Minhla – Letpadan – Tharawaddy – Yangon
⑤ Fifth trip (November 13 to 27, 2002) Shan State
Yangon – Aung Ban – Taunggyi – Yawnghwe – Inlay Lake – Nam Sam – Taunggyi –
Kengtung – Tachile – Taunggyi – Lawksawk, Pangtara and Kyaukme – Pyin Oo Lwin –
Naungcho – Hsipaw – Lashio – Hsenwi – Kutkai – Mu-se – Lashio – Hsipaw – Pyin Oo
Lwin – Kyaukme – Mandalay – Yenangyaung – Yangon
⑥ Sixth trip (December 16 to 24, 2002) Rakhine State
Yangon – Pyi – Minbu – Ann – Mrauk Oo – Kyauktaw – Ponnagyun – Minbya – Sittwe
– (Pandauk) – Taungup – Thandwe – Ngapali – Yangon
⑦ Seventh trip (April 3 to 13, 2003) Chin State
Yangon – Aunglan – Pwintbyu (Magwe Division) – Gangaw (Magwe Division) –
Hakha – Kale (Sagaing Division) – Kyaukhtu – Mindat – Mawoi Mountain – Matupi –
Kanpetlet – Chauk – Yangon
⑧ Eighth trip (May 6 to 30, 2003)
Mandalay – Shwebo – Khin Oo – Kantbalu – Kawlin – Wuntho – Katha – Indaw –
Phakant – Myitkyina – Bhamo – Mogok – Mandalay – Monywa – Butalin – Depayin

100 km

map: Per Sander

Map of Aung San Suu Kyi's travel routes, 2002–3. (Per Sander)

Pictures showing Aung San Suu Kyi and U Tin Oo being hosted by the government during their visits to the construction site of a bridge near Magwe (June 23, 2002) and the Paungdaung Dam near Pyinmana (June 29, 2002). (Photos: Ministry of Information)

took no notice of such efforts made by the government to solicit Aung San Suu Kyi's cooperation.

The next trips, to Mon State (July 20–24, 2002) and Pyay (Prome)—Ne Win's birthplace—at the banks of the Ayeyarwady (October 14–17, 2002), as well as a long trip in Shan State (November 13–27, 2002) also took place without incident. According to the NLD spokesperson, up to five thousand people attended the ritual inaugurations of the party offices and the general secretary's speeches. She visited another dam in Mon State as well as one of the government's many bridge projects aimed at modernizing the country's infrastructure. She was also passionately received by the population in Mawlamyine, the largest city in Mon State. In her address she stressed that the NLD would persevere in fighting for a democratic system, no matter what. The hope for change was echoed by a local party member, who was cited as saying that democracy was in sight.

The travels went smoothly; however, the government and Aung San Suu Kyi—together with her domestic and international supporters—had different interpretations and expectations of what freedom of movement entailed. The government tried its best to allow the trips to take place without any hindrance. In doing so it again projected itself as the keeper of order in the country. In addition, by demonstrating its infrastructure achievements, the government hoped to co-opt Aung San Suu Kyi into its vision of national renewal. These hopes were expressed by young allegedly former members of the NLD in a series of restrospective articles, published in in September 2003, on the events between May 2002 and May 2003 as follows:

> We had at first expected that after visiting one development project after another, she would come to understand and appreciate the extent of the efforts that had been made, and that her attitudes would surely become more flexible to lean towards cooperating with the government. Sadly, things did not turn out as expected.[8]

Aung San Suu Kyi took part in the events organized by the government but in her speeches lost no words on the development projects. Instead, she reiterated her resolve to bring democracy to Myanmar and with it, her own project to a conclusion.

The party office inaugurations were occasions for pushing her own agenda. By regarding her as a symbol of hope, the people in the places she visited were at the same time expressing their rejection of the military regime. Her supporters read this public approval as the impending victory of her movement. More skeptical observers, however, had a sense of foreboding. There was eruptive potential in the growing wave of enthusiasm.

The first major problems started during a trip to the west of the country, in Rakhine State (December 16–24, 2002). According to the NLD, state officials were increasingly hindering the public from attending Aung San Suu Kyi's events. The gatherings were also disrupted more frequently. On the other side, the junta complained that Aung San Suu Kyi's statements about the government were becoming increasingly negative. This was seen as a breach of the agreement reached before her release—to no longer levy attacks on each other. The government had also been trying to tackle the issue of international sanctions for a long time, and Aung San Suu Kyi's continued support of the sanctions pitted her against them.[9]

The NLD media spokesperson told the world of an incident that took place on December 18 in Mrauk-U, the former capital of the old Arakanese Kingdom. He stated that the authorities used sticks and water cannons to try and disperse some twenty thousand people who had gathered to listen to Aung San Suu Kyi. Aung San Suu Kyi subsequently climbed on to a water cannon, gave a speech on democracy, and asked the people gathered to go home. She was quoted as follows: "I am here in the name of democracy which puts the people ahead of everything else. Our first priority is to serve and support the people—the police as well as other officials have the same responsibility. I cannot stand by and watch my people being bullied by [sic] this manner."[10] The media spokesperson took the opportunity to also recall Aung San Suu Kyi's brave stance against a group of soldiers in 1989, when she had unflinchingly stepped towards armed men who had been ordered by an army captain to shoot at her.

The disruptions continued during the next trip, in Chin State (April 3–13, 2003). When asked why the coordination with state authorities went amiss, the NLD spokesperson stated that some disagreement must have existed between the local officials—with whom he had contact—and their superiors in Yangon. He insinuated that the obstruction had been ordered from above. In contrast, the government let it be known that it retained its "complete trust" in Aung San Suu Kyi. It played down any reported hurdles to her journey. The government continued to claim that it welcomed Aung San Suu Kyi's travels and conversations with the citizens. It praised the fact that after all the years of house arrest, she was now able to get back in touch with her country, which had clearly improved.[11]

The mutual trust that both sides had started off with at the beginning of the year had already suffered significant damage by this point. After the trip to Chin State, Aung San Suu Kyi said at a press conference that she and her party had to doubt the SPDC's integrity. She was cited as saying, "National reconciliation is change. They don't want change, but change is inevitable."[12] The next day, the speaker for the government rejected the accusations. General Than Tun, the intermediary between her and the junta who had lead the talks that eventually led to her release, said,

> I would like to question the reasons behind these senseless accusations and cannot help but wonder if it is a deliberate act aimed at discrediting the Myanmar military in the eyes of the world. If that be the case, it will not serve the purpose of national reconciliation. I can only say that this kind of thinking is very outdated . . . and should have been left behind in 1988.[13]

Clearly, there were two opposing points of view on the question of national reconciliation. Each side accused the other of not taking steps forward and of not being seriously interested in an agreement. It was a reminder of the differences between the two sides before Aung San Suu Kyi's house arrest, albeit in language that was less confrontational.

It is no wonder that the situation eventually escalated. On May 6, 2003, the anniversary of her release from the second house arrest, Aung San Suu Kyi set out on her longest trip yet, to the north of the country. As in early 1989, Kachin State, too, had to be visited. The Kachin Independence Organisation was an especially strong autonomy-seeking political association. Their powerful military arm had agreed to a ceasefire with the government in 1994.

The trip again was like a ballooning victory parade. Government officials made futile attempts to convince people not to welcome Aung San Suu Kyi. They also tried to disrupt the trip with counter-demonstrations by USDA members and other measures. Despite the intimidation and the activities of government-mobilized demonstrators, thousands of people lined the streets to receive Aung San Suu Kyi and her travel companions. The small motorcade that had set off from Yangon was joined by more and more motorcycles, on which local NLD members and others accompanied her on her journey. The large numbers that turned out were essentially voting with their presence and showing their support for the NLD leader.

During the last trip, Aung San Suu Kyi had set out her conception of an ideal government in the following way:

> It is said that a government despised by its people is the worst kind of government. The next kind of slightly better government is one that is feared by the people. A government praised by the people is a better one. The best kind of government is one [where] the people do not have to think about its existence. It means the country is very peaceful.[14]

The country was in no state of peace. To the contrary, after the victory parade through Kachin State, the tension escalated and ended in violence.

Aung San Suu Kyi's party returned to Mandalay on May 27, 2003. Some twenty monks accompanied the traveling convoy to protect it from assaults. At a meeting near Mandalay some of them shot with slingshots at USDA members who had tried to disrupt a gathering with loudspeakers. The timing of the visit was poignant as it was on May 27 that the NLD had won the elections thirteen years previously. One eyewitness attested that it was thanks to the monks' intervention that Aung San Suu Kyi went on to receive a jubilant reception, undisturbed by USDA members, on May 29 in Monywa, near Mandalay.[15] Aung San Suu Kyi expressly defended the monks' actions in her Monywa speech:

Aung San Suu Kyi with some bodyguards, on her tour in Mandalay. (Photo: Laif)

"The monks did that because they could not stand the bullying. They did that because they could not accept the injustice. Another thing, they did that because they pitied the NLD."[16]

What happened after dusk on May 30, 2003, in the town of Depayin, further north of Monywa, went far beyond government obstructionism or political antagonism. To this day, it is not clear who specifically was responsible for the violence that followed. The events are interpreted differently by the two sides; Aung San Suu Kyi's supporters and global human rights observers described what happened as a "massacre," while the government saw the events as the culmination of a long series of "incidents."

The United Nations special rapporteur on human rights in Myanmar came to the following conclusion when he published his findings in November 2003 and January 2004: the "violent incident at Depayin in May that led to many arrests could not have happened without the connivance of state agents."[17] According to the rapporteur's findings, Aung San Suu Kyi's pickup truck was leading the convoy of at least eleven cars and around 150 motorcycles.[18] When the convoy arrived near Kyee village, two or more monks, or individuals dressed as monks, appeared in front of it and asked Aung San Suu Kyi to address the people. When the motorcade stopped, the robed individuals and around fifty people riding in trucks that had been trailing the motorcade began to attack. The attackers used sharpened bamboo stakes and iron rods to target the convoy and the villagers who had gathered to welcome Aung San Suu Kyi and her party. The vehicle at the head of the convoy that carried Aung San Suu Kyi managed to break away in a controlled move but was stopped at a roadblock a few kilometers further. The security forces took the opposition leader into custody and brought her to Insein Prison. After spending June to September 2003 in the infamous prison, Aung San Suu Kyi was sent home but under a newly imposed house arrest, which would only end in November 2010.

The security forces that arrived shortly after the outbreak of violence at the scene in Depayin arrested a number of people connected with the NLD. There are no reliable accounts of the number of deaths and injuries. According to the government, which presented its version of events at a press conference on May 31, four people died because of an accident involving a car in the NLD motorcade.[19] Opposition circles spoke of seventy killed. The UN special rapporteur could not ascertain an exact number but reported that "according to testimonies, there were between fifty and seventy people lying on the road, either injured or dead."

Depayin was a tragic and bloody climax of—in hindsight—a foreseeable chain of escalation. The situation had begun to worsen from May 2002 onwards. This was the opposite of what had been hoped for at the point of Aung San Suu Kyi's release. In the years that followed, Depayin went on to become a symbol of the junta's brutality. It came to be seen as an organization that did not even flinch at having a Nobel Peace Prize winner killed. But such a conclusion is too imbalanced, just like the government's stance that the Depayin incident was entirely the result of the NLD and its Western supporters' misconduct. A generous interpretation would suggest that both sides underestimated the dynamics of the event, or knowingly risked the escalation in the hope of advancing their own agendas.

The former UN special envoy Razali Ismail described the dynamics that followed Aung San Suu Kyi's release from her second house arrest in a later interview as follows:

> When she was to be released from detention in 2002, one of the understandings was that she would not go out and demonstrate or speak badly of Myanmar outside. She was to help the government bring about good things for the people. But you are talking about an icon—you release her, everybody flocks to see her. She was always particular about not creating demonstrations, but after a while she could see that there was so much to be done yet so little was actually being done. With people pleading to her to help, her visits took on political overtones. She became more of a politician and started traveling farther outside of Yangon [Rangoon]. Everywhere she went, tens of thousands followed. The military leaders were disturbed. I made the point to a minister I knew for some time that it would be a mistake to let Suu Kyi travel around and not begin the critical talks between the government and the NLD.[20]

Razali's colleague and UN human rights rapporteur Sergio Pinheiro's suspicion that the incident could not have taken place without the government's complicity is undoubtedly correct. The government had an interest in bringing Aung San Suu Kyi's victory parade to a halt. But it is unlikely that there was a plan to kill Aung San Suu Kyi, as has been held by numerous opponents of the regime until today. Unlike U Saw, who had Aung San murdered from a position of weakness, it was not necessary for the government to have its opponent physically removed. The murder of the daughter of the national hero would also not have fit in the junta's Buddhist self-perception. It is more likely that the junta set up the incident at Depayin in an attempt to politically sideline Aung San Suu Kyi, given that her release was not panning out as it had envisioned. Once Depayin happened, the junta was going to impose another long house arrest to try to do the job of banishing the symbol of the people's hope.

The role of the monks at the beginning and end of the 2002 and 2003 travels sheds important light on Aung San Suu Kyi as an icon for democracy. The politicization that Razali complains of falls short in its description of actual developments. In reality, the monks' involvement shows that supporting Aung San Suu Kyi was not just about politics, it was also about religion and morality. Just like Thamanya Sayadaw, whose blessings she had sought before setting out on her political travels, Aung San Suu Kyi was seen as a savior. She gave her country—set on the right path by her father but subsequently defiled by his successors—its dignity back. The monks that stepped in to protect her at the end of the trip illustrated that this was about a fight between good and evil; it was about Buddhist virtues. Purely political compromises—like the ones that Razali and other mediators had tried to negotiate—had no chance of success in this context.

The importance of religion and morality was not unknown to the junta. In April 2002, the SPDC leadership inaugurated a new pagoda on a hill near the airport in the north of Yangon. In the center of this pagoda stood a large marble Buddha that had reached this destination two years earlier after a twelve-day procession from Upper Myanmar. At the beginning of the journey, the first secretary of the junta, Khin Nyunt, spoke to more than one hundred thousand people that had gathered at the landing ramps for the barges, built especially for the occasion. In his speech, he compared the situation in Myanmar to the time of King Mindon. The king also had a Buddha statue carved out of a massive block of marble, which formed the center of a pagoda in Mandalay inaugurated in his presence with great pomp.[21] Khin Nyunt said,

> The ceremony to convey [the marble Buddha] image is an auspicious occasion which can be met [only] once during a span of over 100 years, and those who did meritorious deeds in their past existences can meet it; during the reign of King Mindon, the ceremony to convey [the marble Buddha] image from Sakyintaung [the Marble Hills near Mandalay] was held; only after 136 years elapsed, the State Peace and Development Council has the chance to hold the conveying ceremony of [such

a Buddha image again]; the ceremony is held again only after two or three generations passed. . . . In the Union of Myanmar where Sasana [Buddhist religion] is flourishing as it was in the life-time of the Buddha, . . . Chairman of the State Peace and Development Council Senior General Than Shwe gave guidance that [the image] should be conveyed to Yangon for public obeisance.[22]

In other words, Khin Nyunt was comparing the junta's religious merit with that of the revered King Mindon. A great block of marble transforming into an image of Buddha was both a display of wealth and an attestation of religion. At the same time, it served as a showcase for a country on an economically sound path. The religious foundations of the junta's self-identity are exposed here. Aung San Suu Kyi was released from her second house arrest a month after the inauguration of the pagoda. The government felt certain of its place as a successor of the Buddha and the great King Mindon.

The journey of the image of the Buddha along the Ayeyarwady, a river that has traditionally been the lifeline of Myanmar, and the travels

Send-off for the Buddha image, Mandalay, July 2000. (Photo: Hans-Bernd Zöllner)

of Aung San Suu Kyi share a structural semblance that reveals a key to the relationship between religion and politics in Myanmar. Every politician requires Buddhist legitimation for his or her actions.[23] At the same time, such moral elevation of the political office makes compromise and conciliation difficult. There is either total victory or total defeat. With neither side willing to back down, one can start to understand how Depayin could have happened. In addition, the parallel reveals something about the people's mode of thinking. They gathered in masses at the twelve stations where the great barge carrying the junta's marble Buddha was moored on its way from Mandalay to Insein. But politically, they followed Aung San Suu Kyi.

A compromise between the military regime and Aung San Suu Kyi—something that many had hoped for—had completely failed. She ended up spending the next seven-and-half years under house arrest after a few months in Insein Prison.

Razali Ismail visited Aung San Suu Kyi in prison, where she had been assigned to a special building. The authorities did not reveal her location to the public. Razali painted a detailed picture of his visit:

> It was like one of those detective stories—they changed cars, changed drivers, I had no idea who the guy behind the wheel was. I got into the car and I thought, 'What on earth am I doing?' I was driven farther and farther and I was all by myself. I thought, 'Am I going to be safe?' There were cars with tinted windows following. Then all of a sudden, we had arrived. And what a destination it was, Insein Prison, the general prison where all manner of crooks and criminals were gathered. Pronounced like "insane," the irony of the prison's name was certainly not lost on me. Inside the compound, I was driven first to the left, then to the right, then finally, to a concrete hut.[24]

Only very little information escaped to the public after that. On September 19, Aung San Suu Kyi's doctor stated that she had undergone a "big operation."[25] According to an official announcement she was allowed to return to her house on University Avenue a week later for "humanitarian reasons." Another long house arrest was issued on November 18, 2003. Razali subsequently visited Myanmar two more times. As of June 2004, he could no longer obtain a visitor's permit. He was replaced by the Nigerian diplomat Ibrahim Gambari in December.

The Roadmap to a Disciplined Democracy

A few months after Depayin, an important change of leadership took place in the government. Khin Nyunt, who had served as the first secretary of the junta for fifteen years, was named prime minister in August 2003. Up until this point, this position had been held by the head of the junta, Than Shwe. The new post was no promotion. It was more of a demotion, which cut Khin Nyunt out of the inner circles of the military leadership.

Khin Nyunt's first official act as prime minister was to announce a "Seven-Step Roadmap to a Discipline-Flourishing Democracy."[26] This set the guiding principles for the junta's politics in the coming years.

Step one saw the reconvening of the national convention that had been interrupted in its work of drafting a new constitution in 1996. The constitution itself was to be adopted in step four. Elections were to be held following that, leading to the transfer of responsibility to a government elected in accordance with the constitution. The seventh and final step saw the building of a "modern, developed and democratic nation."[27]

The plan was executed with military precision up to the sixth step, irrespective of all Western critique and domestic protests. The military element in the implementation of the roadmap was reflected in the fact that although the individual steps of the plan were made generally available, hard deadlines were only revealed at short notice. This method left little room for any external resistance to the process. After a deadline was announced with short notice, the military was unswerving in its execution to meet it.

Thus, after the national convention's deliberations, the referendum on the constitution was held as planned on May 8, 2008, although the country had just been hit with a national catastrophe. Cyclone Nargis had ravaged the Ayeyarwady Delta on May 2. More than one hundred thousand people died. Yet the vote was only postponed in the regions hit hardest by the storm. Aung San Suu Kyi was forced to play a marginal role during the entirety of this process. As it happened, the violent culmination of her trips in May 2003 was the starting point for something else: the process that has led to the current political system of Myanmar.

Aung San Suu Kyi and her party only sporadically aroused international attention in the years following the imposition of her third house arrest. The first time was when the NLD refused to take part in the elections held on November 7, 2010—step five of the road map. This decision could not have been made without Aung San Suu Kyi's acquiescence. The NLD's justification for this boycott was that the constitution adopted in 2008—with step four of the roadmap—was just as unacceptable as the election law under which the elections of 2010 were to be held. Among other points of contention, the constitution provided that a quarter of the seats in all elected parliaments would be determined by the upper command of the military.[28] The disagreement on this provision continues until today.

The NLD was removed from the list of registered parties because of its boycott, in accordance with the election law. It thus lost the status that it had held since 1988 as one of the ten officially registered parties. After an intense debate within the party, the National Democratic Force (NDF) was founded. The NDF was made up of NLD members that had been against the election boycott.

Khin Nyunt, who had been the architect and founder of the roadmap, was long out of the picture by this time. He had lost his position in October 2004 and was given a prison sentence, which he was permitted to serve under house arrest. He benefited from an amnesty granted to a number of political prisoners by his successor and later president, Thein Sein, in January 2012. He now has an art gallery, two souvenir shops, and a café on his property.

Khin Nyunt in July 2013 in a pavilion on his property, which now houses an art gallery and a café. (Photo: Hans-Bernd Zöllner)

The transfer of power took place on March 30, 2011. The military could step back into the second row. The SPDC dissolved and handed over government responsibility to the new government under former military general Thein Sein. Thein Sein had previously held Khin Nyunt's long-term position as first secretary of the junta. Shortly before the 2010 election—which was boycotted by the NLD—he ended his military career and took over the leadership of the Union Solidarity and Development Party (USDP), the successor to the mass organization of the USDA.

The Monk Protests

Aung San Suu Kyi appeared in the limelight for some time in September 2007 in the context of the monk protests. The protests came to be known as the Saffron Revolution and dominated international headlines for a short period of time.[29] The demonstrations were preceded by a drastic increase in the price of compressed gas, which had led to an equally drastic increase in the price of bus tickets in Yangon. The hike hit low-income earners the hardest. The protests by civil activists, led by the 88 Generation Students Group, were brought to an end through arrests. The monks started demonstrating on the twentieth anniversary of the SLORC coming to power.[30] One group of monks had handed in an ultimatum to the government after unconfirmed reports that a monk had been killed in the demonstrations in the city of Pakokku in central Myanmar. Besides calling for withdrawal of the price hike, the monks were also demanding Aung San Suu Kyi's release.

At the beginning, the monks had requested the civilian population to refrain from participating in the protests. The government did not intervene for a week. The situation changed when a group of monks filed to the house on University Avenue on September 22 and Aung San Suu Kyi briefly opened the gate to greet them. The monks' visit to the leader of the opposition proved to be a turning point.

Aung San Suu Kyi greeting the monks on September 23, 2007. (Photo: Reuters)

In Theravada Buddhist theory, the sphere of the political world is supposed to remain strictly separate to the sphere of the religious supra-world. Now, the touching of these two spheres gave a new dimension to the demonstrations that ultimately prompted the government into action. The government had the highest council of monks announce that the meddling into political affairs was inconsistent with the ordinances of the monk community. The law enforcement authorities ended the demonstrations after that by raiding the monasteries that were the starting points for the marchers. At least thirty-one people died and many were injured. Despite several reports to the contrary, there were no monks among these numbers.[31] The Saffron Revolution ended without any tangible consequences.

The Swimmer

The story of the "swimmer," John William Yettaw, would certainly take a leading spot in any ranking of surreal and absurd tales (of which there are plenty) from recent Burmese history. The American citizen and Vietnam veteran swam from the South Korean embassy, also located on the shores of Inya Lake, to Aung San Suu Kyi's house on the early morning of May 4, 2009. He was welcomed and taken care of by the house employees and Aung San Suu Kyi herself. He stayed till the late evening of May 5. He was apprehended by the security forces on his attempt to swim back across the lake to the western bank.

It appeared that he had already paid an earlier visit to the property in November 2008 and had left behind a copy of the *Book of Mormon*. The incident had been reported by Aung San Suu Kyi's doctor four days later but Yettaw had already left the country by then. During his visit in May 2009, he left behind two black chadors and veils as well as four sunglasses for Aung San Suu Kyi. Besides that, according to the police report, he also gave her fifty-three sheets of paper, each with a sentence written by his ten-year-old daughter, which read, "I love you. Please don't kill her!"[32]

The officials claimed that Aung San Suu Kyi had broken the terms of her house arrest by receiving the American in her home. On May 13, charges were pressed against her and both her house employees who had helped the visitor. This happened exactly fourteen days prior to the date beyond which legal provisions prohibited any extension of her house arrest. The incident raises the question as to whether the oddly behaving American was not employed to cause harm to Aung San Suu Kyi. The security forces in turn speculated whether the American had a network of helpers.

Aung San Suu Kyi during a trial at Insein Prison on May 20, 2009. (Photo: Reuters)

During the hearing, Aung San Suu Kyi defended her act of receiving the confused swimmer with her political conviction that people who were at risk of unjust imprisonment had to be given protection. When she asked the visitor to leave her property, he expressed the fear of being arrested. This is why she let him stay at her house overnight, so that he could escape unnoticed the next night. She compared Yettaw's potential arrest with the long-term prison sentences levied on many of her colleagues "without the protection or leniency of law."[33] Besides, Aung San Suu Kyi could argue that the problem in this case appeared to be deficient security arrangements put in place by the authorities for the protection of her house.[34]

The court ruled against Aung San Suu Kyi and added eighteen months to her house arrest, with the new end date now set to November 13, 2010. And indeed, Aung San Suu Kyi was released on precisely that day. It was no coincidence that elections had taken place one week earlier, without incident. It is obvious that the NLD leader's date of release played a part in the setting of the election schedule. The SPDC's precision planning in realizing its roadmap towards its own version of democracy would certainly not overlook this detail.

CHAPTER 10

Course Correction or U-turn?

If you want to bring an end to long-standing conflict, you have to be prepared to compromise.

The junta leadership had reason to rejoice on March 30, 2011. Thein Sein, who had until recently worn a general's uniform, was being sworn in as president after a parliamentary vote. The military junta had pressed forth on all fronts. The first six hurdles to a "Discipline-Flourishing Democracy" had been crossed as per the plan. The head of state was one of the junta's very own, and a formally legitimate one at that. Thein Sein took over the role through a formal, watertight democratic process. He had held important official positions over the years and thus appeared to be qualified to take on this final stage as per the military leadership's plans. Unlike the preceding six, however, the seventh and final step of the Roadmap—"building a modern, developed and democratic nation by the state leaders elected by the Hluttaw [parliament]; and the government and other central organs formed by the Hluttaw"—did not lend itself to strategic military planning. It was by its very nature an unpredictable enterprise with an unknown outcome. In any case, the military's involvement in key areas was guaranteed through the constitution. Accordingly, it was supposed that stability would prevail in the country. But whether the people of the country could be convinced that Myanmar would now become modern, developed, and democratic remained to be seen. From a Western perspective, this required letting the voters reach a verdict on the government's success every four to five years.

Thein Sein had been a somewhat colorless military bureaucrat. He had made a civilian impression even while wearing a uniform. He had served the regime in a series of political posts without ever leaving his

Swearing in of the president, Thein Sein, March 30, 2011. (Photo: Myanmar Times*)*

own mark. Thein Sein was held to be one of Than Shwe's yea-sayers. The idea that old rulers continued to hold the strings to power and have their puppets dance on the political stage was, and is, widely accepted both in Myanmar and by Western critics of the regime. For many this resembled Ne Win's retreat in 1988. Ne Win's successors, Saw Maung and Khin Nyunt, were held to be just executors of his ideas. In hindsight this was—at least in part—a misinterpretation. The view was nurtured by the conviction that power-hungry generals by their very nature wanted to keep power for power's sake. This perception undoubtedly undermined the legitimacy of all of Ne Win's successors and also Thein Sein's credibility to some extent. The new president, however, had one thing that worked in his favor: neither he nor members of his family were involved in any scandals. The family was held to be one of the few uncorrupted ones from the higher ranks of the military.[1]

In fact, the new head of state had numerous surprises in store for his skeptics during his first period in office. He not only managed to uphold his clean image but also introduced a comprehensive agenda for reform. This agenda was announced in Thein Sein's inaugural speech and was going to touch all aspects of society.[2] In the first part of the speech, when talking about political power, he stated that the unity of the nation was the highest goal and that changes to the constitution were imaginable in order to achieve that goal. This threw off those who believed Than Shwe to be the puppet master. Than Shwe was held to be a cunning man, but the statements could not be easily reconciled with the idea that he was still pulling the strings in the background. Such a reform program seemed simply incompatible with the former junta strongman.

A Binding Victory

Then Sein's comprehensive plan must also be understood as a response to the colossal task placed by the former military rulers on their alleged stooge. Accordingly, Ko Ko Hlaing—who was appointed chief advisor to the president shortly after Thein Sein took office—said roughly the following in June 2013: "Myanmar suffers from four major shortcomings: lack of trust, lack of skills, lack of unity and lack of political culture. But we accept these big challenges. Who can say that in the world but us?"[3]

According to this evaluation, Myanmar was once again starting from scratch. There are notable parallels here to Aung San Suu Kyi's assessment of 1988, when she called for a second struggle for Burma's national independence.

The president and his advisors were very aware that the final goal of unity—propagated for years by the military leadership but never realized—was only achievable if certain concessions were made. To achieve real union based on national reconciliation within the Union of Myanmar came at a price. The government knew that it also had to approach those who held the new constitution to be undemocratic. These critics were headed by Aung San Suu Kyi—and her party, which should really be understood as an organization held together by the grace of its leader—who had expressly rejected the constitution in the 2009 Shwegondine Declaration. Following Aung San Suu Kyi's advice, the NLD had approved the declaration back then and subsequently paid for it by a party split.

Challenges for the Challenger

Aung San Suu Kyi also found herself in a conflicted position after her release. On the one hand, she was free and once again had access to her elixir of life: the contact with her supporters. She embraced this immediately in her first speech after the end of her house arrest.[4] On the other hand, she had no official political party left. According to the Party Registration Law, each of the ten legally existing parties had until May 6, 2010, to reregister. The NLD had refused to do so because it regarded the law as undemocratic. It was consequently deregistered on May 7, 2010. It must, however, be noted that the government did not take any measures against the various branches of the NLD. They continued their work.

This legal issue did not come up in Aung San Suu Kyi's initial postrelease activities. Upon being reunited with her supporters, she continued in the spirit of her 1995 and 1996 speeches. She asked them for their help in her efforts to make democracy a reality and called on her public to take matters into their own hands. As before, she reiterated that she held no contempt for those who had imprisoned her. She had been treated well. Never were any direct attacks made against the sitting military government, except for a little quip of a comment that the NLD wanted to win people's trust, not their votes. The applause showed that the crowd had clearly understood the reference to the questionable electoral victory of the USDP. In the calls that reached her from the public, a new form of reverence was now to be heard: "Mother Suu." She had come one step closer to the status accorded to her father Aung San, who was after all also "the father of the nation." By this time, Aung San Suu Kyi's age was more suited to the role of the head of the family. She was sixty-six years old at the time of her release but appeared, as many observers have noted, much younger.

Aung San Suu Kyi during her first speech after her release on November 14, 2010, in front of the NLD headquarters. (Photo: AFP/Getty)

During the first days following her release, Aung San Suu Kyi met with friends of the party, visited an AIDS clinic run by a member of the party youth, and gave a series of interviews. In the latter, she stressed that she remained prepared for further dialogue with the junta but had not yet received a signal suggesting that the other side was open to engaging with her.

The first real political act took place a week after her release. She met with the members of the shadow parliament (Committee Representing the People's Parliament or CRPP). The CRPP had been conceived by the opposition in 1998 as an alternative to the 1990 parliament that was never convened. The key issue for the meeting was the support of an initiative—long advocated by ethnic leaders—to arrange a conference aimed at resolving ethnic conflicts. The 1947 Panglong Conference was to serve as a model.

The CRPP was indirectly criticizing the 2008 constitution with this proposition. After all, the constitution also claimed to regulate relations between different ethnic groups in a peaceful manner. For the first time in Myanmar's constitutional history, the 2008 constitutional text established parliaments in all fourteen regions and states of the country. The chief ministers, however, were to be appointed by the president. The representatives of the ethnic minority groups were critical of this last requirement. The NLD adopted the critique and added that if such a conference were to make sense, the military must also participate. The NLD's approach was clever. Aung San Suu Kyi's party reached out to the military with one hand and with the other it approached the ethnic groups. Until now, Aung San Suu Kyi's camp had made only very general statements in relation to the central question of coexistence in the multinational state of Myanmar. In the end—at least for now—the initiative led to nothing.[5]

On top of that, Aung San Suu Kyi advised the party to concentrate its efforts on youth work. A party website was launched for the first time. Aung San Suu Kyi was encouraged by the events in the Arab world and the Arab Spring. She drew comparisons with the situation in Myanmar and hoped that a similar spirit of change would spread in Myanmar with the help of the social media used by young people.[6] Maybe tweets would soon also overwhelm Myanmar's media space. In an interview with a Canadian newspaper, Aung San Suu Kyi noted that she now had an internet connection at home for a thousand US dollars. It had been installed by a company close to the government, but the connection was apparently very slow.[7]

As to the legal status of the NLD, Aung San Suu Kyi challenged the law that had resulted in the party's deregistration. The case was brought before Myanmar's Supreme Court. At some point the high commissioner for human rights was considered as a portal for complaints. However, these moves were more symbolic than anything else. They demonstrated Aung San Suu Kyi's fundamental opposition to the military's attempt to use the law to legitimize its rule. The idea of Aung San Suu Kyi's "democracy movement" as a "government in waiting" was confined to symbolic politics whereas Thein Sein's actual government continued to lack legitimacy despite the changes and the president's programmatic initiatives.

Pragmatic Course Correction

It was the political incumbents that finally took the first steps towards mending the relationship. They demonstrated that they took their commitments seriously and were doing everything they could for national reconciliation and unity. The NLD, on its part, was under pressure to play along with the government because of the upcoming by-elections. There were forty-eight parliamentary seats at stake, vacated by members of parliament who had taken over ministerial positions since the 2010 elections. Not participating again could result in the NLD being pushed further aside.

Cooperation between the two sides was the pertinent issue. This message was delivered to the NLD in no uncertain terms by Aung Kyi, the minister of labor and of social welfare. Also former military, Aung Kyi had already been labor minister under the SPDC government and had the reputation of being a dependable negotiator. After the 2007 monk unrest, he was charged with an additional task and named "minister of relations"—meaning exclusively building and nurturing a good relationship with Aung San Suu Kyi. Since his appointment, the two had met around ten times.

Aung Kyi met with Aung San Suu Kyi on July 25, 2011, and conveyed the government's desire to allow for the party to reregister. Aung San Suu Kyi rejected the idea. After all, it would have involved acknowledging the deregistration as a legitimate act. Despite these opposing views, the two stood before the media after their meeting and confirmed that they would continue to meet in the interests of the nation and the people of the country.

A second meeting ensued on August 12, after just over two weeks. It was followed by a joint statement that the state media also published; both sides agreed to refrain from voicing opposing views in public and to focus on cooperation. Aung San Suu Kyi then received an official invitation to Naypyidaw, to participate in a workshop on the economic development of the country. President Thein Sein was also present here,

Aung San Suu Kyi and Aung Kyi after their meeting at a press conference on October 30, 2011. (Photo: The Voice)

Aung San Suu Kyi and Thein Sein after their conversation on August 19, 2011. (Photo: Reuters)

and he and Aung San Suu Kyi met for an hour on the sidelines of the conference.

The photo published after the meeting is remarkable. The representatives of the two competing political visions for the country— Thein Sein's Myanmar and Aung San Suu Kyi's Burma—stand under an image of Aung San, depicting the father of the nation in civilian clothing. President Thein Sein wears no symbols of his power. The only thing that gives away a difference in rank between him and Aung San Suu Kyi is the latter's name badge, identifying her as a participant in the workshop. Unlike in many other images, she stands here not as an icon for democracy but as "citizen Suu," allowing herself to be photographed with a civilian president.

The government's charm offensive continued and showed effect. At the end of September, it came to be known that a Chinese dam project in Kachin State, which had been the focus of protests by environmentalists, numerous NGOs, and also the NLD, was temporarily halted.[8] Almost simultaneously, the NLD announced that it was considering registering as a political party again. However, this depended on further steps by the government and—according to Aung San Suu Kyi, after a third meeting with Aung Kyi in October—on further consultations within the party.[9] At the end of October, parliament approved a change in the party registration law promulgated by the SPDC before the 2010 elections. Following this, the NLD announced that it would make a decision on the question of registration within a week.

The change of the registration law, signed into effect by President Thein Sein on November 9, addressed two issues. First, until now, party leaders had to pledge to "safeguard" the 2008 constitution upon party registration. This was changed so that party leaders had to "respect" and "obey" the constitution. The NLD's rejection of the constitution was dealt with in this way without changing any provision of the highly contested document. Second, the stipulation that "convicts" could not become party members and thus political candidates was removed. This was, however, just a cosmetic gesture, as according to the definitions at the beginning of the law, "convicts" were persons actually serving a jail sentence. The provision therefore did not prevent Aung San Suu Kyi or any other NLD members who had been released from prison from participating in the elections.

Finally, on November 18, 2011, the central committee of the NLD decided to have the party reregistered. According to newspaper reports, joyous party members broke into a dance as the announcement was made. "What we are doing now involves a lot of risk but it is time to take the risk because in politics there is no 100 percent assurance of success," Suu Kyi told them and hinted at participating in the elections herself.[10]

A day later, the United States announced that Secretary of State Hillary Clinton would visit Myanmar. This happened after President Obama had spoken to Aung San Suu Kyi on the phone from Bali, where he was attending an Asia Pacific Economic Cooperation summit.

Aung San Suu Kyi and Tin Oo traveled to Naypyidaw once more to formally sign the registration application at the election commission there. The party had already formed an election campaign committee by this point.

Hilary Clinton and Aung San Suu Kyi, December 2, 2011. (Photo: Myanmar Times*)*

On December 30, 2011, the election commission announced April 1, 2012, as the date set for holding parliamentary by-elections. In addition to the forty seats in the lower house, six seats had become available in the upper house, or the house of nationalities, and two in the fourteen regional parliaments. The available seats in the lower house accounted for less than a tenth of all seats in parliament. No measurable change in power relationships was thus to be expected. But that did not matter. What was of import was how the elections would unfold. These were the first elections to be held since Thein Sein's nominally civilian government had stepped into power. People within and outside the country were curious. Could the 1990 and 2010 election experience be left behind? In other words, would these elections be free and fair, and would the result be respected? Of course, there was also much curiosity surrounding Aung San Suu Kyi's participation. This was the first time that she was running for political office, and under the very conditions that she had opposed for decades.

The government had made no substantive concessions to the NLD. The NLD participated, thereby implicitly accepting the 2008 Constitution and the election law because of which it had previously boycotted the 2010 elections. The question as to why the party took this U-turn under Aung San Suu Kyi's leadership was never officially answered by anyone. The one hundred delegates who had gathered to vote on the issue of participation on November 18 agreed unanimously, although a group of "hardliners" opposing the move did exist, as it would accord legitimacy to the constitution put in place by the military.

Most analysts are of the opinion that once Aung San Suu Kyi decided to participate in the elections, the party's central committee just followed her. They argue that not participating would have meant leaving the field open for the military and the government installed by it. Besides this rational explanation, the mood of the people and the party members also played an important role. In a meeting with a German delegation in December 2011, one prominent NLD member expressed his conviction that the 2012 elections would be a turning point in Myanmar's history: "All 48 seats contested would be won by the NLD, the same would happen in 2015 as it had in 1990 just because of the party leader's popularity. After that, Aung San Suu Kyi would become President. The people wanted Aung San Suu Kyi to participate in the elections."[11]

Aung San Suu Kyi's attitude towards the government remained ambivalent nonetheless. After meeting with Thein Sein she was convinced of his good intentions, but doubted whether he had the full backing of the military. She articulated this carefully skeptical attitude at the beginning of January 2012 by commenting that the NLD would not limit itself to parliamentary work.[12] She upheld the NLD's position as extraparliamentary opposition. They were to remain the voice of the entire country and not just the voters who would go on to elect NLD representatives on April 1, 2012.

The turn that the party took by registering itself was not to be conceived of as a belated acceptance of the junta's reforms. Rather, it was a tactical move, a necessary adjustment given the new reality. It was also a concession to the people, who would rather support "Mother Suu" with their vote than participate in a stubborn resistance against the junta as had been proposed earlier in Suu Kyi's "revolution of the spirit."

Assessing the NLD's decision to accept the constitution and take part in the elections is a difficult task. It was certainly a complete U-turn by Aung San Suu Kyi's party when compared to the small concessions made by the government. Yet it was the continuation of a previously adopted stance, namely, to change the entire political system. As for the government, the election victories of the NLD must not have posed any fundamental threat since the constitution ring-fenced the military's role and gave it a decisive say in Myanmar's politics. Later, in October 2012, President Thein Sein went on to state that not only could he conceive of a change to the constitution, but Aung San Suu Kyi herself could also become president.[13] According to the present constitution, however, she could only become a regular member of parliament.

A First Victory for Humility

One commentator noted that Aung San Suu Kyi and the NLD's participation would lend "legitimacy, star power and historic significance" to the by-elections.[14] Aung San Suu Kyi herself played down her star role. "Am I looking forward to it?," she asked at a press conference. "I am not sure I think of it as anything other than hard work. But I am not afraid of hard work."[15] Her humble yet self-assured stance stood out in contrast to the faith placed in her. "Of course I will vote for the NLD, because we love Daw Suu and General Aung San," said a Yangon taxi driver. "We believe in her. She will work for the country and its people."[16]

Aung San Suu Kyi started her campaign trips at the end of January. She planned to visit all forty-eight electoral districts where the NLD had fielded candidates. At the same time, the publication of a party magazine titled *D-Wave* (the "D" stood for "democracy") was announced. Large masses gathered to cheer for and listen to Aung San Suu Kyi's words on the upcoming by-elections. "We will bring democracy to our country," she said in her first campaign speech in Dawei, in southern Myanmar. "We will bring rule of law . . . and we will see to it that repressive laws are repealed. . . . We can overcome any obstacle with unity and perseverance, however difficult it may be."[17]

The crowds and large gatherings again led to run-ins with the authorities as had been the case in 2002 and 2003. The NLD consequently complained of campaign interference. The NLD wanted to hold its events in sport stadiums in order to accommodate the large numbers. However, the minister for sports opposed this in the beginning. He eventually had to give in after a decision was made in favor of the NLD by the election commission.

Fewer people came to the NLD campaign events in the northern and largely Christian Kachin State, where armed conflict continued and where some parliamentary seats were being contested. "I have no idea about the elections. If you want freedom you should fight for it," said a Kachin soldier.[18]

Aung San Suu Kyi visited her constituency in Kawhmu only rarely. It lay in the western part of the Yangon region, about two hours' drive away from her mother's place of birth in the Irrawaddy Delta. A dusty path ran from the city of Kawhmu, where the USDP was headquartered, to her official residence at her official home in Wah-thi-ka. This home was a small house that had been made available to her in a village largely inhabited by Buddhist Kayin.

Entrance to the village of Wah-thi-ka, March 29, 2012. (Photo: Hans-Bernd Zöllner)

A *New York Times* correspondent who visited the village was one of the first to sign the guest book set out in the house. The journalist wrote that this was a dusty, remote place, without electricity and running water. But the people of this far off place sounded as if they had won the lottery. "I cannot describe how happy I was when I heard the news," said a rice farmer in the village. "Some people said if we can only have the chance to see Mother Suu in person we will be satisfied; we can die in peace."[19]

The residents were given this opportunity twice. Aung San Suu Kyi visited the village once before the elections and then on the election evening on April 1. A later visitor wondered what change people could expect here after the elections. "Nothing," was the answer, "She had said during her visit that she could make no promises. We are just happy that she is there. We love her."[20]

Aung San Suu Kyi's official home in her constituency. (Photo: Hans-Bernd Zöllner)

For the rural population, Aung San Suu Kyi was "Mother Suu" and not "the Lady," which had become her nickname in the cities and in conversations with Western visitors. What the title "Mother Suu" really meant is captured in a poem that was circulated in the district of Kawhmu:

The Loving Mother
The dark nights of an evil past
lasted far too long, mother.
The full moon that pushed through the black
lightless midnight hour, mother. When you hear dogs baying in the dark
night
don't get up, mother,
it could rob you of your sleep, I fear.

No matter how much Galon U Saw's coat of arms
brings shame to Kawhmu,
the blood in the peacock's coat of arms
is bright red, mother.
When the hounds howl their hearts away,
make no moves to check to see,
it could rob you of your sleep, I fear.
For Kawhmu's protection
there is the peacock's coat of arms.
Hear me when I tell you,
Kawhmu's tale will never be of disgrace, mother.
Thanks to a mother's love
can entire Myanmar
let flowers bloom instead of bullets.[21]

The poem repeats the split political history of Myanmar. The line of the good kings, together with Aung San and Aung San Suu Kyi, stands on one side, and on the other the evil rulers. The symbol of the good kings is the peacock, also adopted by Aung San and the NLD as their emblem. The opposite is symbolized through the mythical bird Galon or Garuda, which Aung San's murderer, U Saw, had chosen as his coat of arms. The last phrase of the poem plays on the bullets that killed Aung San, but can also be read as a reference to the ongoing battles within the country and the danger to Aung San Suu Kyi's life.

This mythical elevation of Aung San Suu Kyi stands in contrast to the rather sober NLD party agenda that the general secretary delivered though state television on March 14. All parties participating in the by-elections had fifteen minutes of air time to introduce their manifestos. All fifteen speeches were also published in the newspapers. A comparison between them reveals the superior rhetoric of Aung San Suu Kyi, who speaks in a league of her own. She is precise, competent, coherent, and engaging.[22]

The authorities had prescreened all speeches to ensure that there were no direct attacks on the military. Still, Aung San Suu Kyi managed to elucidate a row of criticisms in her speech, for example against the part of the constitution that accorded 25 percent of the seats to military officials. At the same time, invoking the authority of her father, she stressed that the armed forces had to be integrated into a "new Burma."

Once again, Aung San Suu Kyi presented herself and her party as an alternative to the prevailing political system. Three points in her election manifesto clarified this position: advancing the rule of law, restoring peace within the country, and amending the constitution. It was of course not possible to set out clear political steps in relation to these three points within the assigned fifteen minutes. Yet, in contrast to other speakers, who also used keywords such as "democracy," "human rights," and "freedom of speech," Aung San Suu Kyi effectively demonstrated that all of these issues must be dealt with together. Only then could a democratic state, complexly woven together with laws, institutions, and citizenship, truly emerge. The NLD's short foundational text can be described as Western in its terminology and arguments. Suu Kyi does make a reference to "freedom from fear," but references to Buddhism are omitted.

Aung San Suu Kyi was deeply personally engaged with this political program. This became clear shortly before election day when she had to cancel a trip because of being unwell. She only recovered two days before the elections. She could still hold an international press conference in her garden. It appeared that her position in relation to the government remained confrontational rather than collaborative. Journalists were handed a three-page list of "unfair and illegal" measures directed by the government against the NLD when they came to pick up tickets ahead of the press conference at the party's headquarters. During her short speech at the start of the press conference, Suu Kyi expanded on the list with fresh examples. For example, one day earlier, an NLD candidate had had a beetlenut catapulted at him (although the target was missed). In general, her conclusion was that the obstacles placed before her party had overstretched the limit acceptable within a democracy. She called on the election observers to take stock of not only what happened on election

Press conference on March 30 in the garden of the house on University Avenue.
(Photo: Myanmar Times*)*

day but also what happened in the days preceding. Thus, shortly before the elections, a direct challenge was posed to the government after all.

Regardless, the NLD won an overwhelming majority. With the exception of one, the party won all districts in which it had put forward a representative.[23] The electoral commission confirmed the victory. Fears of electoral interference had not materialized. Many saw the by-elections as a test case for the 2015 general elections. NLD members and supporters were certain that Aung San Suu Kyi could now take over the reins of the country.

CHAPTER 11

The Vagaries of Realpolitik

The root causes of all the problems here are political. No more, no less.
Just political.

The by-elections had made it clear that "Mother Suu" continued to represent *the* alternative to the political system that had come into existence under the 2008 constitution. After her party's clear victory, Aung San Suu Kyi took on a dual role. On the one hand, she was now one of 440 members of the Pyitthu Hluttaw, or the lower house, which in its institutional role is not too dissimilar from the UK House of Commons or the US Congress. But in contrast to the United Kingdom and the United States, there is no political fractionalization along party lines in Myanmar. As a result, parliamentary reports referred to Aung San Suu Kyi officially as "Representative Daw Aung San Suu Kyi from the district of Kawhmu." On the other hand, in her second role, Aung San Suu Kyi remained the chairperson of the NLD and thus the leader of the most important opposition party, even though it did not yet see its popularity represented in the parliament. She thus was at the helm of a movement that brought the political system installed by the military into question. Her supporters' hope was that the NLD would go on to win the overwhelming majority of seats in the parliament in 2015, take over the government, and radically change the system put in place by the military.[1]

Her dual role required her to not only navigate the daily ins and outs of parliamentary business but also live up to the great expectations placed on her from inside and outside the country. The question that kept resurfacing was whether Aung San Suu Kyi would be able to lead the country as its president in case of an electoral victory in 2015. Article 59 (f) of the constitution prohibited this. It stated that the highest offices of the state, namely that of the president and the president's two deputies, were reserved for candidates who did *not* have a spouse or children with foreign citizenship. Both of Aung San Suu Kyi's sons are British citizens, thus disqualifying her for the highest office. The relevant legal provision is a legacy from the postcolonial period. Its purpose was to ensure the loyalty of those in the highest office.[2] A change in the provision would require a three-quarters majority in parliament. However, the 2008 constitution guarantees a quarter of all parliamentary seats to military officials, thereby creating a blocking minority. Article 59 (f), together with the military's effective veto on change, was one of the key reasons for the NLD's rejection of the constitution.

This was the tense environment in which the party leader found herself. She had the doubly difficult task of working within a parliamentary framework created by the military and at the same time reforming this very framework through constitutional change. The situation resembled Aung San's political debut of 1936. At that time, the Dobama Asiayone had founded a party that hoped to reframe or even destroy the prevailing constitution from within the system. A balancing act was required both then and now. A well-dosed split between pressure and concession was necessary to achieve the goal of change from within. The controversy surrounding the parliamentarians' oath, which had already erupted before the beginning of the first legislative period, is testament to this.

All parliamentarians in Myanmar must take an oath prior to stepping into their roles. The oath requires them to "uphold" the constitution. This was an unreasonable demand for the NLD, a party that in 2010 had boycotted the elections precisely because it held the constitution to be undemocratic. This is why, ten days after the by-elections, the NLD requested that the wording set out in the constitution be amended. The dispute was fought with great rigor initially. There were reports that the NLD may even boycott the parliament. And indeed, NLD parliamentarians did not show up for the first sitting on April 23. Only forty members of the military, who had been newly appointed to parliament, took the oath.

A few days after the first parliamentary sitting, Aung San Suu Kyi played down the controversy surrounding the oath as a "technicality." According to her, the legal formulation included some inconsistencies that should not be the case in legal matters. She finally declared that the situation had been resolved. The NLD parliamentarians would give in and take the oath in the form set out in the constitution. The reason—it was explained—was the voters. The NLD would not have wanted for the will of the people to be swept under in the nitpicking of representatives.

During a visit to Myanmar at the end of April 2012, UN General Secretary Ban Ki-moon confidently proclaimed that Thein Sein and Aung San Suu Kyi would, also in the future, be able to set aside their inevitable differences in opinion in the interest of the nation. During his meeting with the Nobel Peace Laureate, he expressly thanked Aung San Suu Kyi for her willingness to compromise. Finally, on May 2, all NLD representatives took the oath in the constitutionally prescribed form. As with the reregistration of the party, Aung San Suu Kyi had let her criticisms be known but in the end had pragmatically given in.

Visiting Friends Abroad

Aung San Suu Kyi used the first parliamentary recess to take a series of trips abroad. On May 29, 2012, she boarded a plane and left her country for the first time in almost a quarter of a century. The trip was to neighboring Thailand, where a colorful itinerary unfolded. She visited compatriots at a refugee camp at the Thailand-Myanmar border, gave a speech for a few thousand of the 2.5 million labor migrants in the neighboring country, and participated in the East Asian World Economic Forum in Bangkok. Here, she could have met with President Thein Sein, who had originally planned a visit to Thailand. However, he canceled the trip on short notice because of other urgent tasks. The real reason—or so it was believed—was that he did not want to stand in the shadows of his challenger during the meetings.

Aung San Suu Kyi traveled to five European countries from June 13 to 29. She received some of the honors that had been awarded to her during the long years of her house arrest. She also thanked friends and supporters and publicized her cause. She started off with a visit to the United Nations headquarters in Geneva. On the next day, after recovering from a fainting spell at a press conference, she paid a visit to the Swiss Parliament in Bern. On both occasions, she stressed the importance of "democracy-friendly investment" in her country. She continued to Oslo, to personally receive the Nobel Peace Prize that had been awarded to her in 1991. At the next stop, in Dublin, Ireland, she was handed a 2009 Amnesty International prize by Bono, the singer of the band U2. Bono had supported Aung San Suu Kyi both politically and musically. In England she visited her former college in Oxford and received an honorary doctorate, held a speech before both houses of Parliament in London, planted a tree with Prince Charles and his wife Camilla, and met with the Dalai Lama, who happened to be in the city, too. Three days in Paris followed, where, besides meetings with leading politicians, she also visited the Sorbonne and the Louvre.

Aung San Suu Kyi was received like a head of state at all her stops. The red carpets rolled out for her symbolized a deep admiration for her decades-long struggle against a repressive regime. For many in the West, she was the government leader-in-waiting.

Her appearance before both houses of Parliament in London is a good example of the varying expectations projected on her and the manner in which Aung San Suu Kyi deals with them.

Her appearance at the British Parliament was described as historic. Only heads of states had had the honor of speaking here before her. John Bercow, the speaker of the House of Commons, introduced her to the audience. He contrasted Aung San Suu Kyi's personal virtues with the sinister schemes of her adversaries. The speech operated on the sharp distinction between good and evil. It was in many ways the Western counterpart of the Burmese poem cited at the end of the last chapter.

In that, Mother Suu stood facing "the dark nights of evil history." In Bercow's speech, it is the "legendary" virtues of dignity, fortitude, and resolve that stand face to face with a morally rotten military regime that is "exceptional in its barbarity."[3]

Aung San Suu Kyi did not spend a single word on the black-and-white picture painted by Bercow.[4] Instead, she shared some anecdotes of her relationship and that of her family to Great Britain. In doing so, she made no mention of her father turning down the offer for Burma to be included in the Commonwealth. She also requested assistance with the revival of her country. Within the grand building of the Houses of Parliament in Westminster, Aung San Suu Kyi called for introducing elements of a Westminster-style democracy in Burma at various levels, including, for example, during parliamentary debates. After all, the course of proceedings in Myanmar was far too stiff, there was no heckling, and all men wore traditional headdresses.

In addition, she repeated the three main points from the NLD's election manifesto: amending the constitution, rule of law, and peace between the ethnic minorities. Help for the flailing education system and the economy were welcomed. She closed her speech with, "My country has not yet entered the ranks of truly democratic societies, but I am confident we will get there before too long, with your help." With these words she was clearly taking a different approach to her father. Aung San had always supported a form of government organic to Burma. The daughter was making a case for a Westminster-style democracy as a model for her country and thus was distancing herself from the special Burmese path to democracy advanced by the junta.

Aung San Suu Kyi's speeches were criticized by the state newspapers upon her return to the country. The criticism only marginally touched upon the content of her speeches. The complaint was that in her speeches held in English, Aung San Suu Kyi had always referred to "Burma"—the name used by the former colonial powers—and not "Myanmar." She responded to the accusation by arguing that her choice of words was in line with democratic principles and that the change of name had been implemented by the military in 1989, without the peoples' participation in the decision.

Parliamentary Routine

Aung San Suu Kyi only returned to parliament on the fourth day of sittings in the fourth session of the first lower house. It was a typical workday. The state newspaper reported that 404 of the 440 members were present, and stated, "At the meeting, eight questions were raised, three reports discussed, one proposal discussed, one new proposal submitted, and one bill approved."[5] The draft bill related to an amendment to some paragraphs relating to the work of investigation commissions. One of the questions related to a newly granted amnesty for political prisoners. The reports related to general matters of the house and legal issues. The new proposal related to an improvement of traffic connections between parts of the country. The sitting concluded shortly before four o'clock p.m. When asked by a journalist what she thought of her first day as a parliamentarian, Aung San Suu Kyi replied, "A job is a job."[6]

Aung San Suu Kyi in parliament on July 9, 2012. (Photo: Myanmar Times)

The day described above is representative of the usual, unspectacular parliamentary routine in Myanmar. The procedural rules are partly responsible for this. The procedure is aimed at reducing conflict and producing results based on the broadest possible consensus. The parliamentary seating plan also reveals an intention to avoid confrontation, debate, and fractionalization. The elected parliamentarians are positioned in alphabetical order, resulting in representatives of different parties being thrown in randomly together. Only those in military uniform sit in a separate block, illustrating the special role of the military. And as Aung San Suu Kyi mentioned in passing at the British Parliament, external formality is upheld through the parliamentarians' rigid dress code.

Aung San Suu Kyi's tensely awaited first appearance in parliament was unspectacular but was described by some media as historic. On July 25, she took part in a discussion on a proposed law to protect the rights of minorities. In her speech she stressed that minority rights must extend beyond the strengthening of language and culture of certain ethnicities. She further stated that such rights could only be safeguarded in a genuinely democratic nation. Any new laws, she remarked, should be debated in the spirit of the Panglong Agreement, which was entered into through the efforts of her father.[7]

Shortly thereafter, Aung San Suu Kyi was chosen to lead a parliamentary committee on the rule of law, peace, and tranquility. The committee went on to propose an anticorruption law, which was passed in August 2013. The committee's objective was also to support the fight against corruption with the help of civil society organizations. The new committee—one of twenty-five by this time—had been caught up in a controversy in mid-2012 between the parliament and the constitutional court. The question before the court was on the appropriate legal status of the parliamentary committees under the constitution. When the court ruled that the committees could not have union-level status, the parliament took legal action against the court, resulting in the impeachment of the judges. In this, NLD representatives voted together with their USDP counterparts. The episode led some observers to question whether this was not an example of parliament overstepping the law—and that with the approval of the NLD, which had always stood for the primacy of the rule of law.[8]

Boos and Heckling against Aung San Suu Kyi

The new parliamentarian faced the harsh pitfalls of realpolitik for the first time at the end of 2012. A simmering decade-long conflict around a copper mine in the country's northwest erupted anew. The mine was located in Monywa, where the metal was first discovered in the 1930s. In 2007, there had been a questionable transfer of ownership of the mine from a Canadian firm to another entity called the Monywa Trust. The mining of the copper would have come to a standstill had it not been for a Chinese mining company, Wanbao, which signed a contract with a Burmese military company in 2010 allowing it to restart activities.[9] The new project centered on the inclusion of a new mining area, the Letpadaung mine. The signing ceremony had taken place in June 2010, half a year prior to the parliamentary elections, to coincide with the visit of China's Prime Minister Wen Jiabao. Thein Sein, still prime minister of the junta at the time, received the Chinese guest on the occasion of the sixtieth anniversary of diplomatic relations between both countries. This was thus a prestige project of the highest rank, in which China, the most influential foreign actor in Myanmar, was as deeply involved as the government and the military.

Affected villagers were informed that the copper mining operation would require resettlement. The Chinese investor agreed to pay the appropriate compensation. The majority of the villagers signed the contracts, but a minority refused to do so. Protests ensued in September 2012. Villagers complained of corruption, unpaid compensation after expropriation of land, and environmental damage. In their protests, the villagers relied on a law newly enacted by the parliament that permitted peaceful demonstrations and assembly.[10]

The incident was followed closely by national and international observers. The situation was seen as a litmus test for the new civilian government. How would it deal with some core principles of democracy and the rule of law? Thein Sein had halted an earlier Chinese-financed dam project in 2011 after the eruption of protests. However, in contrast to that project, he had had a direct hand in negotiating the copper mine, a fact that now restricted his options.

The protests spread quickly. The local demonstrators were joined by supporters from other parts of the country. Among them were around five hundred monks. The work at the mine came to a halt when demonstrators blocked the entrance to the company's offices. The officials' orders to clear protestor camps and the imposition of a curfew were to no avail. Security forces then decided to end the demonstrations by force. The police used water cannons, tear gas, and phosphorous smoke bombs. Numerous demonstrators, including monks, sustained severe burns.

Aung San Suu Kyi was introduced to this minefield as a mediator by a fellow party member. Khin San Hlaing had run as an NLD candidate in 1990, spent time in prison thereafter, and now, after a successful 2012 by-election, represented a district in the vicinity of the mine. In November 2012, she requested that an independent commission be set up to investigate whether mining activities should be continued.

The defense minister was the first to respond to the parliamentarian's proposal. He argued that the concessionary agreements on the land had been granted in accordance with the law for sixty years, that compensation had been paid, and a set of social measures had been put in place. He also pointed out that the military company, Union of Myanmar Economic Holdings, had been set up by veterans and families of soldiers who had died or been injured in the civil war. The profits, he said, were used for their benefit, not for military purposes.[11] He ended his argument by stating that after twenty years of sanctions it was now finally possible to use advanced international technology to protect the environment. Besides, according to him, various other committees, including the human rights committee of the country had already discussed the matter. He said that he still welcomed the parliamentarian's proposal in the hope that it would serve the interests of the nation.[12]

Finally, on December 1, President Thein Sein appointed an investigation commission under Aung San Suu Kyi's chairmanship. Besides a number of parliamentarians, the committee consisted of various other prominent members, such as the student leader Min Ko Naing. He was no stranger to the issue, as he had held a key speech on the Letpadaung mine at a protest in Yangon. The commission was tasked with eight sets of questions, including a review of the security forces' actions. In addition, the commission was to submit a final recommendation on the future of the project.[13] Two days later, the president issued a note reducing the size of the commission from thirty to sixteen persons. He also crossed out the question relating to the involvement of the security forces and the injuries to the monks.[14] These issues were apparently too sensitive.

The commission visited the copper mine from December 5 to 15, 2012, and spoke with official representatives of the mining company, villagers, and monks, as well as members of the security forces. It presented its findings on March 12, 2013.[15] The commission proposed an increase in the compensation amount. Regarding the 108 people who had been injured, it recommended better training for the security forces in dealing with demonstrations. Among others, it found that environmental protection needed improvement. Overall, however, it concluded that the project should continue. Foreign investment was vital to the country and it was considered important to safeguard the country's reputation, which would inevitably sustain damage from such a breach of contract.

The report was a classic form of political compromise. It responded in part to the local humanitarian and environmental interests but at the same time took account of the macrointerests of the country. The report received mixed reactions. Unsurprisingly, the spokesperson from the Chinese foreign ministry welcomed the outcome and encouraged Chinese investors to continue investing in Myanmar.[16] Wanbao issued a press release stating that the company "will continue contributing to the sustainable development of our local community and of Myanmar as a whole."[17]

At the same time there was sharp criticism by those affected and by protestors both within and outside the country. The commission was accused of prioritizing China-Myanmar relations above the interests of the population. Aung San Suu Kyi met with her critics in Salingyi Township and asked for their understanding. She explained that halting a mining project could hurt Myanmar if China was led to believe that Myanmar was unreliable when it came to economic issues. She added, "We have to get along with the neighboring country, whether we like it or not."[18]

Aung San Suu Kyi and demonstrators in Salingyi on November 30, 2012. (*Photo:* Myanmar Times)

Yet the critics of the project remained unconvinced. Their reactions pointed to something more fundamental. Aung San Suu Kyi's speech was interrupted by heckling and shouting. Some wept and complained that Aung San Suu Kyi had stepped off the path that Aung San had carved out for her and the people. "We feel that Mother Suu doesn't have sympathy for us. We are fighting for the truth," one woman was cited as saying.[19] Another said, "Before, everyone here loved Mother Suu like the Buddha, but no more."[20] The incident goes to show how quickly the emotional connection between Aung San Suu Kyi and her supporters could be broken.

Activists from abroad expressed a fundamental critique of a different nature. One member of the Lawyers' Network, which had published its own report shortly after that of the investigation commission, was cited as saying, "It is a war crime that should be dealt with by the international court."[21] In the same article, a monk states, "The commission failed to protect our interests. We do not accept the recommendation that the project should continue, without saying anything about the violent attack on monks."[22]

The report by the Lawyers' Network sets out the background for such radical rejection of the official committee report. It starts by showing photographs of protesting people, a monk with burn injuries, and then an image of ninety-nine monks standing under a Buddhist flag on the grounds of the mine. The following verse stands on top of the image:

Re Borne on Letpadaung Hill
99 monks sitting steadfast in circles,
One heart beating true for land-loving peoples,
Channeling the power of powerlessness,
Flutt'ring on butterfly-wings of compassion,
Chanting peace sutras under fire-bombs flying,
Tossed like sticks amist [sic] storms of sacred suff'ring,
Flames and flesh, blood and water, inter-mingling,
Just!—As an all-mighty oceans' ceaseless roar!—
Can such devotion ever be defeated?[23]

The text elevates the protest against the copper mine to the ranks of a holy duty. As a result, Aung San Suu Kyi, as part of the investigation commission, is reduced to being a mere mortal. Those affected no longer love her "like the Buddha" given her sober statements. The religious dimension of the fight against the project contributes to the uncertainty over the copper mine's extension.[24]

The police chief of Sagaing Division apologizes to the monk community during a religious ceremony on December 1, 2012. (Photo: Reuters)

Criticism from Abroad on the "Rohingya Issue"

Aung San Suu Kyi also drew critique from abroad when violence broke out in the Western state of Rakhine shortly after the NLD's victory in the by-elections. In early June 2012, there were riots between the majority Buddhist population and the Muslim minority known internationally as Rohingya.[25] The riots broke out after a Buddhist woman was robbed, raped, and murdered on May 28 by three Muslim men, and a minibus carrying ten Muslim passengers was attacked by a Buddhist mob, killing everyone on board.[26] From June 8 onwards, there were riots in many parts of Rakhine State. The victims were overwhelmingly Muslim, although no exact figures were published.[27] According to the finding of a state commission, 192 people lost their lives in two waves of violence between June and October. In addition, more than 265 were injured and 8,614 houses were destroyed. The riots resulted in the displacement of many Muslims, most of them Rohingya. Many ended up depending on foreign aid organizations that faced difficulties providing adequate care given the anti-Muslim sentiments of the majority Buddhist population.[28] A report by Amnesty International, published in November 2017, concluded that the government had set up an "apartheid-regime" in Rakhine State after the violent events of 2012.[29]

In an interview given to the BBC in early November 2012, Aung San Suu Kyi refused to condemn any one side in the conflict by relying on the moral authority attributed to her. She sided neither with the Rakhine nationalists nor with the Rohingya: "I am urging tolerance, but I do not think one should use one's moral leadership, if you want to call it that, to promote a particular cause without really looking at the sources of the problems. I know that people want me to take one side or the other, so both sides are displeased because I will not take a stand with them."[30]

Shortly before the second escalation of violence, in October 2012, President Thein Sein had set up an investigation commission.[31] This commission included prominent former critics of the military regime, such as Ko Ko Gyi of the 88 Generation and popular comedian Zarganar. In an interview given during that time, Ko Ko Gyi stated, "If powerful countries are to keep pressuring us, then we, the democratic forces of Burma, will view this as a national affair and will resolve this issue by joining hands with the Tatmadaw." He was convinced that the Rohingya were "absolutely not an ethnic race of Burma."[32]

The commission published its findings in April 2013.[33] The detailed report tried to be fair to all sides and included a set of practical recommendations. However, it also concluded that the two sides of the conflict were not yet ready for peaceful coexistence. The affected Muslim population were referred to as "Bengali," following the Buddhist majority's view that the Rohingya are in fact immigrants from neighboring Bengal or their descendants.

The outbreak of violence in 2012 was unanticipated. The quick escalation of the riots and the vicious acts from both sides exposed the deep-rooted and unresolved resentments between the Buddhist and Muslim communities in Rakhine. This was not the first time that Myanmar had seen violence directed at its Muslim community. There had been incidents of anti-Muslim acts and behavior in central Burma in 1997 and in 2001. As was the case then, once again the speculation was that hardliners within the military had created the unrest in order to distract the public from internal political problems. This is not surprising in a country where suspicions took on a reality of their own and where the junta was generally mistrusted. In 2012, for example, the general sentiment was that it was noteworthy that the riots "suspiciously" happened shortly after the NLD's election victory of April 1. This was very timely in serving to thwart both the reforms and Myanmar's opening to the world. The unrest could even have been aimed at jeopardizing the 2015 general elections.[34] On the other hand, it could be argued that the vehemence of the violence and the alleged reluctance of the security forces to suppress the fighting were byproducts of the new spirit of "people's power," unleashed by the election frenzy gripping society in the aftermath of Aung San Suu Kyi's and her party's victories. Thein Sein's political reforms had led to liberalization, for example of the media, which now set loose previously suppressed conflicts.

Aung San Suu Kyi's victory in the by-elections was still very fresh at the time of the riots. She was just a newly elected parliamentarian of a still-small opposition party that lacked real power. During her travels to Europe in late June, she gave a very reserved response when asked whether the stateless Rohingyas should be granted citizenship: "I do not know." The journalist citing her commented that a "firmer response" was needed to address the communal problems in Rakhine and other parts of the country.[35] In September, during a visit to the United States, she stated that she did "not want to criticize the government just for the sake of making political capital" and promised to support the government to "bring about peace and harmony in the Rakhine State." She further reiterated one of her mantras, that the "rule of law" must prevail, without elaborating on the controversial citizenship law.[36]

These first statements and many later ones were made on Aung San Suu Kyi's trips abroad. They show that she needed to explain her stance to foreign observers, not to people at home. This necessity for an explanation makes it clear that the Rohingya issue had created a rift between her and her foreign audience from the very beginning of the conflict. Unlike her Western interviewers, Aung San Suu Kyi took an impartial position: "But don't forget that violence has been committed by both sides. This is why I prefer not to take sides. Also, I want to work toward reconciliation between these two communities. I am not going to be able to do that if I take sides," she had said during a visit to India in November 2012.[37]

In the year that followed this comment, anti-Muslim riots broke out in central Myanmar. At least forty-four people died because of violence that erupted following a fight in a shop in the city of Meiktila. Aung San Suu Kyi sought to explain the situation in her country by relying on one of the catchwords that had made her famous: "fear." In an interview given in October 2013 she said, "This problem arose last year, and this is to do with fear on both sides. The fear is not just on the side of the Muslims but also on the side of the Buddhists as well. Muslims have been targeted but also Buddhists have been subjected to violence. . . . Global Muslim power is very great and certainly, that is a perception in many parts of the world and in our country as well."[38] These statements reflect the deep-seated antagonism between the Buddhist and Muslim communities of Myanmar, the latter mainly of Indian origin, stemming back to the colonial period. Aung San Suu Kyi's remarks point to the complex mix of political, economic, and religious factors that—unnoticed by many foreign observers for a long time—contributed to the outbreak of violence in 2012 and 2013 both in Rakhine State and in central Myanmar.

Long-term supporters of Aung San Suu Kyi, the NLD, and the struggle for democracy suddenly found themselves being attacked by the very people whom they had spent over two decades fighting for. For example, Burma Campaign UK, which supported the cause of the Rohingya right from the beginning of the crisis in July 2012, was the target of defamation and insults by Burmese anti-Muslim activists. The organization was accused of being supported by Middle Eastern states and advocating the establishment of an independent Rohingya state. Its director, Mark Farmaner, defended his organization and finally resorted to asking some rather desperate questions:

We are a human rights organization working on Burma. How could anyone disagree that the Rohingya people are entitled to full human rights and the normal rights and protections under international law?

But some people see that statement as such an outrage that Burma Campaign UK staff deserve to be raped and killed. . . . All these views and many more—many vicious and obscene—have been emailed to us or posted on YouTube and Facebook.

The level of abuse, hatred and anger directed against Burma Campaign UK and other organizations who say that Rohingya should have human rights, and which work with Rohingya to defend their human rights, has been astonishing.[39]

It was not only this campaigner for democracy and human rights who was puzzled about the hatred towards the Rohingya that suddenly became visible in Myanmar.[40] The international community, too, opened its eyes to this phenomenon and had to learn that the ideas about democracy and freedom have always had a very different meaning in the West and in Myanmar. The international community came to attribute the visible hatred towards Muslims to the actions of certain individual monks. For example, a formerly entirely unknown figure, the monk Ashin Wirathu, suddenly took the media limelight when he was labeled "the face of Buddhist terror" on the cover of *Time* magazine in July 2013. It came to be publicly known that he agitated against Muslims through inflammatory pamphlets warning of Muslim domination, jihadists, and the targeted marrying of Buddhist women by Muslim men. Under the banner of the 969 Movement—the numbers referring to the Buddhist trinity of Buddha, dhamma, and sangha—Wirathu and his supporters called for the boycott of Muslim-run shops and demanded that interreligious marriage be banned.[41] In January 2015, Wirathu called the UN special rapporteur on Myanmar Yanghee Lee a "whore."[42] One of Ms. Lee's tasks was to gauge the situation of Muslims in Myanmar. The organization MaBaTha, made up of monks and laypeople, successfully pushed parliament to adopt four laws aimed at the "protection of race

Monks demonstrate against the Rohingya in 2012. (Photo: The Voice)

and religion."[43] It must be noted, however, that the majority of NLD parliamentarians voted against the laws.

Over time, criticism towards Aung San Suu Kyi's attitude grew and became ever more aggressive. Different voices had different reasons to be critical. The human rights activist David Mathieson stated, "I think everyone agrees now she has been a disappointment when it comes to human rights promotion."[44] A Rohingya woman living in India gave a verdict that left no hope for the future: "Nothing would ever help us, not elections, not military, not Daw Aung San Suu Kyi."[45] A Kachin analyst stressed that a democratic leader needs the support of all ethnic minorities.[46] A Bangladeshi journalist wrote that she was shocked to learn of the violence and asked herself how different Aung San Suu Kyi's government could be from one of military rule.[47] And Aung Zaw, the founder of the Irrawaddy media group, wrote in October 2012, "The opposition, including democracy icon Aung San Suu Kyi and other prominent figures, has hopelessly failed to intervene or calm the situation. Many, especially in the international community and human rights organizations, were disheartened to see such inaction from those who still claim to represent the democracy movement."[48] Other commentators concluded that the reasons for her "silence" were related to the forthcoming 2015 elections, in which she did not want to risk losing the Muslim vote. It was even debated whether it was "foolish to criticize Aung San Suu Kyi."[49] But the prevailing answer was no.

Aung San Suu Kyi was thus caught up in a flux of antagonistic expectations both inside Myanmar and abroad. This is inherently a reflection of the reality of Myanmar politics, which she and others inherited from the country's past. This heritage—largely unobserved by the international community—had already led to the eruption of violence and the movement of refugees in the past. In 2016 and 2017 it would lead to further escalations, reflected both in the numbers of fleeing Muslims as well as the public reactions within and outside Myanmar.

Part of this heritage was an old predicament. The full interests of all ethnic groups in the country could not be catered to without, at the very least, jeopardizing the unity of the state. No politician since the time of independence of the country has succeeded in producing this frequently invoked "unity." With this reality as a point of departure, Aung San Suu Kyi opted for a political solution that appealed to the majority but precluded the interests of a given ethnoreligious group. Her position became especially visible when no Muslim candidate was put forward in the NLD list of parliamentary candidates for the November 2015 elections, even though there had been several Muslim applicants who had supported Aung San Suu Kyi for a long time and even spent time in jail as a result.[50]

Aung San Suu Kyi still tried to keep balancing on the tightrope by assuming an unbiased approach towards the country's Muslims. In a meeting with leaders of Muslim organizations, she reiterated her message that only the rule of law could solve the problem.[51] "The law in our country has to be just. Everyone must be treated fairly under the existing laws. I want all our people to feel proud for being citizens of Burma."[52] She also refused to criticize the armed forces and their methods, and continued to maintain an "independent" stance on the issue. This disappointed many, for example, the Rohingya community in Japan, who ended up being excluded from a welcome meeting of Myanmar citizens during her state visit to the country.[53]

This political choice aided in securing the 2015 election victory. The problem was shifted out of view. Of course, this did not mean that the problem had disappeared. It remained lurking in the background and could break out at any moment.

Pre-Election Battles

The main theme of the time preceding the November 8, 2015, elections was the election itself. Would the elections be free and fair? Tin Aye, chairman of the government-installed electoral commission, was the focal point of these discussions. His independence was put to question time and again. He had been a general before winning a seat for the USDP in the 2010 elections. When President Thein Sein named him chairman of the electoral commission in 2011, Tin Aye left the party and his elected office in accordance with the protocol. During one newspaper interview, he pointed to the 2012 by-elections as proof of his independence—after all, the NLD had prevailed over the USDP in that instance. He admitted to irregularities during the 2010 elections and said that improvements had been made. If former fellow party members asked him for election favors, he would now respond with a simple "sorry."[54]

The debates on the role of the electoral commission were mainly focused on the drawing up of an accurate voter register, in part because of the large number of internally displaced people. The role of internal and external observers was also discussed at length. One disputed question was whether areas where civil war–like conditions prevailed and where no elections had been held since colonial times should now be allowed to vote. The other open question related to the length of the campaigning period. In relation to this, Tin Aye had announced that campaigning would last two months instead of one as per the parties' request. Some restrictions were, however, deemed necessary to ensure smooth proceedings. These included restrictions on aggressive or insulting electoral advertising.

There was one initiative to reform the electoral law in parliament. This came from the NDF, which had split from the NLD in 2010. Some of the USDP supported the proposal, which aimed at introducing elements of proportional representation, as is the case in Germany for example. The NLD rejected the proposal. Changing the first-past-the-post system acquired from the British would mean a weakening of the NLD's position. Its decisive 1990 and 2012 electoral victories were only possible because of it. One commission drafted a total of eight different options of voting systems.[55] No decision was reached, however, mainly because a fundamental reform of the voting system would have required more time. So, in May, the electoral commission announced that the country would keep the old system. The issue of Rohingya participation was also discussed on the sidelines of a debate around the referendum required for a change in the constitution. Here the NLD supported the opposition to any such possibility, which was being considered by the government.[56]

A fiercer debate centered around the question of whether the constitution could be amended so as to allow Aung San Suu Kyi to become president after an electoral victory. However, as mentioned, this option would require a change in the constitution—an unlikely possibility given that this could only happen with the approval of the military. But the NLD continued to stress that the will of the people to see Mother Suu as their president should be respected. On May 24, 2014, the anniversary of the 1990 elections, the party thus started a petition together with veterans of the 1988 student movement. Some five million signatures were collected by Martyrs' Day on July 19, according to the NLD. The signatures were presented to parliament in August, but nothing changed.

During President Barack Obama's visit in November 2014, Aung San Suu Kyi once again repeated that the constitution was "unfair, unjust and not democratic" due to the notorious Article 59 (f). Later on she considered boycotting the elections.[57] This speculation came to an end when she registered herself as a candidate at the end of July 2015 in the presence of large crowds of journalists and supporters who shouted, "Long live Mother Suu!"

When parliament rejected a change in the constitution at the end of June 2015, it was definitely clear that Aung San Suu Kyi would not become president after the elections. Small student protests followed in Yangon after this decision. There were fears that the elections would be postponed or even canceled given the likelihood of an NLD victory. The pre-election atmosphere was ridden with expectation and nervousness.

Painting depicting Aung San Suu Kyi as president. Upper left: Banknotes showing her father. (Photo: Hans-Bernd Zöllner)

Election Victory for a Lone Fighter

On July 8, 2015, the electoral commission announced that the elections would take place on November 8. It asked the parties to name their candidates within one month. The deadline was extended to August 14 after heavy rainfall had led to devastating floods in the country at the end of July. By this point, seventy-three parties had been admitted to participate in the election. The applications of fourteen others remained under consideration. A total of ninety-one parties finally took part in the elections. About two-thirds of them only fielded candidates in certain regions of the country.

Many of the parties made optimistic statements about their showing ahead of the poll. In December 2014, the NDF, for example, had announced that it wanted to win a hundred seats. Its preparations focused on identifying appropriate candidates for particular districts. In Shan State, the Shan National League for Democracy (SNLD) declared that its target was to win seats for at least half of its candidates in order to have a majority in the Shan parliament. In this way it could respond to local needs and work towards a "genuine federal union."[58] At the same time the party promised to build bridges to other Shan parties, in order to avoid a fragmentation of votes. Other parties made similar promises, yet effective alliances never came to be.

The parties focused less on content and manifestos and much more on the presentation of their candidates. This was particularly true for Aung San Suu Kyi's NLD. Aung San Suu Kyi used her seventieth birthday celebration on June 19, 2015, to encourage her supporters to aim for a "landslide" victory as in 1990. Later she announced that there were plans for the presidential office, which she could not yet share. Just a few days before the election, she made an announcement that has been cited often since: "If we win, and the NLD forms a government, I will be above the president. It's a very simple message."[59] This was in line with the idea of the mythical first ruler, the Maha Sammata, and confirmed her earlier statements on the unique social contract between the people as a whole and one qualified leader. At the same time, the statement stood at odds with the constitution, according to which the president elected by the parliament represented the country. During a press conference two days before the elections, she set out her position on the constitution as follows:

> Constitutions are made by people and they are not eternal. There is no law that says the Constitution is eternal. Even in this Constitution, there are provisions for changing it, but with great difficulty, I admit. But I don't think that is something that should be seen as an impossible obstacle. If the support of the people is strong enough, I don't see why we should not be able to overcome a "minor problem" like amending the Constitution.[60]

Aung San Suu Kyi's statement on standing above the president lends itself to be interpreted as follows: The people would elect the new leader who would then take care of all else, including a new constitution. This was a convincing electoral objective in the context of the Buddhist traditions of the country.

Furthermore, the NLD used the focus on the election of the "super-president" to cover up a number of controversies regarding its candidate selection. Various prominent applicants, such as the popular leader of the 88 Student Generation Ko Ko Gyi, did not appear on the final candidate list. It was rumored that Aung San Suu Kyi had made this and other decisions herself. Supposedly, the applicants' loyalty to Aung San Suu Kyi was the key selection criteria, and the applicants' competency or their local party support made no difference. During the contest for the candidate list, party members from various districts resigned and others were barred by the party after they openly protested. One of them described the situation as follows: "At least they should have done an investigation. We joined the NLD as we hate dictatorship, but what they are doing now is worse than dictatorship."[61] The accusation was that Aung San Suu Kyi was running for a "democratic dictatorship."

Shortly before the deadline for candidate nominations on August 12, Shwe Mann, the USDP chairman, suddenly lost his post. What really happened is yet unclear. Shwe Mann had been treated as a potential successor to Thein Sein. It was suspected that he had good relations with Aung San Suu Kyi. Rumors had a deal running between the two of them, under which Shwe Mann would become president to subsequently pass on his post to Aung San Suu Kyi once appropriate constitutional amendmends had been made. His proximity to the opposition leader is what allegedly led to his downfall. He did, however, keep his influential position as the speaker of the lower house until the elections. His political career ended for the time being when he wasn't able to win his constituency.

At the end of the registration process on August 14, a total of 6,189 candidates had registered for the 1,171 available seats in the sixteen parliaments. From these, eighty-eight—including a number of Muslim candidates—were subsequently disqualified by the electoral commission for various reasons. After strong protest from abroad, eleven of them were resubmitted. However, no Muslim candidate went on to win a parliamentary seat.

Campaigning officially started on September 8, opened by Aung San Suu Kyi with a message on Facebook: "For the first time in decades, our people will have a real chance of bringing about real change. We hope that the whole world understands how important it is for us to have free and fair elections."[62] The word "change" really captured the central message of her election campaign, which was elaborated upon in a twenty-eight-page manifesto a few days later.

A day before the official campaign launch, the NLD filed a complaint against a USDP candidate for bribing voters. The government party retaliated with a complaint against NLD candidates, arguing that they had started campaigning too early. Such mutual accusations continued for two months until election day. Such taunts are symptoms of a typical focus on form over content in Myanmar election campaigns. Just a few days before the election day, Aung San Suu Kyi cautioned her supporters to look out for fraud. As for herself, she led the election campaign as her father had done for the 1947 constituent assembly elections; she traveled from one place to another to the point of exhaustion. She spoke to enthralled crowds and asked them to vote for the local candidate from her party. As the candidate selection process had demonstrated, the party was hierarchical through and through. Aung San Suu Kyi made the final and most important decisions, but she also carried the biggest weight of the campaign.

Critical observers noted that the NLD's election agenda, which was in any case kept very general, played no great role in the election campaign. It was the motto personified in Mother Suu that shone through: "time for change." This was not envisaged as a gradual change. It was to be a fundamental rupture in the system, the rejection of a military regime that had not achieved any real change after all. One NLD candidate, who was running in Yangon against the former mayor of the city, expressed the difference between his agenda and that of his opponent's: "We will work for real change. For my constituency, I would like to promise that in parliament and also outside, I will boldly speak out on what is right and what is wrong, and I won't support those cases that would harm the people."[63] The opponent responded by pointing to the practical successes achieved through his efforts in roadworks and access to water. In the end, the USDP mayor lost the vote.

The parts of the sangha that had successfully put race and religion laws in place also became involved with the election campaign. They sharpened the contest between good and evil. The radical monks' campaign focused on maintaining the "purity" of Buddhist Myanmar and openly criticized the NLD. They claimed that if the NLD were to win, foreigners—especially Muslim South Asians—would take over the country. The accusation was also indirectly leveled at Aung San Suu Kyi, who, after all, had been married to a foreigner.[64] There were suggestions that the government and the military were the ones behind the monks' offensive. This could, however, never be proven. The smear campaign even ended up benefiting the NLD. Many Burmese were disgusted by the MaBaTha's aggressive rhetoric and its attempts to throw dirt on Aung San Suu Kyi's image.

The Big Day

Tensions before election day clearly ran high. On the afternoon before the big day, a young Burmese woman declared, "On Sunday we will be given justice for 1990."[65] The polling stations in Yangon appeared to be well prepared. The voter lists were published, the ballot boxes were ready, and the polling station staff were diligently preparing themselves.[66] Bright posters clearly set out the voting method, easily understandable to all. The man in charge of the polling station on Anawrahta Road in Chinatown explained that there were some mistakes in the voter lists but that they should be 98 percent accurate. Obvious typing errors in the spelling of names or transposition of numbers would not disqualify people from voting, assured the elderly man in a white shirt and longyi.[67]

The polling station on Anawrahta Road, like others throughout the country, opened at six o'clock a.m. sharp. Almost fifty voters were already waiting. They broke into applause as the doors opened. The faces of many shone with obvious pride for having voted as they left the polling station. They held up their election-inked, violet fingers like a victory sign. One young man said, "Now I am free."[68]

Myanmar newspapers one day before the elections. (Photo: Rodion Ebbighausen)

It remained unclear till the last moment whether the military would vote in their compounds or regular polling stations. There were concerns that military personnel voting at the compounds might be under undue influence. In the end there were only scattered complaints in this regard. The voting procedure was generally free and fair, even if it did not—as the German head of the election monitors Alexander Graf Lambsdorff commented in a somewhat know-it-all manner—meet all requirements. One Myanmar journalist observed, "The election was a great success especially compared to regional standards."[69] As had their predecessors in 1990, Tin Aye and his people of the electoral commission had done a good job—and with no interference. The election victory was doubtlessly the fruit of Aung San Suu Kyi's labor. The holding of elections, however, was to the credit of Thein Sein's government, which had organized them.[70]

CHAPTER 12

Dual Rule

We should not pin our hope on one individual leader or organization.

The election results left nothing to doubt; the NLD was the clear winner. Leading USDP politicians acknowledged their defeat even before the final results were announced. The military had let it be known before the elections that it would respect the outcome, come what may.

More than thirty-four million people were eligible to vote, and 69 percent of them cast their ballot. After the counting, six percent of the votes were declared invalid.[1] The NLD won 77 percent of all electoral districts, landing the majority of seats in almost all sixteen parliaments of the country. As had been the case in the 2012 by-elections, the NLD even came out as the clear winner in the capital, Naypyidaw. Only one electoral district there went to the USDP.[2] Only in Rakhine, northern Kachin, and Shan State did the voters show a marked preference for ethnic minority parties. The USDP won the most seats in Shan State. The results indicate that the NLD was not seen as capable of dealing with ethnic conflicts in these states. In Rakhine, for example, it was the Arakan National Party (ANP) that won the most seats. The ANP was a coalition of two parties, one of which took an especially hard stance against the Rohingya.[3]

The British first-past-the-post system again came to the NLD's advantage. This winner-takes-all approach works in Britain to ensure both a strong government and opposition. In Myanmar, however, the system has a different effect. In accordance with the myth of the Maha Sammata, there has always been a tendency towards the domination of one political movement by one charismatic leader, resulting in the marginalization of all other aspirants of political office, thus leaving little room for a strong parliamentarian opposition.

Post-Election Agonies

The exultant mood during and just after the elections quickly sobered. Cardinal Charles Bo, who had spoken of a "'sacred pilgrimage' towards democracy and freedom"[4] before the elections chose more somber words some months later: "There is a very, very long way to go; there are many, many challenges to confront; and no one should think that the election of the new government means that our struggle is over. It is just the very beginning."[5]

The new struggle started with a many-months-long process of power transfer. Public interest continued to focus on Aung San Suu Kyi. The central question remained open: what would her formal role be given that the constitution barred her from the presidency? Throughout the process, she claimed de facto leadership of the new government. In an interview before the publication of the final election results, she explained that a new president would be named, "just to meet requirements of constitution. He will have to understand this perfectly well that he will have no authority, that he will act in accordance with the decisions of the party [sic]."[6] The same interview also suggested that the new president would directly receive instructions from her. Aung San Suu Kyi thus made it clear that only she represented the party. When asked whether this could be a prelude to authoritarianism, she replied that no such thing could happen; the party did after all have the people's support.[7]

On numerous occasions, Aung San Suu Kyi expressed her concern that the transfer of power would not happen without friction—she had learned this much from her dealings with the military over time. The USDP minister for information tried to allay such concerns and stressed that his government would do everything to guarantee a smooth transition. He said that this would be Thein Sein's last victory.[8]

Aung San Suu Kyi met with Thein Sein and then with Min Aung Hlaing, the highest commander of the armed forces, on December 2, 2015. The second meeting was a first between the two individuals and carried some significance. Suu Kyi had spoken to the leaders of the military—identical with the government—in 1994, but now the meeting took place on a level playing field between the civilian and military leadership of the country. A prominent NLD representative acknowledged that the much longed-for dialogue between the two sides was now finally taking place, twenty-seven years later. The minister for information of the outgoing government said that the meeting demonstrated that Myanmar was now cultivating a "dialogue culture," which had been lacking in the past.[9] The contents of the conversations at these highest echelons were not revealed to the citizens of Myanmar. Thant Myint-U, grandson of the former Burmese United Nations secretary-general, saw a seamless continuation of a typically Burmese political pattern in this exchange, noting, "personalities of leaders are often more important than the institutions they lead."[10]

Aung San Suu Kyi also met with former head of state Than Shwe in December. During this meeting, Than Shwe is reported to have endorsed Aung San Suu Kyi's role as the leader of the country, while she suggested that they let the past rest in its place and focus instead on the future of the country.[11] The conciliatory tone follows another pattern in Burmese political rhetoric—letting bygones be bygones. The stance stems from the Buddhist tradition of focusing on the here and now. The belief is that engaging oneself with the sufferings of the past only brings new suffering.

The NLD leadership's decision to describe their parliamentarians as "elected" rather than as the "winning candidates" can also be understood in the Buddhist tradition.[12] "Victory" and "defeat" are just fleeting phenomena in the basic Buddhist belief of impermanence (*anicca*). The NLD may also have chosen its words carefully for fear of the military's response. Making a great show of its victory could well have led to tensions with the military, which could still impede the transfer of power.

After these meetings, the sitting USDP government and the NLD announced that they had set up a commission to organize the details of the transfer.[13] The committee was composed of four confidants each of Thein Sein and Aung San Suu Kyi.

As usual in Myanmar, rumors as to the political appointments that would be made abounded. The long-standing NLD speaker Nyan Win added fuel to the speculation machine by mentioning potential candidates for the influential post of speaker of the house in an interview. As a result, the NLD banned its members from commenting on future political appointments. The party also announced that until the inauguration of the new president, only Aung San Suu Kyi could speak on behalf of the party.

Despite the ban, the NLD's plan to appoint Htin Kyaw as president seeped out. He had been a leader of Aung San Suu Kyi's Khin Kyi Foundation. An IT specialist by training, Htin Kyaw was not one of the early members of the NLD. His father and much respected author Min Thu Wun had successfully run as an NLD candidate in the 1990 elections at the age of eighty-one. Htin Kyaw was married to U Lwin's daughter, Su Su Lwin. U Lwin had been the NLD's press representative from 1988 until his death in 2011. Su Su Lwin had won a seat for the NLD in both the 2012 by-elections and the 2015 elections. However, the man tipped for the presidential post had never run for office himself. He had known Aung San Suu Kyi since his school years and only later got involved with her party. He had been arrested once in September 2000, when he accompanied the party leader on a failed attempt to travel to Mandalay.[14]

The rumor turned out to be true. Htin Kyaw was elected president by the Union Parliament, comprising both houses, on February 15, 2016. The posts of his two deputies were filled by Henry Van Thio, a Christian Chin nominated by the House of Nationalities, and Myint Swe, the former chief minister of Yangon, nominated by the military. The newly elected president gave a short speech after being sworn in on March 30, 2016, in which he took a solemn oath "to pursue a constitution in accordance with democratic norms that will be suitable for our country. I believe that I will have to be patient in implementing this political aim, which the people have wished to see for years."[15] Htin Kyaw thus put himself in the full service of Aung San Suu Kyi's program for introducing a "genuine democracy" in Myanmar. He added no flourishes of his own, making it clear that he was first and foremost a "placeholder president." He thus distinguished himself from Thein Sein, who had kicked off his time in office with a key speech announcing a reform program that had taken many international observers by surprise.

Just four days after Thein Sein's stepping down as head of state, social media was abuzz with photos of him with a shaved head and an orange robe. The former president had had himself ordained as a monk.[16] This shows how Thein Sein, like many traditional Buddhists, was primarily concerned with his *kamma* and less with the fruits of his worldly position. He had fulfilled his duty and sometimes taken measures that conflicted with Buddhist virtues. The time had now come for him to seek balance.

The question of the presidency had now been answered, but it was still not clear what formal role Aung San Suu Kyi would take.[17] The majority of observers were certain that she would become foreign minister. This position would secure her place on the influential, eleven-seat National Defence and Security Council, in which the military occupies a constitutionally guaranteed majority.[18]

On the same day as Htin Kyaw's swearing in, Aung San Suu Kyi took over the government with no less than four posts simultaneously: foreign minister, minister in the president's office, minister for electric power and energy, and minister of education. She gave up the latter two shortly afterwards when the parliament created a new post specifically for Aung San Suu Kyi in early April, namely that of "state counsellor." President Htin Kyaw signed the law creating this position on April 6, which specifically names Aung San Suu Kyi and guarantees her authority over all ministries, departments, organizations, associations, and individuals and makes her accountable to the Pyidaungsu Hluttaw. Her role thus resembled that of a prime minister. Her tasks were "to promote a flourishing multiparty democratic system, a real market-oriented economy, a federal union, and peace and development. The term of the office for the State Counsellor is equal to the term of the current president."[19] This tailor-made law was the arrangement that allowed her to make good on her promise of "standing above the president."

The parliamentarians appointed by the military tried to obstruct the law, but without success. They argued that the term "'state counsellor' in the name of the bill was tantamount to granting such a person both executive and legislative powers, which was against constitutional provisions."[20] Khin Zaw Win, a prominent former political prisoner and social activist, made a fundamental objection: "Aiming to become Paramount Leader in Myanmar is not only setting a dangerous precedent, it can be downright disastrous for the country. It is far more prudent just to do the obvious, that is to get down to putting a country in order after the chaos of a failed dictatorship."[21]

The first moves of the new government set forth old political patterns. Decisions were made at the top of the ruling party, which now happened to be the NLD. The base was left out of the decision-making process, resembling the military practice of making the lower ranks the recipients and executors of orders. As Robert Taylor put it, "Dialogue and discussion, explanation and response, disagreement and discord, are at the heart of effective government. The military administrations that shaped Myanmar's current bureaucracy discouraged if not prohibited this process."[22] However, Aung San Suu Kyi's government appeared to be no different in this regard. She and her military counterparts alone defined the transition process. All decisive meetings and conversations took place behind closed doors. Only very general information, if any, made it to the public realm. Decisions on personnel appointments within the NLD—which now largely dominated the political sphere—were ultimately made by Aung San Suu Kyi herself.

From Human Rights Icon to Power Politician

With Thein Sein's departure, Htin Kyaw's election, and the institutionalization of Aung San Suu Kyi as state counsellor, the formal political transition was complete. It was interpreted in two different ways; the outgoing government spoke of continuity whereas the incoming government spoke of a revolutionary change. According to the first interpretation, the change in government was no more than a regular transition within the constitutional framework set by the military. In Aung San Suu Kyi's interpretation, however, this was the start of a fundamentally new kind of politics.

Various critics saw a threat to democracy and a concentration of political power in Aung San Suu Kyi's lone hands, which could not be reconciled with the image of her as a human rights icon. To such critics, she replied that she had always been a politician and not a human rights icon. She emphasized this as early as October 2013, when she was chairperson for the commission on the Letpadaung Mine: "I'm always surprised when people speak as if I've just become a politician. I've been a politician all along. I started in politics not as a human rights defender or a humanitarian worker, but as the leader of a political party. And if that's not a politician then I don't know what is."[23]

At the same time, she challenged the common view that politics was a dirty business revolving solely around the pursuit of power.[24] She, for one, held herself to have firm convictions on politics: "This was the way I was brought up to think of politics, that politics was to do with ethics, it was to do with responsibility, it was to do with service, so I think I was conditioned to think like that and I'm too old to change now."[25]

Aung San Suu Kyi stresses her sense of duty with which she hopes to serve her people. The statement is reminiscent of the vow she took upon her mother's death on January 2, 1989, which is reproduced at the beginning of this book. She stands for a politics that is in the service of her country and its people. At the same time, she sees herself—as her father before her—as a pragmatic politician whose task is not to save humanity but to make compromises that lead to the betterment of life of those whom she represents.

One problem with this self-definition as "just a regular politician" was that it invoked very different perceptions from both within her country as well as from abroad. The image that people had of her—with or without she herself condoning any such thing—did not fit with the business of politics. There was a fundamental contradiction here in the eyes of observers, particularly those coming from a Western perspective, where religious charisma has a lot less significance than in Myanmar. For Aung San Suu Kyi's supporters, she remained the nation's "Mother Suu" and was never a regular politician seeking power and charting pragmatic paths to achieving certain political ends. This is most obvious from the Letpadaung mine incident (see chapter 11). In that case, the disappointment that people felt because of Aung San Suu Kyi's pragmatic pro-China approach had no impact on the election results of the district. The NLD won that seat without difficulties. What is more, its political competitors did not even try to bring up the controversy around the mine in an attempt to gain electoral advantage.

All Quiet in Naypyidaw

Aung San Suu Kyi's decision to take over various political offices at the beginning of the new government demonstrated the fundamental problem with Myanmar's political culture. Right before the elections, the journalist Zeya Thu had said, "If Aung San Suu Kyi wins, she will hopefully surround herself with the best brains in the country and the whole world. This country has massive problems. To resolve them, one needs a lot of knowledge and practical experience."[26] However, both the party and the country lacked such experts. Even if there had been such people available, they would not have been able to transform Myanmar overnight. Since the country's independence in 1948, it has been difficult to reconcile only a partly functioning bureaucracy with a meaningful involvement of experts. It is simply not enough to have clever brains. Just as important is a functioning coexistence of institutions, a political system, and a political culture.[27] Myanmar had to be reinvented as a political entity—once again. Aung San never had the opportunity to transform his ideas into reality. U Nu and Ne Win failed to establish a new Myanmar. Aung San Suu Kyi had now been given another chance; however, she had to—like her predecessors before her—start practically at zero.

The new beginning had to furthermore unfold in cooperation with the military. The only parliamentary opposition worth mentioning was the quarter component appointed by the military high command in all parliaments. This minority was also capable of blocking constitutional change. Even more importantly, the military controlled certain central ministries, such as the Ministry of Home Affairs, which is responsible for the country's police force. Aung San Suu Kyi and her party thus have to cooperate with their former adversaries in various decisive political spheres. Recalling Aung San Suu Kyi's many years under house arrest, this meant that the former prisoner now had to sit at the same table with her former captors to discuss the future of the country. Given her exceptional personality, the NLD's leader was certainly capable of dealing with this difficult task. It is, however, different for many other members of the NLD who paid for their loyalty to Aung San Suu Kyi with repression by the junta. It would perhaps be most difficult to convince the electorate—who had borne the brunt of military rule for years—that such a compromise would be a historic achievement.

Under these circumstances—lengthy transfer process, lack of leading personnel, and the difficult but necessary cooperation with the military—it is no surprise that the government under Aung San Suu Kyi's leadership had no great achievements to speak of in its first two years in office. When challenged with this after one year in power, Aung San Suu Kyi responded in an interview, "The first nine months have been difficult because we've had to clear away a lot of debris from previous practices and now only, we're beginning to make a little bit of headway."[28] The reference to the "debris" inherited from the past plays on the party's election motto "time for change." In Burmese, the slogan makes a reference to the new year festival of Thingyan.[29] The water fights and religious rituals that take place on this day symbolically wash away the old year, cleaning away the debris so that a fresh new start can be made.

What might be possible in private life, however, cannot succeed in Myanmar's political reality. The debris that had heaped up over the decades—right there in the public eye—could first of all not be cleared away with a wave of the hand for its sheer amount. Second, the military was solidly entrenched within the country's political system. The new era could only be a modified version of the old one. In other words, it could only be an evolution, not a revolution. It had to be a continuation of the reforms initiated by the military instead of a complete about-face.

This challenge dominated the new government from early on. This comes to light through two examples. The first relates to the government's efforts to bring about positive economic development, and the second to its endeavors to end the armed conflicts in the country. Yet both of these central challenges faced by the new government were quickly overshadowed by escalations at the country's peripheries. As a result, Aung San Suu Kyi's takeover of the government and thus increased responsibility for the country unfurled with both domestic and international unexpected tensions.

Investment and Economy

Even before taking over the government, Aung San Suu Kyi had been promoting investment in her country during all her foreign visits.[30] She stressed the importance of ethical and responsible business.[31] Such investments would benefit not a small group of cronies—as had been the case in the past—but the largest possible part of the population. In a different context, Aung San Suu Kyi had expressed this understanding as follows: "Concepts of development are more meaningfully divided into 'people centered' and 'government centered', than into 'western' or 'eastern.'"[32] She wanted her country to have people-centered economic policies that empower its citizens.[33] Foreign direct investment was to play a contributing part in this vision. Since coming into power, she has only intensified her calls for investment, for example during her visits to the USA, Singapore, Thailand, Japan, and China.

These appeals are Aung San Suu Kyi's way of dealing with the issue of economic growth, which a number of foreign observers hold to be the key to the success of the country's political reform process. The belief that a democratic system under the NLD's leadership is better for the people can only be upheld if large parts of the population see a marked improvement in their standard of living, or so the narrative runs. However, this logic of a free-market economy and democracy together taking hold in Myanmar lends itself to much doubt. First, the neighboring country Thailand—which in many respects resembles Myanmar—is a clear example of how modernization theory does not always work. Here, economic growth did not result in the growth of participatory political structures. Second, Myanmar's election results show that there is little value placed on competition between political ideas. The political system is monopolistic in nature, and the same is true of the economy. Anyone who speaks to the NLD's voters and supporters would see that economic aspects play a subordinate role in their voting decisions. Far more important are what could be termed "spiritual" elements. With Aung San Suu Kyi in power, the country is finally led by someone who deserves the highly revered title of "mother of the nation" by virtue of her moral qualities.

Myanmar has always been presented to the world as a place of great economic potential. Institutions such as the World Bank or the Asian Development Bank support this position to this day. The country's great strengths are its richness in fertile land and forests, the large fresh water reserves, as well as deposits of gas, oil, and other minerals. In the long term, the geographic location itself could prove to be an economic advantage. Myanmar could be the bridge between India and China— the two most populous countries in the world.[34] Finally, with more than fifty million inhabitants and a large proportion of young people who may be prepared to work for relatively low wages, the country could—at least for a given period of time—benefit from a comparative competitive advantage.[35] Experts thus predict a medium-term average GDP growth rate of 8.2 percent.[36]

There are, however, considerable obstacles in exploiting this great potential. According to experts, the country's entire economic system is in need of a structural overhaul. The financial sector is still in its infancy, there is a lack of professionals, the infrastructure—such as electricity supply and the transport system—remains underdeveloped. Although power cuts in Yangon are becoming less frequent, the system is still nowhere near what would be required for large-scale industrial production. The internet, too, is slow and unreliable. The bureaucracy, such as in customs clearance or the founding of a company, is full of red tape and takes up a lot of time. The legal enforcement of contracts is lacking.[37] Furthermore, the ongoing battles in some regions scare many investors away. Inflation of around 9 percent in 2016 affects the poor rural population disproportionately. To date, they have felt little of Myanmar's economic boom. The kyat has declined in value.

Some success stories signal hope. One example is the rapid development of the mobile phone network. Mobile phones were a rare sight in Myanmar just six years ago. Telephone stalls lined the streets, where customers from the surrounding residential blocks could make phone calls. Today mobile coverage extends to more than 90 percent of the population and the prices for SIM cards have dropped dramatically.[38]

Still, Western observers repeatedly expressed their doubts as to the new government's ability to bridge domestic realities and international standards of a modern economy.[39] For example, the NLD's program for the economy did not appear for a long time. It was only in July 2016 that the government published its twelve-point paper.[40] The paper covers almost all fundamental aspects of the economy but only in a short and fleeting way. The highest priority is placed on the project of national reconciliation, which is to be achieved through a fair and sustainable use of natural resources in a way that profits all citizens equally. The paper also states that the mineral resources sector—central to Myanmar's economy—is to become more transparent. The NLD embraces a free-market economy in the paper and aims to fight against corruption and monopolies. It strives for price stability, simplification of the tax system, development of infrastructure, better access to finance, and so on. The list bears a fatal resemblance to the big plans set out by U Nu and Ne Win at the start of their terms in office, all of which failed.

The enormous challenges that the new government faces are perhaps best exemplified in the agricultural sector, which, by employing more than 70 percent of the population, remains the most important economic sector. Like the governments that preceded it, the new government also places great weight on this segment of the economy. So far, the country has not been able to transform what is essentially subsistence farming into a for-profit market structure. This is partly because Myanmar's economy plays by different—what may, again, be referred to as "spiritual"—rules. Studies by an American anthropologist from as far back as the 1960s revealed that between 25 and 40 percent of family income in rural areas was spent on religious ends.[41] Until today, a "*dāna* economy" has prevailed in Myanmar. *Dāna* (religiously motivated giving) is the highest virtue in Buddhism. Through giving, an individual invests in his or her next life, not in the economic betterment of this life and society. Empirical studies as to how the *dāna* economy has evolved in recent years are lacking. On first sight, it appears to be ubiquitous in the rural areas and still important in the cities. Introducing free-market ideals and incentives in such a society cannot be straightforward.

The current discussions, however, do not focus on fundamental social challenges such as that of the *dāna* tradition. The questions discussed center instead on land reform, given that a number of small farmers have lost their land because of debt, engagement of large agribusiness firms, and expropriation by the military.[42] The legal system remains weak, and despite prescriptive calls for the "rule of law," it is unlikely that the proposed measures will lead to an improvement even in the medium term. If the NLD were to follow through with its intention of a serious land reform program addressing past unjust expropriations, it would quickly run into confrontations with the military and its cronies.

It is worth noting that even without any major changes to economic policy, Myanmar is likely to experience a rise in its standard of living, especially in the cities. The inflow of foreign direct investment and development funds will certainly boost economic growth, even if the benefits of this growth are not spread as evenly as the NLD may have hoped in its vision of a "clean economy."

It is no surprise, then, that the economic elite of the country are in high spirits. On election day, one business representative stated, "One could sense the tremendous positive energy brimming under the surface."[43] Another nationally known businessman with good connections to the military and a member of the USDP—a prototypical "crony"—who had lost his seat in parliament after the elections spoke of "business as usual." The man was on the United States' blacklist but based his confidence on the following explanation: "When the investments come in, there is no one else apart from us, the 'cronies,' who will be able to work on the same level as the foreign investors."[44] The property developer supported Aung San Suu Kyi's government and even spoke of his "friendship" with Aung San Suu Kyi to a journalist, comparing his relationship to her as one between siblings.[45]

Also, in the economic sphere, Aung San Suu Kyi and the government that she leads can only achieve the change and cleaning up of the "debris" with the help of the very forces that represent the old system. The irony is that if she sets out to break the monopolies of cronies in order to achieve a "clean economy," she risks slowing down economic growth by pushing away their economic expertise. There is still a wide gap between a fundamental renewal of the country, as symbolized by the Thingyan festival, and political realities.

Peace and Reconciliation

The NLD's election manifesto prioritized ethnic affairs and striving for internal peace. The primary method for achieving this aim was identified as follows: "Hold political dialogue based on the Panglong spirit in order to address the roots of internal armed conflict and enable people to live in security and tranquillity."[46] The party's program thus tied together the memory of the 1947 Panglong Conference—the founding myth of the Union of Myanmar—together with the word "dialogue"—a word that Aung San Suu Kyi had used during her times of confrontation with the military as a signal of overcoming differences. Back then she was facing *one* other party, that is, the military. Now Aung San Suu Kyi represented the government and was confronted with a task of entirely different proportions: a far more complex dialogue with multiple groups who often had varying and contradicting interests. To find a balance here was and remains a challenge of the highest order, not least because some of the armed ethnic groups view Aung San Suu Kyi's practical alliance with the military with deep-seated suspicion. The battles that had started with the founding of the country are not forgotten and continue in various locations.

The military had held a series of dialogues with the armed groups since the 1988 coup. In many cases, this had led to more or less stable ceasefire agreements. In addition to the seven regions for the country's ethnic majority, the 2008 constitution provided for seven states for the large "national races" as well as the Union Territories around Naypyidaw and "self-administrative areas," in which ethnic political organizations had a say together with the state institutions. This was a practical recognition of the fact that there were border areas in the country that had been de facto autonomous for a long time.[47] The upshot of this arrangement was that a quasi-independent state formed in the northeast of the country; the Wa Special Zone 2 was ruled over by an up to 30,000-strong army, the United Wa State Army (UWSA), which had good connections to neighboring China. A second region over which the government has no real control lies in the north of Kachin State, around the city of Laiza, where the Kachin Independence Organisation and its army, the KIA, are headquartered. The KIA has a Christian leadership and is the best-trained rebel army in the country. It is fighting for the autonomy of the entire Kachin State and actively training members of other rebel groups.

In October 2015, shortly before the elections, Thein Sein's government had hoped to conclude its peace talks with a universal signing of the Nationwide Ceasefire Agreement (NCA). However, only eight of the fifteen invited groups signed the agreement with the government in October 2015. Among these eight was the Karen National Union, which in January 1949 had been the first ethnic group to wage civil war.[48] The organization of the peace process in Myanmar is still based on the principles laid out in this agreement. The principles include the territorial integrity of the state, democracy, and federalism. They also prescribe a military code of conduct for all parties and armies, and point finally to a process of legal adjustment to the constitution in order to create a federal union.[49]

Two committees were set up two days after the signing of the agreement to bring the agreement to life. The Joint Ceasefire Monitoring Committee (JMC) is supposed to monitor compliance with the agreement. The eighteen-seat Union Peace Dialogue Joint Committee—consisting of members of rebel organizations, the government (including representatives of the military), and the parties—is supposed to advance the political path to peace and reconciliation. On December 15, 2015, the committee proposed a framework for political dialogue, setting out a highly complicated process. The first step under this process was the convening of a Union Peace Conference in which seven hundred delegates were to participate.[50] This conference then took place in January 2016. Aung San Suu Kyi, who had been absent at the signing of the NCA, participated and gave a speech.

Many hoped that the new government under Aung San Suu Kyi would not only continue with the peace process but also give it new direction. Her party had, after all, also received support from large parts of the non-Bamar population. Such hopes quickly received their first blow. Just a few hours before the swearing in of the new president, fighting broke out in Shan State between the Tatmadaw and one of the groups that had not signed the October 2015 agreement. The installation of the new head of state had no impact on the continuation of hostilities. That is just one example. The JMC received five hundred complaints in its first six months of operation.[51]

At the end of April 2016, Aung San Suu Kyi used a meeting with the JMC to announce the Union Peace Conference, which she referred to as a Second Panglong Conference. The conference took place four months later, from August 31 to September 3 in Naypyidaw. Its official title was the "Union Peace Conference—21st Century Panglong," which evoked the memory of the historical conference organized by Aung San in 1947.

Around 1,600 people participated in the conference, including United Nations secretary-general Ban Ki-moon. Various parties, organizations, and groups, including some of the rebel armies that had refused to sign the NCA, were represented. Three armies that had been founded relatively recently and that were primarily active in Shan State were barred from the conference. As had been the case in the run-up to the NCA, there were battles about the choice of words. Rebels and conference organizers could not reach an agreement on the wording of an eventual promise by the armed groups to one day lay down their weapons.

The delegation of the UWSA left the conference on the second day. It did not feel fairly treated by the conference organizers. This again was about a detail, namely the correct description of the UWSA delegates; they had been assigned "observer" and not "speaker" status by the conference organizers.[52] Such incidents go to show the high value placed by different groups on being recognized and respected before engaging in any dialogue.

The war of words points towards a fundamental problem for the peace process. None of the rebel armies can imagine laying down its arms in the foreseeable future. Over the decades, the weapons have become part of their identities. The Tatmadaw also cannot give up its claim to a monopoly on the use of force. The minority armies will not lay down their weapons without trust in the army and credible guarantees of their security. One concrete—albeit far in the future—solution could, for example, be the integration of the rebel armies into the Tatmadaw. That would of course also mean allowing generals from armies such as the Wa State Army or the KIA to hold key commanding positions in the Tatmadaw. Such an idea, however, has not yet appeared on the agendas of the peace-process meetings.

Several speeches were given on the first and second day of the 2016 conference. Almost all of these speeches invoked the "spirit of Panglong." Military representatives—as always—stressed the importance of the unity of the nation whereas ethnic groups emphasized the importance of a "truly federal union," articulating their desire for autonomy. Contentious issues were not discussed. There was also no concluding statement as, in essence, no decisions had been made. In her closing speech, Aung San Suu Kyi called the conference a success and "urged all participants to make the Conference go down in history of the country in the same way . . . the Panglong Conference did in 1947."[53]

In reality, the 2016 conference could never meet such high a bar—it is always difficult to convert a myth into concrete politics. The remodeled Union Peace Conference was to now meet every six months, flanked by regional political dialogues.[54] A second "Panglong Conference of the 21st Century" took place from May 24 to 29, 2017, in Naypyidaw. The outcomes of this meeting were mixed. Progress included the development of a forty-five-point declaration of the Union Peace Dialogue Joint Committee (UPDJ). However, groups that had not signed up to the NCA were not represented in the UPDJ. Out of the forty-five points, thirty-seven were adopted. Among others, the central question of secession from the union remained contentious.[55] A date for the signing of a much longed-for nationwide peace agreement remains far in the future.

Escalation and the New Rakhine-Rohingya Crisis

On the last day of the first 21st Century Panglong Conference in early September 2016, former United Nations secretary-general Kofi Annan arrived in Myanmar in his new role as chairman of the newly created Advisory Commission on Rakhine State.[56] This commission had been set up by the government to find a solution to the Rohingya problem. The nine-person commission was largely composed of citizens of Myanmar. Kofi Annan immediately set off for Sittwe, the capital of Rakhine State, where he was whistled at and booed. Buddhist groups had already been protesting the appointment of three foreigners to the commission. Emotions in Rakhine State obviously ran high.

The situation was rapidly worsening. On October 9, 2016, shortly after the commission had taken up its tasks, Muslim insurgents attacked a number of police posts in the border area and killed nine police officers. The security forces responded with so called "clearance operations" aimed at arresting the attackers based on their own statements. These operations led to further armed clashes, where—according to official government information—about forty persons were killed.[57] But all such figures are not without flaws. An International Crisis Group report finds that the insurgent group, which a year later came to be known as the

Arakan Rohingya Salvation Army (ARSA), was being directed by a group of Rohingya émigrés in Saudi Arabia.[58]

These attacks added a new dimension to the conflict. The mass exoduses of 1977–78 and 1991–92 had each seen a quarter of a million Rohingyas fleeing Myanmar. These displacements were caused by state acts, which led Muslims in the region to fear the worst. The first, in 1977, was a crackdown on citizenship status; the second, in 1991, was repressive measures undertaken by the military. The outbreak of violence in 2012 had to do with the acts of civilian groups on both sides. This time, however, it was a Muslim insurgent group that declared war on the state of Myanmar. Given the global dialogue on Islamic terrorism in the Middle East, South Asia, Southeast Asia, and elsewhere, the conflict was now placed in a new international context. While in Myanmar and some other countries like China and India the focus was blankly placed on Islamic terror, in the West the focus was just as simply placed on the victimization of the Rohingya.[59]

After the conflict came to light, there were multiple reports on the human rights offences committed by the state, such as mass shootings, rape, and burning down of entire villages. The government continued to deny such reports.[60] Fighting broke out again in November with casualties on both sides. According to the government, sixty-nine Muslim insurgents and seventeen members of the country's armed forces lost their lives.[61] At the end of November 2016, John McKissick, head of the United Nations refugee agency at the Bangladeshi border town of Cox's Bazar, told the BBC that troops were "killing men, shooting them, slaughtering children, raping women, burning and looting houses, forcing these people to cross the river" into Bangladesh.[62] This evoked an outraged response from the spokesperson for Myanmar's President Htin Kyaw: "I would like to question the professionalism and ethics which should be followed and respected by UN staff."[63] Some 60,000–70,000 Rohingya fled over the border to Bangladesh following the disputes.

Like in 2012 and 2013, these events led to strong criticism of Aung San Suu Kyi, especially from abroad. The Malaysian Prime Minister Najib Razak used the term "genocide"—long adopted by human rights activists—to call for an end to the plight of the Rohingya.[64] In Indonesia, two thousand activists gathered in protest outside the embassy of Myanmar.[65]

Kofi Annan again traveled to Myanmar in December 2016 and tried to quell the storm. He warned that observers should be "very, very careful" in using the word genocide.[66] Aung San Suu Kyi asked the international community for its understanding for the difficult position that the current government found itself in: "I would appreciate it so much if the international community would help us . . . to make progress in building better relations between the two communities instead of always drumming up calls for bigger fires of resentment."[67]

Western media predominantly focused on the crisis in Rakhine State in its coverage of Myanmar. The situation was declared to be the litmus test for Aung San Suu Kyi and the new government. Human rights activists were quick to conclude that the NLD and its leader had failed. The decades-long conflict and the complex involvement of the military in the region since independence was, in reality, something that could not be resolved overnight. But this is something that most international commentators conveniently overlooked.[68] The old black-and-white lens employed by observers to gauge good versus evil in the country was back. This time, however, Aung San Suu Kyi, who had been shouldered forth as the carrier of hope just a few months ago, was now painted as the wrongdoer by the very same people.

Largely unnoticed and far from Rakhine State, the situation in Shan State, in the east of the country, also worsened. A coalition of four groups started an offensive against the army and made the following public announcement: "Despite the fact that our alliance of the Northern Brotherhoods truly wants a genuine peace and wishes to solve political problems through political means, we have inevitably launched such a joint military operation after constant military pressure from the Burma Army."[69] The statement speaks of peace and political solution but ultimately serves as a declaration of war. A few days later, the defense minister called for parliament to declare the alliance a terrorist organization. However, such a label would have signaled a failure of the peace process. The defense minister's request was rejected. Still, the label of terrorism would soon become popular.

The commission led by Kofi Annan published an interim report on the crisis in Rakhine on March 16, 2017.[70] The report contained a number of recommendations. The commission's chair expanded on the report as follows:

> These recommendations include a renewed call for unimpeded access for humanitarian actors and journalists to the affected areas in Northern Rakhine and for independent and impartial investigation of the allegations of crimes committed on and since October 9, 2016.
>
> We strongly believe that perpetrators of these crimes must be held to account.
>
> Our recommendations, of course, go beyond the current situation in Northern Rakhine and include proposals relating to: the protection of rights, freedom of movement, enhanced economic and social development and the edification of Rakhine's cultural heritage.
>
> The Commission is aware of a number of unresolved concerns surrounding the verification of citizenship and recommends that they be clarified and resolved without delay.
>
> We also stress that inclusive access to healthcare and education for the all the people in Rakhine requires attention and improvement.[71]
>
> Aung San Suu Kyi welcomed the interim report and promised to implement its recommendations. Amnesty International was not impressed. The organization encouraged the immediate implementation of the recommendations but remained critical of the report, finding that "unfortunately, the commission's recommendations go not far enough to address the increasingly dire situation on the ground."[72]

Kofi Annan presented the interim report to the president of Myanmar, Htin Kyaw, on August 23, 2017. It was passed on to Aung San Suu Kyi one day later. On the same day, one UN spokesperson welcomed the fact that the report also addressed the root causes of the conflict and promised to study its recommendations in detail.[73] But before that could happen, there was another attack by Muslim insurgents. On the morning of August 25, 2017, the ARSA carried out numerous attacks. At the same time it posted a declaration on Twitter:

> Rohingya Community in Rathedaung [a township with many Rohingya residents] has been under a Burmese government sponsored atrocities and blockade for more than 2 weeks which is starving them (the Rohingya people) to death. Over the last 2 days, Burmese security forces together with Rakhine extremists killed over a dozen people in the township.
>
> As they plan to do the same in Maungdaw; and conducted raids and committed atrocities in some Rohingya villages in the township last night (24 August night), we had eventually step up [sic] in order to drive the Burmese colonizing forces away.
>
> Currently we have taken our defense actions against the Burmese marauding forces in more than 25 different places across the region. More soon![74]

One day later, ARSA accused the Burmese army of attempting, "to derail the 'Kofi Annan Report and Recommendations' by triggering an unrest in the state. Therefore, we have tried our best to avoid any potential conflict meanwhile [sic]."[75] The attacks by the group consisted of a seemingly well-coordinated assault on thirty police stations, resulting reportedly in the death of twelve members of the Burmese armed forces. The number of casualties on the insurgents' side is unknown.

The army responded to the ARSA fighters' attacks with further clearance operations. According to the government, these lasted till September 5.[76] Around one hundred purported insurgents were reportedly killed as a result. Aung San Suu Kyi condemned the insurgents' attacks and set out her position in an official statement: "It is clear that today's attacks are systematically planned and are intended to cripple the efforts for peace, stability and co-existence of the local communities. Our determined efforts would not waver in any way due to atrocious acts of brutality of extremist terrorists."[77] Three days later, ARSA was declared to be a terrorist group under the country's Anti-Terrorism Law.[78]

The start of the fighting set a refugee movement in motion, causing dramatic scenes at the border. Refugees were sent back by soldiers at the border, but some managed to make it to refugee camps on the other side. From there they reported of the atrocities of "armed Buddhists." On the Myanmar side, thousands of non-Muslims were evacuated from the conflict zone by Burmese armed forces.[79] An unprecedented escalation of the conflict followed. By the end of October, over six hundred thousand Rohingyas had fled to Bangladesh. That is more than half of the Muslim population that had been living in Rakhine.

Media on both sides of the border were overwhelmed with opposing accounts of events. The international media once again portrayed the Burmese military as an inhumane force that would not shy away from committing any scale of atrocities in the name of ethnic cleansing or even genocide. A large number of reports by well-known human rights organizations such as Amnesty International or Human Rights Watch relied on the same methodology, namely interviewing Rohingya refugees in Bangladesh, to come to the same conclusions: the Tatmadaw and Buddhist Arakanese had brutally and systematically advanced against the Rohingya. Shootings, gang rapes, and the burning down of entire villages were the chosen methods.[80]

On the other side, Myanmar's social media in particular was rife with a new wave of hate campaigns. Mark Farmaner of Burma Campaign UK had already lamented these a few years ago, but now the phenomenon took off with an increased intensity and in higher numbers. The campaigns were targeted at both Muslims and the international media. Within Myanmar, it was rumored that some foreigners who sided with the Rohingya were bullied out of the country. Open discussions on the causes of the conflict were not possible.[81]

Aung San Suu Kyi's alleged silence in the face of the Rohingyas' suffering meant that criticism targeted at her personally grew. Foreign supporters who had idealized her in the past now debased that image. This included, for example, the musician and Live Aid concerts' organizer Bob Geldof.[82]

The only excuse offered for her misconduct was her dependence on the military. A process of understanding unfolded in the West. It became clearer that the 2015 elections had not led to the military losing power and the victory of democracy. However, not all came to this realization. Archbishop Desmond Tutu, a recipient of the Nobel Peace Prize like Aung San Suu Kyi, argued that political compromises could not be without limits: "If the political price of your ascension to the highest office in Myanmar is your silence, the price is surely too steep."[83] With this, he implied that Aung San Suu Kyi was clinging onto power. Other commentators suspected that she was hoping to assume the presidency in 2020 with the help of the military. All else had to be subordinated to this goal.[84] International travelers considered whether travel to Myanmar should be boycotted. This reflected a stance promoted by Aung San Suu Kyi herself while she was under house arrest.

Aung San Suu Kyi responded to her critics in a televised speech delivered to foreign diplomats and Myanmar officials on September 19, 2017.[85] She defended her government's position and promised to investigate allegations of human rights abuses and to punish wrongdoers. She also stated that those who had fled could return if—as was agreed with Bangladesh in the previous displacement of people in the 1990s— they could prove that they had been living in Myanmar. The speech did not satisfy her critics but received full support in Myanmar.

Hurried negotiations with the government of Bangladesh followed. On November 23, the parties signed an agreement setting out the details for regulating return.[86] The poor English of the text already indicates that the agreement was drawn up in haste. Human rights organizations were already criticizing the agreement a few hours later. Knut Ostby, the highest UN representative in Myanmar, expressed his doubts as to the country's honest intentions to facilitate a return for the refugees.[87]

Violent Disappointment, Entrenchment, and Realpolitik

It remains unclear whether and how the agreement can be translated into the real return of the Rakhine Muslims that have fled the country. What is clear is that in this case, as in all other aspects of Burmese politics, no quick and straightforward results are to be expected. At the end of 2017, as before, the country finds itself in a state of "stable limbo."

The course of Burmese politics can be understood by thinking of a theater production in which the actors' roles differ depending on whether the director comes from a Western tradition of from a Burmese one. At the end of 2017, two versions were available.

Since the mass movement of the Rohingya, what plays center stage in the West is the mass misery of the Muslims who fled Rakhine and who are seen as the victims of an inhumane Myanmar military. That this flight was sparked by a Muslim insurgent group is only marginally acknowledged in this interpretation. The new actors, with the impersonal acronym of ARSA, did not yet have a part. On the other hand, the character of the former protagonist now sees a turnaround. For the international public, Aung San Suu Kyi is no longer the glimmering heroine that she was in the earlier acts of this drama. She is now a cool, calculating politician, a kind of Lady Macbeth of Myanmar who is willing to sacrifice the lives of others in the name of her own ambitions. In this, she is now playing into the hands of the former villain—the military—once so forcefully fought against. Largely unnoticed, the people cheer in the background. They unconditionally support Aung San Suu Kyi and do not accept the Rohingya as citizens of Myanmar.

A different interpretation is offered on the national stages of Myanmar. Flashbacks are used to portray the Rohingya as a threat to Buddhism and the entire country. Aung San Suu Kyi keeps the role of queen of hearts, beacon of hope. The previous act of the Burmese interpretation had ended with joyous scenes of the November 2015 election night. Then, the military had appeared to be defeated. Now, however, it is making a gradual comeback. The role of the villains has shifted from those in uniform to the international community, which does not understand Myanmar and makes false accusations.

In both interpretations, disappointment and frustration prevail.[88] Internationally, many are disappointed that the democratization process, in which so many hopes had been placed, seems to have come to a standstill so quickly. Instead of advancement, the set is dominated by scenes of a humanitarian catastrophe. All calls to Aung San Suu Kyi and her government, voiced by a choir of human rights organizations and UN employees, seem to fall on deaf ears. The "true" villain, Min Aung Hlaing, commander-in-chief of the army, remains unchallengeable.[89] The Western audience had previously clad the heroine in Western clothes. Now they are disappointed that she dons Burmese attire and seems to also follow the political logic of her country. Only a few spectators realize that what is at play here is the manifestation of a psychological defence mechanism; every idealization is followed by a devaluation.

The people in Myanmar are disappointed that the world that had been so well-wishing towards them in the past has now revoked its affection and support. Most of them are defiant, perhaps more scornful of Muslims than they previously were, and are waiting for the happy end that Mother Suu will surely deliver to them.

That means, to put it bluntly, that after some two years under Aung San Suu Kyi's government, Myanmar finds itself negotiating the cobwebs of realpolitik. The political charisma that was accorded Aung San Suu Kyi abroad is as good as gone. Internally, she has to proceed in a large coalition with an undesirable partner, but can always rely on the support of the majority of her Buddhist voters. Externally, she has lost a number of friends and not made any new ones. At best one can witness a rapprochement with China.[90] Under her leadership, Myanmar has reached a point of international normality. The fairy tale narrative of "the beast and the beauty" that had been reproduced both internationally and nationally, and the tense expectations that came with it, have been done away with. The military no longer stands in opposition to Aung San Suu Kyi, and Myanmar is at the same political point as many other countries in South Asia and beyond. The dream of a great political rebirth has faded away; realpolitik and crisis management are the terms of the day.

That does not have to be a disadvantage. The Rohingya crisis disappointed inflated expectations. Perhaps in this way it has created room for the consistent efforts for smaller steps, which have also been made. For example, there has been improvement in relation to freedom of opinion and the press. It is unlikely that the Rohingya crisis will be resolved in the foreseeable future. The return of almost 250,000 Muslims in 1992 had still not been completed ten years later.[91] In relation to the economy, the peace process, legal system reform, and the building of democratic institutions, progress can only be achieved in the long run. Various small steps are needed in the political and social spheres, as is the effort to avoid further escalations.

Epilogue

"Cycles of Change" was the title of the first chapter of the book that Dr. Maung Maung, socialist Burma's last president, wrote as a retrospective on 1988, the year that Aung San Suu Kyi began her stellar ascent into the country's politics. The first sentences read as follows:

> Change happens in cycles, patterns and rhythms, sometimes seemingly regular and obeying some law of nature, sometimes seemingly erratic, unshackled by law, entirely wild and free. . . .
>
> Cycles of change in Myanmar since independence was recovered from Britain in 1948 seem to have run in cycles lasting ten to fifteen years.[1]

This observation is made in the spirit of Buddhist historical philosophy and may be unusual for a Western reader who is used to a more linear, progressive telling of history. Yet this cyclical interpretation can be applied to this book's understanding of Aung San Suu Kyi's political career. The first cycle runs for fifteen years from 1988 until the introduction of the "Seven-Step Roadmap" in 2003. This phase can be described as one of confrontation between the military junta on the one side, and Aung San Suu Kyi together with her domestic and international supporters on the other. Then—from 2003 to 2016—follows the step-by-step transformation towards a disciplined democracy, as conceived and implemented by the military. At the end of this cycle, Aung San Suu Kyi becomes state counsellor and de facto head of state with Htin Kyaw as president. The third cycle in this interpretation of Burmese politics has thus just commenced. This is the cycle of dual rule between the military and the NLD.

All signs indicate that the current phase of Myanmar's development is inextricably connected to Aung San Suu Kyi's personal fate. It is she alone that holds the NLD together, and the fragile task of political cooperation between segments of the civilian population of the country and the military essentially rests on her shoulders. Aung San Suu Kyi's key role bears a fateful resemblance to that of her father's.

Myanmar's politics remains—as before—clearly predicated upon Buddhist patterns. The prevalence of cycles is fundamentally connected to the personalization of politics, going back to the concept of the Maha Sammata. Individuals are more important than institutions. It follows that the country's political history can be told through the life stories of its protagonists, be they Aung San, Ne Win, or Aung San Suu Kyi.

One consequence of such personalization is that the country's development is marked by unexpected, even magical, moments as well as tragic turning points, just as these mark the lives of individuals. Both illustrate the foundational Buddhist belief in the impermanence of all things (*anicca*). How tragic, then, that Aung San was murdered just at the beginning of the first cycle after independence. How coincidental that Khin Kyi fell ill just at the moment that the students took to the streets against the socialist regime. Or that shortly thereafter Ne Win stepped down, to everyone's great surprise.

With Aung San Suu Kyi, local conceptions of politics were supplemented with a Western imagination of democracy, without there ever having been a successful amalgamation of these two models. For the majority of the population, politics remains a duel. There is either victory or defeat, which leaves little room for the kind of compromise required to allow for a change of government and opposition.

Aung San Suu Kyi realized early on how difficult it is to reconcile both political models in Myanmar while doing justice to the challenges of a multiethnic nation-state that did not historically exist. The country owes its current relative stability largely to the constitution drafted by the military and Aung San Suu Kyi's (albeit reluctant) willingness to play according to the rules. In many ways, this constitution contradicts Western expectations of a democratic order.

The political realities of Myanmar on the one hand and of international agents—such as the UN, the foreign governments involved in Myanmar, international NGOs, and media—on the other thus stand disconnected. Media and political actors outside of Myanmar have time and again ignored the country's political culture. Conversely, the majority of the country's population does not quite know what to do with Western models of democracy.

Both sides' illusion that the two political models could be reconciled with Aung San Suu Kyi's intervention remained untested until the 2015 election victory. Only then did the carrier of hope first have the opportunity to actually make administrative decisions. Disillusionment was especially quick to set in among foreign observers, but the seeds had already been sown earlier given Aung San Suu Kyi's stance towards the country's Muslims. Real progress in the attainment of peace, economic development, or the rule of law is yet to materialize.

The Rohingya refugee crisis then decisively demonstrated that Aung San Suu Kyi's tenacity in fighting for her people's freedom did not in any way equate to a Western conception of a free democratic order, in which the rights of minorities are also protected. In her self-understanding, Aung San Suu Kyi was and still is, first and foremost, the people's voice. Her stance towards the Rohingya has less to do with her considerations for the military but rather with the fact that she respects her supporters' opinion, for whom the Rohingya never were and still are not equal citizens of the country.

Given the traditional dominance of a political culture shaped by Buddhism, it is certain that Aung San Suu Kyi's eventual withdrawal from politics will initiate a new cycle. It is highly unlikely that the NLD will retain its strong position without Aung San Suu Kyi. The open question is to what extent the current key players in Burmese politics—the civilian factions around Aung San Suu Kyi, and the military—will prepare for the impending new beginning. That there is even a chance of a new beginning is to Aung San Suu Kyi's credit and will be her legacy. In any case, the international community will come to play a central role, as it has from the time that Aung San Suu Kyi's entry on to the political stage introduced the world community to the problems of Burma/Myanmar. One hopes that it will learn from the miscalculations and inflated expectations with which the media, foreign governments, and activists have often approached the country in the past and continue assisting the many Myanmar initiatives working for the improvement of the lives of the people.

In order to achieve this, it will be necessary to concentrate on the actual circumstances in Myanmar rather than on the personhood of the head of state. Perhaps this would also fulfill one of Aung San Suu Kyi's wishes that she expressed at the end of 2016: "I hope that I'll be able to make myself totally dispensable, that they will not need me to go on—neither my party, nor my country."[2] Perhaps one day, the world, too, will not need Aung San Suu Kyi or the magical moments associated with her in order to grant Myanmar the attention it deserves.

Notes

Prologue

1. Conversation with Rodion Ebbighausen on election night (November 8, 2015).

2. Patrick Greenfield, "Oxford college drops Aung San Suu Kyi from common room's name," *The Guardian*, October 19, 2017, https://www.theguardian.com/world/2017/oct/19/oxford-college-drops-aung-san-suu-kyi-as-name-of-common-room.

3. Patrick Greenflied, "Aung San Suu Kyi loses Freedom of Oxford over Rohingya crisis," *The Guardian*, November 7, 2017, https://www.theguardian.com/world/2017/nov/27/aung-san-suu-kyi-loses-freedom-of-oxford-over-rohingya-crisis.

4. Zachary Abuza, "Who Are the Arakan Rohingya Salvation Army?," *Radio Free Asia*, January 9, 2017, http://www.rfa.org/english/commentaries/arsa-commentary-09012017155658.html; International Crisis Group, "Myanmar: A New Muslim Insurgency in Rakhine State," Asia Report No. 283, 2016, https://d2071andvipowj.cloudfront.net/283-myanmar-a-new-muslim-insurgency-in-rakhine-state.pdf; Carlos Sardina Galache, "Inside view of Myanmar's Rohingya insurgency," *Asia Times*, October 31, 2017, http://www.atimes.com/article/inside-view-myanmars-rohingya-insurgency/.

5. UNHCR, "Mission report of OHCHR rapid response mission to Cox's Bazar, Bangladesh," September 13–24, 2017, http://www.ohchr.org/Documents/Countries/MM/CXBMissionSummaryFindingsOctober2017.pdf; Amnesty International, "'My World is Finished': Rohingya Targeted in Crimes Against Humanity in Myanmar,"

October 11, 2017, https://www.amnestyusa.org/wp-content/uploads/2017/10/Amnesty-My-World-Is-Finished-Myanmar-18.10.20171.pdf.

6. United Nations, "UN human rights chief points to 'textbook example of ethnic cleansing' in Myanmar," September 11, 2017, http://www.un.org/apps/news/story.asp?NewsID=57490#.WhPkAoriY2w.

7. "Myanmar denounces UN's 'ethnic cleansing' suggestion," *BBC*, September 12, 2017, http://www.bbc.com/news/world-asia-41248029.

Chapter 1. Peacock from the Ashes

Opening quote from Gustaaf Houtman, *Mental Culture in Burmese Crisis Politics: Aung San Suu Kyi and the National League for Democracy* (Tokyo: Tokyo University of Foreign Studies, 1999), 16.

1. Ne Win was especially concerned that Myanmar might be drawn into the Cold War. See Robert Taylor, *General Ne Win: A Political Biography* (Singapore: ISEAS, 2015).

2. The government later ended up dropping this proposition and started preparations for multiparty elections.

3. Aung San Suu Kyi, *Freedom from Fear and Other Writings*, ed. Michael Aris (London: Penguin, 1995), 192–97.

4. Thaw Ka went on to be one of the founding members of the NLD, was imprisoned, and convicted. He died in custody in 1991. See Bertil Lintner, "A Tribute to Maung Thaw Ka," *The Irrawaddy*, February 12, 2014, http://www.irrawaddy.org/feature/magazine-feature/tribute-maung-thaw-ka.html.

5. A video with footage from the event is available at "Daw Aung San Suu Kyi's firt [sic] ever public speech 1988," YouTube video, 14:01, posted by DVB TVnews, https://www.youtube.com/watch?v=gJV7fw577wk. Translation by Frankie Tun.

6. See "Speech to a Mass Rally at the Shwedagon Pagoda," *Online Burma/Myanmar Library*, burmalibrary.org/docs3/Shwedagon-ocr.doc.

7. The name Khin Thida Tun appears as number 476 of 568 in a list of names titled "Enemies of Burmese Revolution." The three-time winner of a Myanmar film prize is stated to be "pro–military junta." See "Enemies of Burmese Revolution," *Burma Compatriots*, May 27, 2006, https://www.scribd.com/doc/13005730/Enemies-of-Burmese-Revolution.

8. Interview with Soe Moe, Yangon, January 26, 2015.

Chapter 2. The Incomplete Hero

Opening quote from Houtman, *Mental Culture in Burmese Crisis Politics*, 373.

1. See Heinz Schütte, *Yangon: Ein historischer Versuch* (Berlin: regiospectra, 2017).

2. From Website Aungsan, "Problems for Burma's Freedom: Presidential address delivered to the first Congress of AFPFL, January 20, 1946," http://www. aungsan.com/Speeches.htm, accessed December 29, 2014.

3. Cited in Susanne Prager, "Nationalismus als kulturelle Reproduktion" (PhD diss., University of Heidelberg, 1998), 149.

4. Friedrich Nietzsche, ed., Giorgio Colli and Mazzino Montinari, *Morgenröthe: Idyllen aus Messina; Die fröhliche Wissenschaft*. Kritische Studienausgabe, vol. 3. (Berlin/New York: dtv/de Gruyter, 1999), 526. Translation by the authors.

5. The photos were taken by photographer U Kwalt (1913–88). In February 2015, on the ocassion of Aung San's one hundredth birthday, U Kwalt's grandson organized an exhibition of his photographs at the Think-Gallery in Yangon. He granted Hans-Bernd Zöllner persmission to reproduce the photographed image of the photos taken by his grandfather and all images exhibited at the gallery.

6. At the end of 1939, a Burmese delegation visited China and there also met with Chiang Kai-shek. Nu, who represented the *Dobama Asiayone* delegation, had a strong desire to also meet with Mao Tse Tung, which was left unfulfilled.

7. Josef Silverstein, ed., *The Political Legacy of Aung San*. Revised ed. with introductory essay (Ithaca, NY: Cornell University, 1993), 83.

8. Prager, "Nationalismus als kulturelle Reproduktion," 149.

9. The first name was Anti-Fascist Organization.

10. Silverstein, *The Political Legacy of Aung San*, 28–29.

11. The Japanese renamed the Burmese Army more than once. See the glossary for further reference.

12. Silverstein, *The Political Legacy of Aung San*, 52. Thakin Soe, the leader of the smaller Communist Party of Burma who lived underground during the Japanese occupation, was involved in multiple sex scandals. On the contrary, Than Tun, the leader of the larger Communist Party and Khin Khyi's sister's husband was—as far as is known—always loyal to his wife.

13. Kyaw Hin Hlaing, "Political Impasse in Myanmar" (working paper series, University of Hong Kong, 2011), 31.

14. Matthew J. Walton, "Ethnicity, Conflict, and History in Burma: The Myths of Panglong," *Asian Survey* 48, no. 6 (2008).

15. Silverstein, *The Political Legacy of Aung San*, 65.

16. In a speech at his hometown Natmauk, Aung San said, "I will govern with *mettā* and integrity. When I am convinced that something is good and correct, I will give my life for it." (See Prager, "Nationalismus und kulturelle Reproduktion," 176).

17. The text is printed in Kyo Van, *The 1947 Constitution and the Nationalities* (Yangon: Universities Historical Research Centre and Inwa Publishing House, 1999), 225–66.

18. Silverstein, *The Political Legacy of Aung San*, 20.

19. Hugh Tinker. *The Union of Burma: A Study of the First Years of Independence.* (London: Oxford University Press, 1957), 26, 286.

20. Silverstein, *The Political Legacy of Aung San*, 161.

21. See Josef Stalin, *Nation and Nationalism* (Moscow: Foreign Languages Publishing House, 1953).

22. Prager, "Nationalismus als kulturelle Reproduktion," 315. See also Website Aungsan, "Speech from 1 May holiday April 26, 1946," http://www.aungsan.com/Speeches.htm, accessed December 29, 2014.

23. The Pali term *loka nibbana* was first coined by mentor of the *Dobama Asiayone* and national poet Thakin Kodaw Hmaing. It had a critical influence on the political thinking of the young revolutionaries.

Chapter 3. A Child of Many Worlds

Opening quote from Eamonn Welsh, "Aung San Suu Kyi: 'I have personal regrets,'" *BBC*, September 23, 2012, http://www.bbc.com/news/magazine-19667956.

1. See, for example, Mark R. Thompson and Claudia Derichs, eds., *Frauen an der Macht: Dynastien und politische Führerinnen in Asien* (Passau: Universität Passau, 2005).

2. Aung San Suu Kyi, *Freedom from Fear*, ed. Michael Aris (London: Penguin, 1995), 195.

3. Aung San Suu Kyi, *Freedom from Fear.*

4. Alan Clements, *The Voice of Hope: Aung San Suu Kyi; Conversations with Alan Clements* (New York: Seven Stories Press, 1997), 77.

5. Relatives, friends, and NLD members, but not Aung San Suu Kyi, attended the funeral ceremony. See "BurmaNet News: April 14, 2014," http://www.burmalibrary.org/reg.burma/archives/200104/msg00055.html, accessed August 21, 2016.

6. Today, Tower Lane is called Bogyoke Aung San Pyadaik [Musuem] Road. As for the house they moved to, 54/56 University Avenue is the official address. Normally only the first house number for the entire plot is mentioned.

7. Clements, *The Voice of Hope*, 67.

8. Dr. Maung Maung, ed., *Aung San of Burma* (Den Haag: Martinus Nijhoff, 1962), 120.

9. Clements, *The Voice of Hope*, 79–80.

10. Claudia Dreifus, "Interview: Aung San Suu Kyi (1995)," in *Interview* (New York: Seven Stories Press, 1997), 43.

11. Myint Kyi, et. al., *Myanmar Politics 1958–1962* (Yangon: Ministry of Culture, Historical Research Center, 2007), 167–68.

12. It is speculated that it was Ne Win who had sent Khin Kyi to New Delhi in order to get the widow of the national hero out of the country and thereby also remove the hero's memory, in order to set forth his own plans for autocratic rule. See Peter Popham, *The Lady and the Peacock: The Life of Aung San Suu Kyi* (New York: Experiment, 2013), 40–41. Khin Kyi traveled to India on May 19, 1960. Ne Win had given up his post to U Nu on April 20, 1960, after the Clean AFPFL's clear victory in the elections organized by Ne Win's government. Besides, Khin Kyi had politically supported U Nu in various ways.

13. Interview with Rev. Ko Lay, Judson Church, in August 2015.

14. Clements, *The Voice of Hope*, 69–70. Ma Than E, a family friend who had taken Aung San Suu Kyi under her wing while she was with the United Nations, describes things differently. She says that it took a long time for the "trauma of this tragedy" to dissipate (Aung San Suu Kyi, *Freedom from Fear*, 246).

15. Ma Than E states that Khin Kyi made her children aware of their father's legacy already in their childhood (Aung San Suu Kyi, *Freedom from Fear*, 246).

16. In Clements's interviews with Aung San Suu Kyi she expresses her hunch that people have transferred the great trust they had in her father on to her. Here, the idealization of her father is mirrored in public opinion. On another occasion she concludes that her father "was a better person than [her]," and adds that she is not just saying that for the sake of sounding modest. She supports the statement by revealing that, in contrast to Aung San, she was often very lazy as a child and young person. However, she concludes that her approach to life is one that she shares with her father. That is something she noticed when she started looking more closely at his life. (Clements, *The Voice of Hope*, 41).

17. Clements, *The Voice of Hope*, 58.

18. Taylor, *General Ne Win*, 235–36.

19. Wintle, *Perfect Hostage*, 194, 225.

20. The "Stable" AFPFL was regarded as being close to the Tatmadaw.

21. Paul Gore-Booth, *With Great Truth and Respect* (London: Constable, 1974), 213.

22. Ibid., 212.

23. Ibid., 224.

24. Ibid., 224–25.

25. Aung San Suu Kyi, *Freedom from Fear*, xix.

26. Wintle, *Perfect Hostage*, 179.

27. Aung San Suu Kyi, *Freedom from Fear*, 286.

28. Ibid., 1–38.

29. Ibid., 39–81.

30. Ibid., 140–64.

31. Ibid., 82–139.

32. See Michael Aris, *Hidden Treasures and Secret Lives: Study of Pemalingpa (1450–1521) and the Sixth Dalai Lama (1683–1706)* (London: Kegan Paul International, 1989).

33. The article on literature and nationalism in the colonial period that came about during her time in Japan does not include any analytical statements but points to different works produced in this period.

34. Aung San Suu Kyi, *Aung San of Burma* (Edinburgh: Kiscadale, 1984).

35. Aung San Suu Kyi, *Freedom from Fear*, 34.

36. Ibid., 34.

37. Ibid., 135.

Chapter 4. The Struggle for the Right Path to Democracy

Opening quote from Houtman, *Mental Culture in Burmese Crisis Politics*, 380.

1. For details of Ne Win's speech and the party congress, see Robert H. Taylor, *General Ne Win*, 522–25.

2. The speech is printed in Dr. Maung Maung, *The 1988 Uprising in Burma*, Yale Southeast Asia Studies (New Haven, CT: Yale University Press, 1999), 86–89.

3. Dr. Maung Maung, *The 1988 Uprising in Burma*, 108–12

4. Article 11 of the 1947 constitution reads, "The State shall adopt a single-party system. The Burma Socialist Programme Party is the sole political party and it shall lead the State." Article 194 (a) states: "The Preamble of this Constitution, Article 1 and 4 of Chapter I, Articles 5, 6, 7, 8, 9, 11, 13, 14, 18, and 21 of Chapter II; Articles 28, 29 and 32 of Section III, Articles 41, 44 and 46 of Chapter VI and Article 194 of Chapter XV shall be amended with the approval of 75 percent of all the members of the Pyitthu Hluttaw [parliament] in a nation-wide referendum only with the majority vote of more than half of those who have the right to vote."

5. "Daw Aung San Suu Kyi issued an announcement," *Working People's Daily*, September 10, 1988, http://www.ibiblio.org/obl/docs3/BPS88-09.pdf.

6. *Working People's Daily*, September 14, 1988, http://www.ibiblio.org/obl/docs3/BPS88-09.pdf.

7. *Working People's Daily*, September 15, 1988, http://www.ibiblio.org/obl/docs3/BPS88-09.pdf.

8. See Aurel Croissant, *Die politischen Systeme Südostasiens: Eine Einführung* (Wiesbaden: Springer VS, 2016), 1–16 and 291–333.

9. *Working People's Daily*, September 15, 1988, http://www.ibiblio.org/obl/docs3/BPS88-09.pdf.

10. *Working People's Daily*, September 18, 1988, http://www.ibiblio.org/obl/docs3/BPS88-09.pdf.

11. It is unlikely that U Nu gave up his position entirely voluntarily. Rather, it had been under pressure from two younger military officials with political ambitions. One of them had been none other than Aung Gyi, who in 1988 again came to be part of the circle of potential heirs to the throne.

12. The elections took place later than originally planned. Ne Win did not see it fit to hold them within half a year, which was the constitutional timeframe set out for a non-parliamentarian to hold a ministerial position. Under this provision, Ne Win had already held the post of deputy minister president as well as defence and interior minister for six months in the civil war year of 1949. In 1959, he stepped down after six months, following which the parliament temporarily removed the relevant constitutional article from force and once again elected Ne Win as minister president. See Hans-Bernd Zöllner, *Konflikt der Welt-Anschauungen: Die "Zwei Birmas" seit Beginn der Kolonialzeit* (Berlin: regiospectra, 2011), 160–63.

13. *Working People's Daily*, September 9, 1988, http://www.ibiblio.org/obl/docs3/BPS88-09.pdf.

14. Burmese numerology plays a role here. The "9" is a lucky number and had also been used as such by Ne Win. In 1987, Ne Win had banknotes with values of 90 and 45 kyat printed, after earlier banknotes were removed from circulation largely without compensation. The opposition to his regime directed itself with another lucky number, the "8," when it carried out a general strike on 8/8/88, which was to start at eight o'clock.

15. A member of the Thirty Comrades, the nucleus of the Burma Independence Army, son-in-law of Ba Maw, the Burmese leader under Japanese occupation who had led the troops assembled in Thailand under Nu's political leadership to topple Ne Win.

16. *Working People's Daily*, September 15, 1988, http://www.ibiblio.org/obl/docs3/BPS88-09.pdf.

17. *Working People's Daily*, September 11, 1988, http://www.ibiblio.org/obl/docs3/BPS88-09.pdf.

18. *Working People's Daily*, September 1988, http://www.ibiblio.org/obl/docs3/BPS88-09.pdf.

19. Dr. Maung Maung, *The 1988 Uprising in Burma*, 223

20. *Working People's Daily*, September 29, 1988; Tatmadaw Researcher, *A Concise History of Myanmar and the Tatmadaw's Role*, vol. 2 (Yangon: Ministry of Information, 1991), 3.

21. "Burma Press Summary 88-10," *ibiblio.org*, October 1988, http://www.ibiblio.org/obl/docs3/BPS88-10.pdf, 8.

22. *Working People's Daily*, October 1988, http://www.ibiblio.org/obl/docs3/BPS88-10.pdf, 9.

23. General Saw Maung, the chairman of the SLORC, stated in a speech on September 23 that the military was bound to loyalty to the nation and the people by oath (*Working People's Daily*, September 24, 1988).

24. Aung San Suu Kyi, *Freedom from Fear*, 208–10.

25. *Working People's Daily*, September 29, 1988; Tatmadaw Researcher, *A Concise History of Myanmar and the Tatmadaw's Role*, 20–21.

26. Peter Popham, *The Lady and the Peacock*, cites the diary entries of Ma Thanegi. From these we learn a lot about Aung San Suu Kyi's apparel but close to nothing about the content of her speeches.

27. The episode is retold in detail in Justin Wintle, *Perfect Hostage: Aung San Suu Kyi, Burma and the Generals* (London: Hutchinson, 2007), 211–16. Aung San Suu Kyi herself has provided a much more sober yet humorous account (Clements, *The Voice of Hope*, 45–46). Rumors that the government had set up a special unit to kill Aung San Suu Kyi had been circulating for a while. Such reports were positively rejected by the government (*Working People's Daily*, April 2, 1989).

28. *Working People's Daily*, June 23, 1989.

29. Aung San Suu Kyi, *Freedom from Fear*, 225.

30. "Hanging in There," *Asiaweek*, October 7, 1988, http://netipr.org/8888/interview-with-aung-san-suu-kyi-by-asiaweek.

31. Aung San Suu Kyi, *Freedom from Fear*.

32. "1991 Nobel Peace Prize for Daw Aung San Suu Kyi," *Burma Alert*, no. 10, vol 2. http://www.burmalibrary.org/docsBA/BA1991-V02-N10.pdf. General Saw Maung tried to explain his relationship to Ne Win to a foreign journalist by saying that in the tradition of the armed forces, the supreme commander—whether it be Aung San or Ne Win—is somewhat like the father that everyone respected, including when he retires. However, that did not mean that one would take directions from him after he had stepped down ("I Saved Burma," *Asiaweek*, January 27, 1989, http://netipr.org/8888/interview-with-gen-saw-maung-by-asiaweek).

33. See "Excerpts from Interview, Articles on 1989 Aung San Suu Kyi House Arrest," last updated November 21, 2010, *Voice of America*, http://www.voanews.com/english/news/asia/southeast/Excerpts-from-Interview-Articles-on-1989-Aung-San-Suu-Kyi-House-Arrest-109999214.html.

34. Alan Clements, Aung San Suu Kyi's Buddhist interviewer, would also go on to use the term "killing field."

35. See Taylor, *General Ne Win*, especially chapters 8–11.

36. For an account of the armed forces, see Tatmadaw Researcher, *A Concise History of Myanmar and the Tatmadaw's Role*, vols. 1 and 2.

37. The full text of the SLORC's declaration 1/88: "1) In order to effect a timely halt to the deteriorating conditions on all sides all over the country and for the sake

of the interests of the people, the Defence Forces have assumed all power in the state with effect from today so as to carry out the following tasks immediately: a. to restore law, order, peace and tranquillity; b. to provide security and to facilitate transport and communications; c. for this organisation to do the utmost to ease the people's food, clothing, and shelter needs, and to render as much help as possible to the cooperatives and the private concerns; d. to stage democratic multiparty general elections after fulfilling all the above-stated responsibilities. 2) The present Elections Commission for Holding Democratic Multiparty Elections will continue to exist for the successful holding of multiparty general elections. 3) In order to be ready for the multiparty general elections, all parties and organizations which will accept and practice genuine democracy can make preparations and form parties beginning now. 4) All presently active organisations, individuals, monks, and all the people are requested to render their assistance.

38. Bertil Lintner, *Outrage: Burma's Struggle for Democracy*, 2nd ed. (Bangkok: White Lotus, 1990), 163.

39. Ibid., 163.

40. "Burmese, Still Under Military, Settle Into a Sullen Waiting," *New York Times*, January 9, 1989, http://www.nytimes.com/1989/01/09/world/burmese-still-under-military-settle-into-a-sullen-waiting.html?pagewanted=all.

41. Aung San Suu Kyi, *Freedom from Fear*, 168–79.

42. The story can be found in the *Aggañña Sutta* of the Buddhist canon. An English translation of the long text is available online at http://www.urbandharma.org/pdf/AggannaSutta.pdf, accessed December 29, 2014.

43. Aung San Suu Kyi, *Freedom from Fear*, 170.

44. Ibid., 173.

45. See note 42 above.

46. "Fighting a Bad King," *Asiaweek*, October 29, 1989, http://www.burmalibrary.org/reg.burma/archives/199810/msg00543.html. The interview took place in October 1988 in the hiding place of the student leader, who was later captured and sentenced to a long prison term.

47. See Taylor, *General Ne Win*, epilogue.

48. Hans-Bernd Zöllner, *The Beast and the Beauty: The History of the Conflict between the Military and Aung San Suu Kyi in Myanmar 1988-2011, Set in a Global Context* (Berlin: regiospectra, 2012), 148–50.

49. This argument was used by Khin Nyunt in a press conference on August 9, 1989, in his attempt to show that the Burmese Communist Party tried to take over power by infiltrating the NLD. "Burma Communist Party's Conspiracy to take over State Power," press conference, August 5, 1989, ibiblio, August 5, 1989, http://www.ibiblio.org/obl/docs/BCP_Conspiracy.htm. Aung San had said in 1946 that "we

must take proper care that we must not make a fetish of this cult of hero worship" (cited in Houtman, *Mental Culture in Burmese Crisis Politics*, 286).

Chapter 5. Birth of a Global Icon

Opening quote from Rowan Callick, "I'm no icon, says Myanmar's hope Aung San Suu Kyi," *The Australian*, November 29, 2013, https://www.theaustralian.com.au/national-affairs/foreign-affairs/im-no-icon-says-myanmars-hope/news-story/3c29fc1b9c9a1b678298854cffb146e9?sv=ba7670b54fb476be5e43a349f07ca5d7.

1. Kyaw Win was a confidant of Than Shwe and was later promoted to general. In the spring of 2002, he led the investigations against members of Ne Win's family, who supposedly had planned a coup against the regime. After the dismissal of Khin Nyunt in October 2004 and the restructuring of the military secret services, he was given an honorable send-off into retirement.

2. In 1992, Than Shwe had replaced Saw Maung, who had not been up to the task by any measure.

3. For the whole statement see "Daw Aung San Suu Kyi Releases Press," *burmalibrary*, July 12, 1995, http://www.burmalibrary.org/reg.burma/archives/199507/msg00116.html.

4. "Press Release Daw Aung San Suu Kyi 11.7.95," *burmalibrary*, July 11, 1995, http://www.burmalibrary.org/reg.burma/archives/199507/msg00124.html.

5. For the whole transcript of the interview see "Transcript of ASSK interview," *burmalibrary*, May 13, 1995, http://www.burmalibrary.org/reg.burma/archives/199405/msg00060.html.

6. "Press Release Daw Aung San Suu Kyi 11.7.95."

7. Barbara Victor, *The Lady: Aung San Suu Kyi; Nobel Laureate and Burma's Prisoner* (New York: Faber & Faber, 1998), 106.

8. Shortly before her release in July 1995, the state newspaper reported that Michael Aris had visited eight times between 1992 and 1994, and had spent 294 days in the country in total (*Working People's Daily*, July 8, 1995).

9. Philip Shenon, "Husband Finds Burmese Dissident Still 'Indomitable,'" *New York Times*, May 18, 1992, http://www.nytimes.com/1992/05/18/world/husband-finds-burmese-dissident-still-indomitable.html.

10. Wintle, *Perfect Hostage*, 348.

11. For details of the travels see Popham, *The Lady and the Peacock*, 93–146. Her first journey outside of Yangon started one month after the foundation of the NLD in October 1988. Accompanied by a convoy of cars, she visited the Burmese heartland, the divisions (renamed "regions" in the 2008 constitution) Bago, Mgwe, Mandalay, and Sagaing. After her mother's funeral in early January 1989, she went to the Ayeyarwady Delta and in February to the Shan, Rakhine, and Kayah States

before returning to Rangoon. At the end of March, she toured another part of Ayeyarwady Division including the place where her mother had stayed before her birth. During the Thingyan festival she stayed in Rangoon and left then for Kachin State via Mandalay. She returned in May.

12. Aung San Suu Kyi, *Freedom from Fear*, 218–23. Popham's description of the travels, based on the diaries of her travel companion, Ma Tanegi, provides a lot of information on her various outfits rather than on the contents of her speeches.

13. Aung San Suu Kyi, *Freedom from Fear*, 222

14. Ibid., 212–13.

15. Ibid. 209–11, 214–16. These letters were addressed to Amnesty International, foreign ambassadors in Burma, and the United Nations Commission on Human Rights.

16. Ibid., 216.

17. "I Saved Burma," *Asiaweek*, January 27, 1989, http://netipr.org/8888/interview-with-gen-saw-maung-by-asiaweek.

18. For a collection of statements of military leaders on the issue of the election see "Chronology of Statements by Burmese Military Spokesmen on Multi-Party Elections, a New Constitution, the National Convention, Transfer of Power etc.," http://www.ibiblio.org/obl/docs/Statements.htm, accessed August 30, 2016. The quotations that follow are taken from this source.

19. "'I Saved Burma': Interview with Gen. Saw Maung," *Asiaweek*, January 27, 1989, http://netipr.org/8888/interview-with-gen-saw-maung-by-asiaweek.

20. "SLORC Press Conference (extract), June 9 1989," http://www.ibiblio.org/obl/docs/SLORC_Press_conf-1989-06-09.htm.

21. Aung San Suu Kyi, *Freedom from Fear*, 233.

22. Shortly before the elections, Saw Maung was reported to have said, "As our current aim is to hold the election as scheduled we cannot yet concern ourselves with the Constitution. . . . A new Constitution can be drafted. An old Constitution can also be used after some amendments. . . . Among the 93 parties . . . five . . . want to use the 1947 Constitution, . . . 77 parties . . . want to draw up a new constitution and . . . 11 parties . . . made no comments. . . . Whatever may be the case, the people will decide with their votes." (*Working People's Daily*, May 10, 1990).

23. For details of the election results see "1990 Multi-Pary Democracy General Elections," *Democratic Voices of Burma*, no date, http://www.ibiblio.org/obl/docs4/1990_multi-party_elections.pdf.

24. Derek Tonkin, "The 1990 Elections: Broken Promises or a Failure of Communication?" *Contemporary Southeast Asia* 29, no. 1 (2007).

25. On Saw Maung's personality, self-assessment, and political position see Zöllner, *The Beast and the Beauty*, 104–8.

26. Sein Win was born in 1944 and held a PhD in mathematics from Germany. He had won a constituency for an NLD-connected party during the 1990 elections. In Manerplaw, he was elected to be prime minister of the National Coalition Government of Burma on December 18, 1990. After the capture of Manerplaw by troops of the central government in January 1995, the seat of the organization moved to the USA. It was formally dissolved on September 14, 2012, after the reform process in Myanmar started.

27. There were two prizewinners in the first year, Nelson Mandela and Anatoli Martschenko.

28. Francis Fukuyama, *The End of History and the Last Man* (New York: Free Press, 1992).

29. The explanatory text of the Norwegian committee is published in Aung San Suu Kyi, *Freedom from Fear*, 236–37.

30. "Vaclav Havel Refused 1991 Nobel Peace Prize Nomination, Says Daw Aung San Suu Kyi," *The Lede*, September 16, 2013, http://thelede.blogs.nytimes.com/2013/09/16/vaclav-havel-refused-1991-nobel-peace-prize-nomination-says-daw-aung-san-suu-kyi/?_r=0.

31. "Aung San Suu Kyi—Acceptance Speech," Official Website of the Nobel Prize, http://www.nobelprize.org/nobel_prizes/peace/laureates/1991/kyi-acceptance_en.html

32. Bertil Lintner, *Aung San Suu Kyi and Burma's Struggle for Independence*, (Chiang Mai: Silkworm Books, 2011), 73–101. In Lintner's view, the NLD should have organized a people's uprising after the election victory and freed Aung San Suu Kyi from house arrest. Then they should have brought her to the nearby state broadcasting central, where she could have given a speech over the radio and television to the people. The overtaking of power would have been accomplished in this way (129–30).

33. "Aung San Suu Kyi—Acceptance Speech" (see note 31).

34. The speech is available at "Aung San Suu Kyi's speech in Norway on June 16, 2012," YouTube video, 51:16, posted by Taang Sianpu, June 16, 2012, https://www.youtube.com/watch?v=HUPfkNXpZvQ.

35. "Aung San Suu Kyi—Acceptance Speech" (see note 31).

36. See Samuel P. Huntington, *The Third Wave: Democratization in the Late 20th Century* (Oklahoma: University of Oklahoma Press, 2012).

37. In the neighboring Asian countries, the dedication to democracy was not as great as in the West. The long-standing prime minister of Singapore Lee Kwan Yew and his Malaysian colleague Mahathir always expressed great doubt as to whether the Western democratic model could directly be applied in their countries' multiethnic societies. The majority of countries of the Southeast Asian association ASEAN are still governed under authoritarian rule.

38. For the letter and other details of the visit see, "US Congressman Visits Daw Aung San Suu Kyi," *Burma Alert*, February 1995, http://www.burmalibrary. org/docsBA/BA1994-V05-N02.pdf.

39. For the whole text of Richardson's statement see "U.S. Rep. Sees Daw Aung San Suu Kyi," *ibiblio.org*, http://www.ibiblio.org/obl/docs3/BPS94-02.pdf.

40. Aung San Suu Kyi had insisted that an American *New York Times* reporter and a representative of the UN be present during the conversation. The origin of the transcripts is unclear. For the public summary see http://www.burmalibrary. org/reg.burma/archives/199405/msg00060.html. Excerpts of the conversation are reprinted in Aung San Suu Kyi, *Freedom from Fear*, 249–59.

41. Richardson returned to Myanmar in 1995 but wasn't allowed to visit Aung San Suu Kyi or any other political prisoner. This time he did not get a chance to see her. He later confessed that this trip had been a complete failure and predicted that Aung San Suu Kyi would not be released any time soon. Upon becoming US ambassador to the United Nations for a year in 1997, he supported sanctions against Myanmar. For quotes, see note 39.

42. For particulars on Rewata Dhamma's personality and mission, see Zöllner, *The Beast and the Beauty*, 386–91.

43. The full original text can be found at "Text of Statement by Aung San Suu K," *burmalibrary.org*, January 25, 1995, http://www.burmalibrary.org/reg.burma/ archives/199501/msg00066.html.

Chapter 6. The People's Voice

Opening quote from Hans-Bernd Zöllner, ed., *Talks over the Gate: Aung San Suu Kyi's Dialogues with the People, 1995 and 1996* (Hamburg: Abera Verlag, 2014), 121.

1. The executive committee of the party in 1995 was composed of only seven people, of whom the youngest was sixty-nine years old. The law on party registration provided that a party would dissolve if the number of members fell under five (Zöllner, *The Beast and the Beauty*, 244).

2. The changes were submitted to the election commission and the commission rejected them. However, this decision had no concrete consequences (see Zöllner, *The Beast and the Beauty*, 244).

3. See the English translation of the press conference provided in "Interview after Release," dassk.org, http://dassk.org/index.php?topic=793.0;wap2, accessed September 2, 2016. We have lightly edited the translated excerpts quoted here for readability.

4. See the end of chapter 5.

5. The 702 members constituted of the following groups: (1) representatives of the political parties, (2) elected representatives, (3) representatives of ethnic

minorities, (4) farmers' representatives, (5) workers' representatives, (6) intellectuals and technocrats, (7) representatives of the state, (8) other invited persons (*Working People's Daily*, October 3, 1992). In total, a solid 107 of the parliamentarians elected in 1990 took part, of which, of course, the majority were from the NLD.

6.   A transcript of the interview can be found at "Transcript of ASSK interview," *ibiblio.org*, http://www.ibiblio.org/obl/reg.burma/archives/199405/msg00060.html.

7.   Kyaw Yin Hlaing, *Prisms on the Golden Pagoda: Perspectives on National Reconciliation in Myanmar* (Singapore: NUS Press, 2014), 152.

8.   For further specifics on her dialogue with her supporters, see Zöllner, *Talks over the Gate*, 14–22.

9.   "BurmaNet News 15th July 1995," *Bangkok Post/burmalibrary.org*, July 12, 1995, http://www.burmalibrary.org/reg.burma/archives/199507/msg00175.html.

10.   "Interview with Daw Aung San Suu Ky," *burmalibrary.org*, July 27, 1995, http://www.burmalibrary.org/reg.burma/archives/199507/msg00265.html (language corrected and edited by authors).

11.   See "Daw Aung San Suu Kyi's speech, 1996." YouTube video, 2:13, posted by tolimoli, April 18, 2007, https://www.youtube.com/watch?v=5JSZ9K2rZRA.

12.   They were published in an appendix of a book on Aung San Suu Kyi's political thought, written by a Japanese researcher. The book was published by a Japanese organization that worked on women's issues in Asia.

13.   Zöllner, *Talks over the Gate*.

14.   Richard Roewer, "Myanmar's National League for Democracy at a Crossroads," *GIGA Focus Asia* , no. 1 (April 2017), https://www.gigahamburg.de/de/system/files/publications/gf_asien_1701_en.pdf.

15.   Zöllner, *Talks over the Gate*, 179.

16.   "Dialogue is the best answer for all," *The Irrawaddy*, August 1998, http://www2.irrawaddy.com/article.php?art_id=535.

17.   All Q & A selections excerpted from Zöllner, *Talks over the Gate*, 112–18.

18.   The building was destroyed by soldiers on July 7, 1962, a few months after the military coup of March 2. The question of who was responsible remains unanswered to this day. Ne Win addressed this question in detail in his farewell speech of July 23, 1988 ("U Ne Win's Speech from the BSPP Extraordinary Congress, *burmalibrary.org*, November 11, 1999, http://www.burmalibrary.org/reg.burma/archives/199911/msg00331.html, accessed January 15, 2015).

19.   The question refers to the USDA, the mass organization set up two years earlier.

20.   Karen Connelly, *Burmese Lessons: A True Love Story* (New York: Doubleday, 2009), 68.

21.   Amitav Ghosh, "University Avenue 54, Yangon," *The Kenyon Review* 23, no. 2 (2001), 165.

22. See Zöllner, *Talks over the Gate*, 272–78.

23. Zöllner, *Talks over the Gate*, 90.

24. Ibid., 164.

25. Even though it was an abiding theme for Ne Win to just mention one example. See Taylor, *General Ne Win*, 110, 331–32, 394, 471.

26. See Aung San Suu Kyi, *Freedom from Fear*, 180–85. The phrase comes from her speech at the reception of the Sakhorov Prize awarded to her in December 1990. She could not give the speech at the award ceremony in July 1991. Instead, her essay "*Freedom from Fear*"—which was also the title given to the book that was published later in the same year when she was awarded the Nobel Peace Prize—was published in a number of newspapers worldwide at the time of the award ceremony.

27. This is true of all elections in independent Burma, but for one exception: the 1956 election. At that time, the opposition coalition won a significant proportion of votes. The ruling AFPFL no longer received the majority of the votes of the people. This occurrence—which would be normal in Western democracies—led to a deep crisis of the state, which eventually resulted in the splitting of the AFPFL in 1958 and the entry of the military into the realm of political governance.

28. Zöllner, *Talks over the Gate*, 50–51, emphasis added.

29. "Suu Kyi 'will be above president' if NLD wins Myanmar election," *BBC*, November 5, 2015, http://www.bbc.com/news/world-asia-34729659.

30. Zöllner, *Talks over the Gate*, 144, 167.

31. Robert Taylor, *The State in Myanmar* (Singapore: NUS Press, 2009), 290.

32. Mary P. Callahan, "Democracy in Burma: The Lessons of History," *Analysis* (May 1998), 21.

Chapter 7. Revolution of the Spirit

Opening quote from Thilo Thielke, "'We Have to Tackle This - With Peaceful Means,'" *Der Spiegel*, November 22, 2010, http://www.spiegel.de/international/world/spiegel-interview-with-aung-san-suu-kyi-we-have-to-tackle-this-with-peaceful-means-a-730390.html.

1. Aung San Suu Kyi, *Freedom from Fear*, 180–85.

2. Ibid., 181.

3. Ibid., 180–85.

4. Aung San Suu Kyi, *Letters from Burma* (London: Penguin, 1997), 187.

5. Ibid., 200–201.

6. Gustaaf Houtman, *Mental Culture in Burmese Crisis Politics: Aung San Suu Kyi and the National League for Democracy* (Tokyo: Tokyo University of Foreign Studies, 1999), 250.

7. Conversation with Reverend Ko Lay on February 8, 2015.

8. The school is today the No.1 Basic Education High School Dagon and located next to the Methodist Church at 63 Alan Phaya Road (Signal Pagoda Road).

9. Popham cites from Ma Thanegi's diaries, according to which, during her travels through the country, Aung San Suu Kyi would use a Buddhist rosary and recite mantras every Tuesday, which was her day of birth (Popham, *The Lady and the Peacock*, 292).

10. "Sayadaw" distinguishes a monk of special status (saya means teacher, the suffix -daw indicates great importance for Burmese society) and abbot of a Buddhist institution. The name "Mahasi" was attributed to him in 1936. That word means "large drum" and refers to the quality of the monk's teachings.

11. Aung San Suu Kyi, *Letters from Burma*, 200–201.

12. Ibid., 159–61.

13. Pandita, *In This Very Life*.

14. Zöllner, *Talks over the Gate*, 52.

15. Our argument follows Houtman, *Mental Culture in Burmese Crisis Politics*.

16. Aung San Suu Kui, *Letters from Burma*, 3–17.

17. Zöllner, *Talks over the Gate*, 72–73.

18. Ibid., 72.

19. One of Aung San Suu Kyi's first calls to the international public was an appeal against the expected forced recruitment of students as porters for the army (Aung San Suu Kyi, *Freedom from Fear*, 209–10).

20. From the perspective of a Japanese researcher who investigated the cult around Thamanya Sayadaw, there is a more sober image of the context in which the good streets in Kayin State came into existence. See Keiko Tosa, "The Cult of Thamanya Sayadaw: The Social Dynamism of a Formulating Pilgrimage Site," *Asian Ethnology* 68, 2 (2009), 139–64.

21. Zöllner, *Talks over the Gate*, 140.

22. The practice was also adopted by Aung San Suu Kyi after her first visit to the monk and given up later. (Houtman, *Mental Culture in Burmese Crisis Politics*, 334).

23. See Ma Thanegi, The Native Tourist: A Holiday Pilgrimage in Myanmar (Chiang Mai: Silkworm Books, 2000). The author was one of Aung San Suu Kyi's closest colleagues before and after her house arrest. She later separated herself from her because she did not agree with Aung San Suu Kyi's support for economic sanctions.

24. For details see Amy Gold May, "Will Thamanya Sayadaw's Body Ever Rest in Peace?" *The Irrawaddy*, June 2008, http://www2.irrawaddy.org/article.php?art_id=12596, accessed December 19, 2014; and Houtman, *Mental Culture in Burmese Crisis Politics*, 336.

25. See Ingrid Jordt, *Burma's Mass Meditation Movement: Buddhism and the Cultural Construction of Power* (Athens, OH: Ohio University Press, 2007).

26. Judith Shapiro, "Burma Road," *New York Times*, June 7, 1998, http://www.nytimes.com/books/98/06/07/reviews/980607.07shapirt.html. See also Victor, *The Lady*.

Chapter 8. One Country, Two Governments

Opening quote from Zöllner, *Talks over the Gate*, 237.

1. Hans-Bernd Zöllner, conversations in Yangon in March 1996.

2. See Robert Heine-Gelder, *Conceptions of State and Kingship in Southeast Asia* (Ithaca, NY: Cornell University Press, 1956).

3. The name was an epithet for Mandalay, the last royal capital of Burma and thus not an invention of the military. *Pyi* means "city"; *daw* indicates a notion of reverence and appreciation as shown for a high-ranking monk (*saya-daw*) royalty in the old times and a grand nation. Nay ("*sun*") refers to the belief that the Burmese kings were descendants of the "sun race" to which the Buddha belonged. The name indicated continuity of Buddhist-Burmese traditions.

4. See Uta Gärtner, "Nay Pyi Taw: The Reality and Myths of Capitals in Myanmar," in *Southeast Asian Historiography: Unravelling the Myths: Essays in honour of Barend Jan Terwiel* (Bangkok: River Books, 2011), 258–67.

5. The owner of the property that housed the NLD headquarters was called upon numerous times to revoke the lease to the NLD. The construction of their new headquarters only started in 2015, once contributions were collected in 2014. There was a conflict over user rights in relation to the house on University Avenue as well. Aung San Oo, Aung San Suu Kyi's brother, made multiple attempts to reclaim rights to half of the house through a Burmese court. The legal proceedings have not yet been concluded.

6. See Hans-Bernd Zöllner, *Konflikt der Welt-Anschauungen: Die "Zwei Birmas" seit Beginn der Kolonialzeit* (Berlin: regiospectra, 2011).

7. "NLD Statement 22 Nov-Full Text," *burmalibrary.org*, www.burmalibrary.org/reg.burma/archives/199511/msg00175.html.

8. Previously, in August, the Thai ambassador to the country and a UN official had been guests at her house.

9. "Press Statement of US Ambassador to the United Nations, Madeleine, K. Albright," *burmalibrary.org*, September 10, 1995, http://www.burmalibrary.org/reg.burma/archives/199509/msg00065.html.

10. "Burma Press Summary 95-11," *ibiblio.org*, November 1995, http://www.ibiblio.org/obl/docs3/BPS95-11.pdf.

11.   See All Burma Students' Democratic Front, ed. *Letters to a Dictator: Official Correspondence from NLD Chairman U Aung Shwe to the SLORC's Senior General Than Shwe, from December 1995 to March 1997* (Bangkok: All Burma Students' Democratic Front, 1997).

12.   One year later, on July 23, 1997, the country was granted full membership status together with Laos.

13.   Aung San Suu Kui, *Letters from Burma*, 179–97

14.   "Burmese Junta Sentences 80 Year Old," *burmalibrary.org*, May 28, 1998, http://www.burmalibrary.org/reg.burma/archives/199805/msg00407.html.

15.   This provision was called the "Habitual Offenders Restriction Act" and was aimed at individuals suspected of repeatedly breaking the law. The colonial law was reformulated under U Nu. Its use in 1998 was supposed to suggest that the elected representatives of the NLD were habitual offenders.

16.   For details see Hans-Bernd Zöllner, *The Beast and the Beauty*, 253–71.

17.   "Committee constituted to act for and on behalf of the 1990 Multi-party General Elections. People's Parliament Statement No. 1," *ibiblio.org*, http://www.ibiblio.org/obl/docs/crpp1998.01.htm.

18.   The legal background of her "house arrest" between September 2000 and May 2002 is not quite clear. Between 1989 and 1995 as well as between 2003 and 2011 the house arrest was based on State Security Law adopted in 1975 by the Burmese parliament (see Zöllner, *The Beast and the Beauty*, 148–50). This was not the case after the confrontation highlighted by the standoffs in 2000. She did not leave the house after that—and this period could be called a "self-imposed house arrest." As we have shown, she was only "half-free" during 1995–2000 and 2002–3, despite the rhetoric of "unconditional release."

19.   Anna Magnusson and Morten B. Pedersen, *A Good Office? Twenty Years of UN Meditation in Myanmar* (New York: International Peace Institute, 2012). Available from http://www.ipinst.org/images/pdfs/ipi_ebook_good_offices.pdf. This assessment was shared by some of her closest allies, as demonstrated by Kyi Maung's resignation from the party in December 1997. Kyi Maung had represented the party during the 1990 elections and participated in the talks over the gate. It is widely held that his decision to leave was based on his disagreement with Suu Kyi's uncompromising approach.

Chapter 9. A Victory Parade Cut Short

Opening quote from Peter Carey, ed., *Burma: The Challenge of Change in a Divided Society* (London: Macmillan, 1997), x.

1.   Seth Mydans, "Burmese Democracy Advocate Is Released From House Arrest," *New York Times*, May 6, 2002, http://www.nytimes.com/2002/05/06/world/burmese-democracy-advocate-is-released-from-house-arrest.html.

2. "Ending Repression in Myanmar" *New York Times*, May 7, 2002, http://www.nytimes.com/2002/05/07/opinion/ending-repression-in-myanmar.html.

3. Zöllner, *The Beast and the Beauty*, 254.

4. Seth Mydans, "Burmese Dissident Strikes New Balance With Junta Leaders," *New York Times*, July 5, 2002, http://www.nytimes.com/2002/07/05/world/burmese-dissident-strikes-new-balance-with-junta-leaders.html.

5. Newspaper reports allow the reconstruction of Aung San's trips and show that between 1946 and the elections in April 1947 he traveled to at least the following places together with the leading members of the AFPFL: In March 1946 he was in Rakhine for several days; one month later he visited laborers on strike in Dala in the vicinity of Yangon. At the end of November, he was in Kachin State. Some photos were taken here that came to be reproduced often in 2015 and were of some significance given the context of actual fighting between Kachin rebels and government troops. During her visit to Kachin State, Aung San Suu Kyi recalled the friendship between her father and Kachin leaders from that time. In December 1946, Aung San was first in Mawlamyine in the Mon region and then traveled to Kayah State, where he was to meet Shan leaders. Further visits to Shan state followed. He traveled there again in February 1947 to conclude the Panglong Agreement on the twelfth of the month. In March he was again in southern Burma and held speeches in Myeik (Mergui) and Mawlamyine. Shortly thereafter he went on a journey to Mandalay and vicinity. There he also visited Monywa on March 20, which had been the last stop during Aung San Suu Kyi's travels before she was forced to abort her trip in Depayin. In her speech in Monywa Aung San Suu Kyi recalled what her father had said in this city in 1947. The newspaper reports of the 1940s resemble those of the 2000s. Both father and daughter had been greeted by exultant crowds. On the journey back, Aung San visited his birthplace Natmauk and some other cities, before returning to Rakhine state once more on April 1. From there, on April 6, 1947, three days before election day, he traveled once more to Kachin State.

6. See the book published after the Depayin incident: Ministry of Information, *Daw Suu Kyi, the NLD Party, and Our Ray of Hope and Selected Articles* (Rangoon: News and Periodicals Enterprise), 2003.

7. Ministry of Information, *Daw Suu Kyi, the NLD Party, and Our Ray of Hope*, 7.

8. "Myanmar junta launches fresh attacks on Suu Kyi, diplomats," *Agence France Press*, July 6, 2002, archived at *burmalibrary.org*, http://www.burmalibrary.org/TinKyi/archives/2003-07/msg00008.html. The press release quotes from a series from the state newspaper. It was published as a brochure by the Ministry of

Information in September 2003 under the title *Daw Suu Kyi, the NLD Party, and Our Ray of Hope.*

9. "Myanmar junta raps Suu Kyi over backing of international sanctions," *Agence France Press*, December 18, 2002, http://www.burmalibrary.org/TinKyi/archives/2002–12/msg00020.html.

10. "Sermon atop fire engine by Suu Kyi to the local junta authorities," *Asian Tribune*, December 21, 2002. http://www.burmalibrary.org/TinKyi/archives/2002-12/msg00028.html.

11. "Myanmar junta says it has 'complete trust' in Aung San Suu Kyi," *Agence France Press*, April 15, 2003, http://www.burmalibrary.org/TinKyi/archives/2003–04/msg00012.html.

12. "Aung San Suu Kyi takes calculated risk in shifting stance against junta," *Agence France Press*, April 24, 2003, http://www.burmanet.org/bnn_archives/2003/20030424.txt.

13. "Myanmar junta says Aung San Suu Kyi criticism 'senseless,'" *Agence France Press*, April 25, 2003, http://www.burmanet.org/bnn_archives/2003/20030425.txt.

14. "Road to Depayin," *Alternative Asean Network on Burma*, May 14, 2003, http://www.altsean.org/Photogalleries/RoadtoDepayin.htm.

15. "Myanmar junta says Suu Kyi causing 'commotion,'" *Reuters*, May 30, 2003.

16. Zöllner, *Talks over the Gate*, 285.

17. "Myanmar's human rights situation has regressed—UN expert," *UN News Centre*, November 12, 2003, http://www.un.org/apps/news/story.asp?NewsID=8867&Cr=myanmar&Cr1=#.WRWojWjyg2x.

18. The following is based on the Report of Sergio Pinheiro "Situation of human rights in Myanmar Report submitted by the Special Rapporteur, Paulo Sérgio Pinheiro," January 5, 2004, available from: http://burmacampaign.org.uk/media/SR-Rept-512004.pdf, paragraphs 12–21.

19. The text of the press conference is contained in a "Preliminary Report of the Ad hoc Commission on Depayin Massacre (Burma), 4 July 2003," *Ad hoc Commission on Depayin Massacre*, https://de.scribd.com/document/26614595/Depayin-Massacre-Preliminary-Report-1, 37–43.

20. Razali Ismail, "Meetings with Aung San Suu Kyi," *The Irrawaddy*, April 2007, http://www2.irrawaddy.com/article.php?art_id=6974&page=3.

21. Both pagodas are known as *Kyauk-taw-gyi phaya*, the Revered Great Stone Pagoda. The pagoda in Mandalay is located on the foot of Mandalay Hill, the Yangon pagoda on Mindhamma Hill.

22. "The New Light of Myanmar (Tuesday, 25 July 2000)," *The New Light of Myanmar*, July 25, 2000, http://www.burmalibrary.org/NLM/archives/2000-07/msg00021.html.

23. See, for the many activities of the junta in this regard, Donald M. Seekins, *State and Society in Modern Rangoon* (Abingdon: Routledge, 2011), 179–97.

24. Ismail, "Meetings with Aung San Suu Kyi."

25. The procedure took place in the reknowned Asia Taw Win Clinic.

26. The roadmap is commonly referred to in the international media as the "Seven Step Roadmap."

27. *New Light of Myanmar*, November 8, 2004, http://www.ibiblio.org/obl/docs/NLM2004-11-08.pdf.

28. Representatives for sixteen parliaments were elected on November 7, 2010: for the house of representatives (Pyitthu Hluttaw) with a total of 440 seats, the house of nationalities (Amyotha Hluttaw) with 224 seats, and fourteen parliaments of the seven regions and the seven states of the union. The fact that the different regions received their own parliaments and governments was a complete novelty in Burmese constitutional history.

29. See Hans-Bernd Zöllner, *Weder Safran noch Revolution: Eine kommentierte Chronologie der Demonstration von Mönchen in Myanmar/Birma im September 2007* (Hamburg: Abera Verlag, 2008).

30. In Burmese counting, the year starts on its first day. The Buddhist calendar, which starts on the day of the Buddha's enlightenment, thus changes from year to year in Thailand and Myanmar.

31. Hans-Bernd Zöllner, *Neither Saffron nor Revolution: A Commented and Documented Chronology of the Monks' Demonstrations in Myanmar in 2007 and their Background* (Berlin: Humboldt University, 2009). Available online at http://www.burmalibrary.org/docs08/WP%2036%20Zoellner%20.pdf and http://www.burmalibrary.org/docs08/WP%2037%20Zoellner-2.pdf.

32. "Press conference on intrusion of US citizen Mr John William Yettaw into Daw Aung San Suu Kyi's residence held," *New Light of Myanmar*, June 26, 2009, http://www.burmalibrary.org/docs07/NLM2009-06-26.pdf.

33. "Trial of Daw Aung San Suu Kyi," *burmalibrary.org*, May 2009, http://www.burmalibrary.org/docs07/NCGUB_Trial_Update27-28-May.pdf.

34. "Chairman of the State Peace and Development Council issues directive dated 10 August 2009 for Ministry of Home Affairs stating upon Court pronouncing sentence to Daw Aung San Suu Kyi, sentence to be served by her under Criminal Procedure Code be amended to be remitted and suspended if she displays good conduct and pardon be granted accordingly," *New Light of Myanmar*, August 12, 2009, http://www.burmalibrary.org/docs07/NLM2009-08-12.pdf, 9. Seekins, *State and Society in Modern Rangoon*.

Chapter 10. Course Correction or U-Turn?

Opening quote from "VOA Interview with Aung San Suu Kyi," *Voice of America*, September 18, 2012, https://www.voanews.com/a/voa-scott-stearns-interview-with-aung-san-suu-kyi/1510542.html.

1. See Taylor, *General Ne Win*, chapter 13.

2. For the text, see "We have to strive our utmost to stand as a strong government while conducting changes and amendments in order to catch up with the changing world," *burmalibrary.org*, *New Light of Myanmar*, March 31, 2011, http://www.burmalibrary.org/docs11/NLM2011-03-31.pdf.

3. Personal communication with Hans-Bernd Zöllner, June 2013.

4. The speech is reproduced in Zöllner, *Talks over the Gate*, 287–96.

5. However, it was immediately taken up again with the NLD's victory in the 2015 elections, highlighting the symbolic meaning of the 1947 agreement adopted as a result of Aung San's efforts.

6. See Hans-Bernd Zöllner, *Fetisch Demokratie: Der Arabische Frühling, von außen betrachtet* (Hamburg: Abera Verlag, 2014).

7. "After Egypt, Myanmar's Suu Kyi wants Twitter," *Deccan Herald* (AFP), February 20, 2011, http://www.deccanherald.com/content/139310/content/196937/a-treat-deccan-heralds-facebook.html.

8. The project remains in a limbo as of June 2017.

9. "NLD considers registering as official political party," *Mizzima News*, September 29, 2011, http://archive-1.mizzima.com/news-91481/prisoner-watch/6002-nld-considers-registering-as-official-political-party.

10. Aye Aye Win, "Aung San Suu Kyi's party to run in Burma elections," *Independent*, November 18, 2011, http://www.independent.co.uk/news/world/asia/aung-san-suu-kyis-party-to-run-in-burma-elections-6264220.html.

11. Interview with Thein Han, a Muslim politician from Mandalay, on December 2, 2011. Thein Han had spent some time in jail together with Min Ko Naing and was confident that there were no plans for retaliation against the Tatmadaw by the winning party.

12. Esmer Golluoglu, "Vote of confidence in Burmese president's appetite for reform," *The Guardian*, April 1, 2012, https://www.theguardian.com/world/2012/apr/01/vote-confidence-burma-president-reform.

13. "Burma's Thein Sein: 'Aung San Suu Kyi could be president,'" *BBC*, September 30, 2012. http://www.bbc.com/news/world-asia-19776164.

14. Aye Aye Win, "Myanmar's Aung San Suu Kyi confirms run for parliament seat, legitimizing elections," *Christian Science Monitor*, January 10, 2012, http://www.csmonitor.com/World/Latest-News-Wires/2012/0110/Myanmar-s-Aung-San-Suu-Kyi-confirms-run-for-parliament-seat-legitimizing-elections.

15. "Myanmar president says 'there's no turning back' on reforms," *Deutsche Welle* (*AP*, *AFP*), January 20, 2012, http://dw.com/p/S7HF.

16. Interview, December 6, 2011.

17. "Suu Kyi campaign sheds light on Burma's political spirit," *Burma Report* (*AP*), February 1, 2012, http://www.burma-report.de/Burma%20report%20pdf/106EBRI12.pdf.

18. Sebastian Strangio, "Myanmar by-elections a hard sell in Kachin conflict zone," *PRI*, April 1, 2012, https://www.pri.org/stories/2012-04-01/myanmar-elections-hard-sell-kachin-conflict-zone.

19. Thomas Fuller, "Election Puts Pressure in Myanmar Dissident," *New York Times*, March 3, 2012, http://www.nytimes.com/2012/03/08/world/asia/in-election-a-new-risk-for-aung-san-suu-kyi.html?pagewanted=all&_r=0.

20. Hans-Bernd Zöllner, *Von Birma nach Myanmar: Ein Zeit-Reise-Führer* (Hamburg: Abera Verlag, 2014), 176. The residents gave similar responses in 2015 during a visit by Rodion Ebbighausen.

21. Thanks to Uta Gärtner for the translation from Burmese to English.

22. "National League for Democracy presents its policy, stance and work programmes," *New Light of Myanmar*, March 15, 2012, http://www.burmalibrary.org/docs13/NLM2012-03-15.pdf, 6.

23. No elections were held in three districts within Kachin State, as the government found the situation in these areas to be too unstable (an assessment disputed by the NLD). One of the candidates had been disqualified by the Electoral Commission because one of his parents possessed a foreign passport. Only in Shan State did a candidate from a large regional party marginally defeat the NLD candidate.

Chapter 11. The Vagaries of Realpolitik

Opening quote from Zöllner, *Talks over the Gate*, 186.

1. Talks with NLD leaders in November 2011.

2. Articles 121 (e)–(g) of the constitution include similar but less strict provisions on parliamentary officials. The provisions date back to the 1947 Constitution. Article 74 (i) includes the vague provision that any person, who in any way is bound to a foreign power, may not become a parliamentarian and accordingly, as per Article 49 (ii), also may not become president of the country.

3. John Bercow, "Address to Aung San Suu Kyi," June 21, 2012, http://www.parliament.uk/business/news/2012/june/speaker-addresses-aung-san-suu-kyi/.

4. Aung San Suu Kyi, "Suu Kyi recalls Nehru in historic speech at UK Parliament," June 22, 2012, http://www.rediff.com/news/column/suu-kyi-recalls-nehru-in-historic-speech-at-uk-parliament/20120622.htm.

5. "Fourth regular session of First Pyithu Hluttaw continues for fourth day. Eight questions raised, three reports discussed, one proposal discussed, one new proposal discussed, one new proposal submitted, one bill approved," July 9, 2012, *burmalibrary.org*, http://www.burmalibrary.org/docs13/PH-NLM2012-07-10-day 04.pdf.

6. "Aung San Suu Kyi takes seat in Burma's Parliament," *news.com.au* (*AFP*), July 10, 2012, http://www.news.com.au/world/suu-kyi-takes-seat-in-parliament/ news-story/c71263cbc6164cc3f69a8afda2f8b4e6.

7. *New Light of Myanmar*, July 26, 2012, http://www.burmalibrary.org/docs 13/NLM2012-07-26.pdf, 6.

8. Aung Htoo, "A constitutional crisis in Burma?," *Democratic Voice of Burma*, September 7, 2012, https://www.dvb.no/analysis/a-constitutional-crisis-in-burma/23662; *New Light of Myanmar*, August 5, 2012, 16.

9. Wanbao Mining belongs to the conglomerate China North Industries Corporation (Norinco). The complex and partly intransparent ownership and rights relationships can be read in Amnesty International, "Open for Business? Corporate Crime and Abuses at Myanmar Copper Mine," May 10, 2015, http://www.amnesty.org/en/documents/asa16/0003/2015/en/.

10. The Peaceful Demonstrations and Gatherings Act of December 2, 2011. See Lawyers Network and Justice Trust, "Submission of Evidence to Myanmar Government's Letpadaung Investigation Commission," January 28, 2013, http://www.burmalibrary.org/docs15/Letpadaung-Lawyers_report-en-red.pdf, 12.

11. Fahrion comes to an entirely different conclusion. Georg Fahrion, "Myanmars Wirtschaft: Ein ewiges Versprechen," in *Myanmar Handbuch*, ed. Ute Köster et al. (Berlin: Horlemann, 2014) 253–65. He finds that military conglomerates like Union of Myanmar Economic Holdings Limited account for a considerable portion of the military budget and create opportunities for an uncontrolled spread of cronyism.

12. "Proposal to send large numbers of scholars to foreign countries approved," *New Light of Myanmar*, November 24, 2012, http://www.burmalibrary.org/docs14/ NLM2012-11-24.pdf.

13. The eight questions were as follows: Did the project meet international standards and was environmental protection adequate? What was the impact of the project on society and the environment? Is the project profitable to the state? What was the cause of the protests that had led to the closure of the copper mine? What was the nature of the involvement of the security forces and the injuries caused to the monks? Should the project continue or should the foreign investment be suspended? Any recommendations on the development of the country and the rule of law? Any other recommendations of the commission? See "Presidential

Notification No. 92/2012," *Myanmar Press Office*, archived at http://www. charltonslaw.com/newsletters/myanmar-law/en/2013/3/nl-mylaw-20130419-3. html, accessed December 14, 2014.

14. "Presidential Notification 95/2012," *Myanmar Press Office*, archived at http://www.charltonslaw.com/newsletters/myanmar-law/en/2013/3/nl-mylaw-20130419-3.html, accessed December 14, 2014.

15. The investigation report is not available in English, but see the presidential notification cited above.

16. "Foreign Ministry Spokesperson Hua Chunying's Regular Press Conference on 13 March 2013," *Permanent Mission of the People's Republic of China to the UN*, March 13, 2013, http://www.china-un.org/eng/fyrth/t1021567.htm.

17. Kyaw Phyo Tha, "Wanbao Welcomes Inquiry Commissions's Verdict," *The Irrawaddy*, March 13, 2013, http://www.irrawaddy.org/burma/wanbao-welcomes-inquiry-commissions-verdict.html.

18. Kate Hodal, "Aung San Suu Kyi faces protesters at copper mine," *The Guardian*, March 13, 2013, http://www.theguardian.com/world/2013/mar/13/aung-san-suu-kyi-mine.

19. Yadana Htun, "Myanmar villagers unhappy that Suu Kyi backs mine," *CNS News*, March 13, 2013, http://cnsnews.com/news/article/myanmar-villagers-unhappy-suu-kyi-backs-mine.

20. Patrick Winn, "Is Aung San Suu Kyi a tarnished idol?," *Alaska Dispatch News*, updated September 29, 2016, https://www.adn.com/nation-world/article/where-aung-san-suu-kyi-tarnished-idol/2013/03/21/.

21. Lawyers Network and Justice Trust, "Submission of Evidence to Myanmar Government's Letpadaung Investigation Commission." See note 10.

22. Ei Ei Toe Lwin, "Fury over Letpadaung copper mine report," *Myanmar Times*, March 18, 2013, http://www.mmtimes.com/index.php/national-news/5175-fury-at-copper-mine-report.html.

23. Lawyers Network and Justics Trust, "Submission of Evidence to Myanmar Government's Letpadaung Investigation Commission," 2. See note 10 above. The English is quoted from this source. The original language and author are not known.

24. Further protests ensued. See, for example, "Fresh protests over Chinese-backed Letpadaung mine," *Frontier Myanmar* (AFP), May 8, 2016, http://frontiermyanmar.net/en/news/fresh-protests-chinese-backed-letpadaung-mine. A demonstrator was killed in December 2014 (see: Amnesty International, "Open for Business?").

25. An extensive study about the events of 2012 and the underlying conflict was published by Francis Wade, *Myanmar's Enemy Within: Buddhist Violence and the Making of a Muslim "Other"* (London: Zed Books, 2017).

26. Three men were given death sentences by a local court on June 18, 2012, one of them having committed suicide before. The two others pleaded guilty. In Myanmar, no death sentences have been enforced since 1988. Nyein Nyein, "Death Sentence for Arakan Rape-Murderers," *The Irrawaddy*, June 18, 2017, https://www.irrawaddy.com/news/burma/death-sentence-for-arakan-rape-murderers.html.

27. "Final Report of Inquiry Commission on Sectarian Violence in Rakhine State," *Online Burma/Myanmar Library*, July 8, 2013, http://www.burmalibrary.org/docs15/Rakhine_Commission_Report-en-red.pdf.

28. Médecins Sans Frontières was forced to close its doors in Rakhine State in February 2014 following a government order. MSF doctors were accused of favoring Muslims. Kate Hodal, "Burma tells Médécins Sans Frontières to leave state hit by sectarian violence," *The Guardian*, February 28, 2014, http://www.theguardian.com/world/2014/feb/28/burma-medecins-sans-frontieres-rakhine-state.

29. Amnesty International, "Caged Without a Roof, Apartheid in Myanmar's Rakhine State," London, 2017.

30. "EU chief Barroso offers new development aid to Burma," *BBC*, November 3, 2012, http://www.bbc.com/news/world-asia-20189448.

31. "President Office Notification No. 58/2012," August 17, 2012. Available from http://www.president-office.gov.mm/en/?q=briefing-room/notifications/2012/08/17/id-561, accessed December 16, 2014.

32. Wade, *Myanmar's Enemy Within*, 126.

33. Republic of the Union of Myanmar *"Final Report of Inquiry Commission on Sectarian Violence in Rakhine State,"* http://www.burmalibrary.org/docs15/Rakhine_Commission_Report-en-red.pdf.

34. Aung Zaw, "Are Myanmar's Hopes Fading?" *New York Times*, April 24, 2013, http://www.nytimes.com/2013/04/25/opinion/will-hatred-kill-the-dream-of-a-peaceful-democratic-myanmar.html.

35. Vikram Nehru, "Aung San Suu Kyi Must Transition Too," *The Wall Street Journal*, June 20, 2012, https://www.wsj.com/articles/SB10001424052702304898704577477991620165070.

36. Lalit K Jha, "Suu Kyi Backs Govt to Diffuse Arakan Tensions," *The Irrawaddy*, September 19, 2012, https://www.irrawaddy.com/news/burma/suu-kyi-backs-govt-to-diffuse-arakan-tensions.html.

37. Anjana Pasricha, "Aung San Suu Kyi Explains Silence on Rohingyas," *Voice of America*, November 15, 2012, https://www.voanews.com/a/aung-san-suu-kyi-explains-silence-on-rohingyas/1546809.html.

38. Haroon Siddique, "Burma sectarian violence motivated by fear, says Aung San Suu Kyi," *The Guardian*, October 24, 2013, https://www.theguardian.com/world/2013/oct/24/burma-sectarian-violence-fear-aung-san-suu-kyi.

39. Mark Farmaner, "Supporting Rohingya human rights draws ugly attacks," *Mizzima*, July 13, 2012, http://www.burmanet.org/news/2012/07/13/mizzima-news-supporting-rohingya-human-rights-draws-ugly-attacks-%e2%80%93-mark-farmaner/.

40. Human Rights Watch, "'All You Can Do is Pray': Crimes Against Humanity and Ethnic Cleansing of Rohingya Muslims in Burma's Arakan State," 2013, 107.

41. The three digits 969 are supposed to symbolize the Buddha's virtues, the teachings of Buddhism, and the Buddhist community. The first 9 stands for the Buddha's nine attributes, the 6 for the attributes of his teachings and the second 9 for the characteristics of the sangha. The numbers were also selected to draw a distinction from the digits 786, used by Muslims throughout Southeast Asia to represent the saying "In the name of Allah, the most merciful, the most beneficient."

42. "Myanmar probes monk Wirathu's comments on UN envoy," *BBC*, January 21, 2015, http://www.bbc.com/news/world-asia-30911124.

43. Wa Lone, "Ma Ba Tha to celebrate passage of race & religion laws," *Myanmar Times*, September 5, 2015, http://www.mmtimes.com/index.php/national-news/16307-ma-ba-tha-to-celebrate-passage-of-race-religion-laws.html.

44. Tim Hume, "Aung San Suu Kyi's 'silence' on the Rohingya," *CNN*, April 15, 2014, http://edition.cnn.com/2014/04/15/world/asia/myanmar-aung-san-suu-kyi-rohingya-disappointment/.

45. Raksha Kumar, "Daw Aung San Suu Kyi Offers Little Hope for Rohingya Refugees," *The New York Times*, November 20, 2012, https://india.blogs.nytimes.com/2012/11/20/daw-aung-san-suu-kyi-offers-little-hope-for-rohingya-refugees/?ref=asia.

46. Pangmu Shayi, "Suu Kyi's silence," *DVB*, September 19, 2012, http://www.dvb.no/analysis/suu-kyi%E2%80%99s-silence/23825.

47. Anushay Hossain, "The Silence of a Laureate: Ethnic and Religious Tensions Rise in Burma," *Forbes*, October 8, 2012, http://www.forbes.com/sites/worldviews/2012/10/08/the-silence-of-a-laureate-ethnic-religious-tensions-rise-in-burma/?

48. Aung Zaw, "Fresh Arakan Strife Bad Omen for Reform," *The Irrawaddy*, October 29, 2012, https://www.irrawaddy.com/opinion/fresh-arakan-strife-bad-omen-for-reform.html

49. Hanna Hindstrom, "Is it foolish to criticise Aung San Suu Kyi?," *DVB*, September 24, 2012, http://www.dvb.no/uncategorized/is-it-foolish-to-criticise-aung-san-suu-kyi/23942.

50. Poppy McPherson, "No vote, no candidates: Myanmar's Muslims barred from their own election," *The Guardian*, November 3, 2015, https://www.theguardian.com/world/2015/nov/03/no-vote-no-candidates-myanmars-muslims-barred-from-their-own-election.

51. "Aung San Suu Kyi on the Rohingya Muslims," *Shingatsu News Agency*, April 20, 2014, https://www.youtube.com/watch?v=Q3WQE-hVucI.

52. Kyaw Phyo Tha, "Promoting 'Rule of Law' Will End Violence, Suu Kyi Tells Muslim Leaders," *The Irrawaddy*, April 11, 2013, https://www.irrawaddy.com/news/burma/promoting-rule-of-law-will-end-violence-suu-kyi-tells-muslim-leaders.html.

53. "Agence France Presse: Myanmar's Rohingya 'barred from Suu Kyi meet' in Japan," *Burmanet*, April 11, 2013, http://www.burmanet.org/news/2013/04/11/agence-france-presse-myanmars-rohingya-barred-from-suu-kyi-meet-in-japan.

54. San Yamin Aung, "Citing Nonpartisan Duty, Election Chief Says 'Sorry' to Former Party," *The Irrawaddy*, June 17, 2015, http://www.irrawaddy.org/burma/citing-nonpartisan-duty-election-chief-says-sorry-to-former-party.html.

55. Htoo Thant, "MPs mull eight paths to democracy," *Myanmar Times*, October 24, 2014, http://www.mmtimes.com/index.php/national-news/12071-electoral-reform-body-submits-second-report.html.

56. Aung Kyaw Min, "Courting of Rohingya in 2010 comes back to haunt USDP," *Myanmar Times*, August 26, 2015, http://www.mmtimes.com/index.php/national-news/16158-courting-of-rohingya-in-2010-comes-back-to-haunt-usdp.html.

57. "Aung San Suu Kyi condemns 'unjust' constitution," *BBC*, November 14, 2014, http://www.bbc.com/news/world-asia-30049266.

58. Nang Mya Nadi, "SNDP sets sights on 50% election success rate," *DVB*, February 18, 2015, http://www.dvb.no/news/sndp-sets-sights-50-election-success-rate/48441.

59. Andrew R. C. Marshall and Timothy Mclaughlin, "Myanmar's Suu Kyi says will be above president in new government," *Reuters*, November 5, 2015, http://www.reuters.com/article/us-myanmar-election-idUSKCN0SU0AR20151105.

60. Kyaw Phyo Tha, "Takeaways From Suu Kyi's Marathon Pre-Poll Presser," *The Irrawaddy*, November 5, 2015, http://www.irrawaddy.org/election/news/takeaways-from-suu-kyis-marathon-pre-poll-presser.

61. Kyaw Phyo Tha, "NLD Leadership Expels Pakokku Party Officials over Protest," *The Irrwaddy*, August 11, 2015, http://www.irrawaddy.org/burma/nld-leadership-expels-pakokku-party-officials-over-protest.html.

62. Peter Popham, "Burma election: Suu Kyi calls for calm in run up to poll that could change the country—if the generals permit it," *Independent*, September 8, 2015, http://www.independent.co.uk/news/world/asia/burma-election-suu-kyi-calls-for-calm-in-run-up-to-poll-that-could-change-the-country-if-the-10492065.html.

63. San Yamin Aung, "Former Rangoon Mayor Hopes New Roads Pave Way to Re-Election," *The Irrawaddy*, September 22, 2015, http://www.irrawaddy.org/election/news/former-rangoon-mayor-hopes-new-roads-pave-way-to-re-election.

64. Sithu Aung Myint, "Ma Ba Tha, USDP: election bedfellows?," *Myanmar Times*, September 30, 2015, http://www.mmtimes.com/index.php/opinion/16738-ma-ba-tha-usdp-election-bedfellows.html.

65. In conversation with Rodion Ebbighausen on November 7, 2015 in Yangon.

66. There was also an advance voting system, intended for voters who were unable to cast their vote on election day in their districts. Such voters could cast an advance vote. The system lent itself to interference. It was difficult to organize and voter lists could be easily manipulated. Each district could not confirm whether a person had already voted using the advanced system or not. Double-counting was also a risk.

67. In conversation with Rodion Ebbighausen on November 7, 2015, in Yangon.

68. In conversation with Rodion Ebbighausen on November 8, 2015, in Yangon.

69. In conversation with Rodion Ebbighausen on November 9, 2015, in Yangon.

70. See Rodion Ebbighausen, "Opinion: Congratulations Myanmar!" *Deutsche Welle*, November 10, 2015, http://dw.com/p/1H2dB.

Chapter 12. Dual Rule

Opening quote from Zöllner, *Talks over the Gate*, 250.

1. R. J. Vogt, "UEC puts election turnout at 69 percent," *Myanmar Times*, December 3, 2015, http://www.mmtimes.com/index.php/national-news/nay-pyi-taw/17948-uec-puts-election-turnout-at-69-percent.html.

2. William R. Sweeney, "Myanmar's Historic 2015 Elections," *IFES*, November 24, 2015, http://www.ifes.org/news/myanmars-historic-2015-elections.

3. Timothy Mclaughlin, "Rising Rakhine party looming threat to Myanmar's Muslim minority," *Reuters*, October 1, 2015, https://uk.reuters.com/article/us-myanmar-election-rohingya/rising-rakhine-party-looming-threat-to-myanmars-muslim-minority-idUSKCN0RV5RO20151001.

4. Francis Khoo Thwe, "For Myanmar cardinal, elections are a "sacred pilgrimage" towards democracy and freedom," *AsiaNews.it*, November 4, 2015, http://www.asianews.it/news-en/For-Myanmar-cardinal,-elections-are-a-sacred-pilgrimage-towards-democracy-and-freedom-35780.html.

5. "'Myanmar, now stands on the threshold of hope' Cardinal Charles Maung Bo," *Mizzima*, March 16, 2016, http://www.mizzima.com/news-opinion/'myanmar-now-stands-threshold-hope'-cardinal-charles-maung-bo.

6. May Wong and Sujadi Siswo, "Appointed president will take instructions from me if NLD wins: Suu Kyi," *Channel News Asia*, November 24, 2015, http://

www.channelnewsasia.com/news/asiapacific/appointed-president-will-take-instructions-from-me-if-nld-wins-s-8225564.

7.   May Wong and Sujadi Siswo, "Appointed president will take instructions from me."

8.   Lally Weymouth, "Aung San Suu Kyi: 'I'm going to be the one who is managing the government,'" *Washington Post*, November 19, 2015, https://www.washingtonpost.com/opinions/aung-san-suu-kyi-im-going-to-be-the-one-who-is-managing-the-government/2015/11/19/bbe57e38-8e64-11e5-ae1f-af46b7df8483_story.html?postshare=5611447950678539&tid=ss_tw.

9.   Timothy Mclaughlin and Aung Hla Tun, "Mum's the word as Myanmar's Suu Kyi starts military rapprochement," *Reuters*, December 3, 2015, http://www.reuters.com/article/us-myanmar-politics-idUSKBN0TM0HP20151203; Hein Ko Soe, "Suu Kyi meeting with Commander-in-Chief produced good results," *Mizzima*, December 3, 2015, http://www.mizzima.com/news-domestic/suu-kyi-meeting-commander-chief-produced-good-results.

10.   Thomas Fuller, "Aung San Suu Kyi and Myanmar General Meet, Taking Steps Toward Sharing Power," *New York Times*, December 2, 2015, http://www.nytimes.com/2015/12/03/world/asia/myanmar-aung-san-suu-kyi-meets-president-army.html?&_r=0.

11.   Hnin Yadana Zaw, "In Myanmar, political mood sours as transition talks hit a snag," *Reuters*, February 2, 2016, http://www.reuters.com/article/us-myanmar-politics-idUSKCN0VL16I.

12.   Bni, "NLD instructs candidates to refer to themselves as elected candidates," *Mizzima*, December 14, 2015, http://www.mizzima.com/news-domestic/nld-instructs-candidates-refer-themselves-elected-candidates.

13.   Tin Htet Paing, "Bipartisan Transition Committee Holds First Meeting in Naypyidaw," *The Irrawaddy*, December 16, 2015, http://www.irrawaddy.com/burma/bipartisan-transition-committee-holds-first-meeting-in-naypyidaw.html.

14.   Ei Ei Toe Lwin, "Who is President U Htin Kyaw?" *Myanmar Times*, March 30, 2016, http://www.mmtimes.com/index.php/national-news/nay-pyi-taw/19714-who-is-president-u-htin-kyaw.html.

15.   "Transcript: President U Htin Kyaw's inaugural address," *Myanmar Times*, March 30, 2016, http://www.mmtimes.com/index.php/national-news/19730-transcript-president-u-htin-kyaw-s-inaugural-address.html.

16.   "Myanmar's ex-president Thein Sein becomes Buddhist monk," *The Guardian* (AP), April 5, 2016, https://www.theguardian.com/world/2016/apr/05/myanmars-ex-president-thein-sein-becomes-buddhist-monk.

17.   Some weeks before the transfer of governmental responsibility to the NLD, one of the party's legal advisors, Ko Ni, stated that the party could introduce

an entirely new constitution. Such a constitution could include a high political office designed for Aung San Suu Kyi. Ko Ni, a Muslim man, was murdered near Yangon airport at the end of January 2017. (Ei Ei Toe Lwin, "NLD could draft new constitution," *Myanmar Times*, April 22, 2016, http://www.mmtimes.com/index. php/national-news/nay-pyi-taw/19910-nld-could-draft-new-constitution.html).

18. Hnin Yadana Zaw and Timothy Mclaughlin, "Myanmar's Aung San Suu Kyi set to steer cabinet as minister," *Reuters*, March 22, 2016, http://www.reuters.com/ article/us-myanmar-politics-idUSKCN0WO0BL?rpc=401.

19. Wa Lone, "NLD to ram through state counsellor law," *Myanmar Times*, April 4, 2016, http://www.mmtimes.com/index.php/national-news/nay-pyi-taw/19807-nld-to-ram-through-state-counsellor-law.html.

20. Timothy McLaughlin, "Suu Kyi's state counselor bill passes vote despite military protest," *Reuters*, April 5, 2016, http://www.reuters.com/article/us-myanmar-politics-idUSKCN0X217N.

21. Wa Lone, "NLD to ram through state counsellor law." See note 18.

22. Robert H. Taylor, "Discord, not devotion, will help Aung San Suu Kyi succeed," *Nikkei Asian Review*, March 30, 2017, https://asia.nikkei.com/Viewpoints/ Robert-H.-Taylor/Discord-not-devotion-will-help-Aung-San-Suu-Kyi-succeed.

23. "Suu Kyi: I started as a politician not a human rights defender," *Equality Myanmar*, October 29, 2013, http://equalitymyanmar.org/suu-kyi-i-started-as-a-politician-not-a-human-rights-defender/.

24. Matthew J. Walton, *Buddhism, Politics and Political Thought in Myanmar* (Cambridge: Cambridge University Press, 2017), chapter 3.

25. "Full transcript: My farewell message for my husband was too late, says Aung San Suu Kyi to NDTV," *NDTV*, update November 15, 2012, http://www.ndtv. com/article/india/full-transcript-my-farewell-message-for-my-husband-was-too-late-says-aung-san-suu-kyi-to-ndtv-292831.

26. Conversation with Rodion Ebbighausen on August 7, 2015 in Yangon.

27. Daron Acemoglu and James Robinson, *Why Nations Fail: The Origins of Power, Prosperity, and Poverty* (New York: Random House, 2012).

28. "Exclusive: Success is determined by how dispensable I can make myself, says Suu Kyi," *Channel News Asia*, December 8, 2016, http://www.channelnewsasia. com/news/singapore/exclusive-success-is-determined-by-how-dispensable-i-can-make/3352100.html.

29. This information was provided by Zeya Thu on January 23, 2017.

30. Michael Peel and Lucy Hornby, "Myanmar's Suu Kyi heads for China in first big foreign trip," *Financial Times*, August 17, 2016, https://www.ft.com/ content/bca71e4e-6442-11e6-8310-ecf0bddad227. After the USA lifted further sanctions in September 2016, Aung San Suu Kyi repeated her calls for investment

in her home country. See Timothy McLaughlin, "Aung San Suu Kyi Calls for More Investment in Burma Following U.S. Sanctions Relief," *TIME* (*Reuters*), September 16, 2016, http://time.com/4496468/aung-san-suu-kyi-obama-sanctions-relief-investment/; Minami Funakoshi and Elaine Lies, "Myanmar's Suu Kyi visits Japan, seeking investment, as crisis builds at home," *Reuters*, November 1, 2016, http://www.reuters.com/article/us-myanmar-japan-idUSKBN12W3JO.

31. "Aung San Suu Kyi would welcome 'ethical' UK investment in Burma," *The Scotsman*, June 18, 2012, http://www.scotsman.com/news/politics/aung-san-suu-kyi-would-welcome-ethical-uk-investment-in-burma-1-2360900.

32. Aung San Suu Kyi, "Heavenly abodes and human development," *Trócaire Development Review 1997*, https://www.trocaire.org/sites/default/files/resources/policy/1997-aung-san-human-development.pdf.

33. See Nilanjana Sengupta, *The Female Voice of Myanmar: Khin Myo Chit to Aung San Suu Kyi* (New Delhi: Cambridge University Press, 2015), 311.

34. Thant Myint-U, *Where China Meets India: Burma and the New Crossroads of Asia* (New York: Farrar, Straus and Giroux, 2012).

35. Asian Development Bank, *Myanmar: Unlocking the Potential*, Country diagnostc study (Mandaluyong City, Philippines: Asian Development Bank, 2014), https://www.adb.org/sites/default/files/publication/42870/myanmar-unlocking-potential.pdf, 13ff.

36. World Bank, *Myanmar Economic Monitor: Anchoring Economic Expectations* (Washington, D.C.: World Bank Group, 2016), 39.

37. "US Businesses: Myanmar Investment Challenges Persist," *VOA News*, June 6, 2016, http://www.voanews.com/a/united-states-business-myanmar-investment-challenges/3364356.html.

38. Roland Berger, "Myanmar: A wave of optimism—will it last?" December 2016, http://www.ntccthailand.org/images/articles_reports/Roland-Berger-Myanmar.pdf.

39. Richard Cockett, "Can Aung San Suu Kyi save Burma's economy?," *Foreign Policy*, April 12, 2016, http://foreignpolicy.com/2016/04/12/can-aung-san-suu-kyi-save-burmas-economy/.

40. Aye Thidar Kyaw and Clare Hammond, "Government reveals 12-point economic policy," *Myanmar Times*, July 29, 2016, http://www.mmtimes.com/index.php/business/21664-nld-12-point-economic-policy-announcement.html. In fact, most of the laws relating to the improvement of the economic framework had already been passed under the USDP government. This included, for example, the Myanmar Comprehensive Development Vision or the National Comprehensive Development Plan 2011–2013

41. Melford E. Spiro, *Buddhism and Society: A Great Tradition and Its Burmese Vicissitudes* (Berkeley: University of California Press, 1982).

42. Brian McCartan, "Myanmar: Land Grabbing as Big Business," *CETRI*, March 11, 2013, http://www.cetri.be/Myanmar-Land-grabbing-as-big?lang=fr; "Burma: Farmers Targets of Land Grabs," *Human Rights Watch*, November 3, 2016, https://www.hrw.org/news/2016/11/03/burma-farmers-targets-land-grabs. A good overview and a collection of articles is available at www.farmlandgrab.org/. For relatively contemporary basic information see G. Henley, "A Case Study on Land in Burma," *Department for International Development*, January 1, 2014, https://www.gov.uk/dfid-research-outputs/case-study-on-land-in-burma; see also Aubrey Belford, Hnin Yadana Zaw, and Antoni Slodkowski, "Suu Kyi tackles military land grabs in test of new Myanmar government," *Reuters*, August 3, 2016, http://www.reuters.com/article/us-myanmar-military-land-insight-idUSKCN10E0JU.

43. Clare Hammond, "Investors relieved, optimistic after provisional results," *Myanmar Times*, November 10, 2015, http://www.mmtimes.com/index.php/business/17523-investors-relieved-optimistic-after-provisional-results.html.

44. Hnin Yadana Zaw and Antoni Slodkowski, "Former Junta 'Crony' sees business as usual after NLD Win," *The Irrawaddy* (*Reuters*), November 18, 2015, http://www.irrawaddy.org/election/news/former-junta-crony-sees-business-as-usual-after-nld-win.

45. Moe Myint, "Win Htein: Suu Kyi can be President within 5 Years," *The Irrawaddy*, December 5, 2015, http://www.irrawaddy.org/election/news/win-htein.

46. "National League for Democracy 2015 Election Manifesto," *Burma Library*, http://www.burmalibrary.org/docs21/NLD_2015_Election_Manifesto-en.pdf.

47. The details of the complicated issue are set out in articles 275–83 of the 2008 constitution

48. "The Nationwide Ceasefire Agreement Between The Government Of The Republic Of The Union Of Myanmar And The Ethinic Armed Organizations," http://www.peaceagreements.org/wggsite/downloadAgreementMasterDocument/id/1436

49. International Crisis Group, "Myanmar's Peace Process: Getting to a Political Dialogue," No. 149, October 19, 2016, https://www.crisisgroup.org/asia/south-east-asia/myanmar/myanmar-s-peace-process-getting-political-dialogue.

50. "The Framework for Political Dialogue," *Ethnic Peace Resources Project* (*EPRP*), December 22, 2015, http://www.eprpinformation.org/files/recent-events/the-framework-for-political-dialogue-unofficial-translation--22dec2015--eng.pdf.

51. Nyein Nyein, "Joint Ceasefire Monitoring Committee To Extend Mandate," *The Irrawaddy*, April 1, 2016, http://www.irrawaddy.com/news/burma/joint-ceasefire-monitoring-committee-to-extend-mandate.html.

52. Myo Thant Khine, "Myanmar Peace Commission Apologizes to Wa State Army For Badge Snafu," *Radio Free Asia*, September 2, 2016, http://www.rfa.org/english/news/myanmar/myanmar-peace-commission-apologizes-to-wa-state-army-for-badge-snafu-09022016145105.html.

53. "The Heart of the Nation State Counsellor calls for constant efforts to keep up momentum for peace and reconciliation," *Burma Library*, September 4, 2016, http://www.burmalibrary.org/docs23/GNLM2016-09-04-red.pdf.

54. "21st Century Panglong to be held every six months," *Mizzima*, August 16, 2016, http://www.mizzima.com/news-domestic/21st-century-panglong-be-held-every-six-months.

55. Nyan Hlaing Lynn and Oliver Slow, "Mixed results at latest Panglong peace conference," *Frontier Myanmar*, May 30, 2017, https://frontiermyanmar.net/en/mixed-results-at-latest-panglong-peace-conference.

56. By Aung San Suu Kyi's office of the state counsellor in August 2016.

57. Michelle Dozier, "In-depth analysis of Rohingya insurgency in Myanmar," *Muir Analytics*, November 16, 2016, http://muiranalytics.com/?p=372.

58. International Crisis Group, "Myanmar: A New Muslim Insurgency in Rakhine State," Asia Report No. 283, Brussels 2016, https://www.crisisgroup.org/asia/south-east-asia/myanmar/283-myanmar-new-muslim-insurgency-rakhine-state.

59. Subir Bhaumik, "Why do China, India back Myanmar over the Rohingya Crisis?" *South China Morning Post*, October 18, 2017, http://www.scmp.com/week-asia/geopolitics/article/2115839/why-do-china-india-back-myanmar-over-rohingya-crisis.

60. Fiona Macgregor, "Dozens of rapes reported in northern Rakhine State," *Myanmar Times*, October 27, 2016, https://www.mmtimes.com/national-news/23326-dozens-of-rapes-reported-in-northern-rakhine-state.html.

61. Antoni Slodkowski, "Myanmar army says 86 killed in fighting in northwest," *Reuters*, November 15, 2016, https://in.reuters.com/article/myanmar-rohingya/myanmar-army-says-86-killed-in-fighting-in-northwest-idINKBN13A11N.

62. "Myanmar wants ethnic cleansing of Rohingya - UN official," *BBC*, November 24, 2016, http://www.bbc.com/news/world-asia-38091816.

63. "Ethnic cleansing by Myanmar: UN," *Straits Times*, November 26, 2016, http://www.straitstimes.com/asia/se-asia/ethnic-cleansing-by-myanmar-un.

64. Michelle Nichols, "Malaysian PM urges intervention to stop 'genocide' of Myanmar's Rohingya Muslims," *Reuters*, December 4, 2016, http://www.reuters.com/article/us-myanmar-rohingya-malaysia-idUSKBN13T07I; Rodion Ebbighausen, "Rohingya conflict: What constitutes genocide?" *Deutsche Welle*, January 13, 2017, http://dw.com/p/2Vm3Q.

65. "Indonesians protest at Myanmar embassy over Rohingya cause," *AP*, November 24, 2016, http://bigstory.ap.org/article/e15decb9efe74a0498977bf0dc 3f44af/indonesians-protest-myanmar-embassy-over-rohingya-cause.

66. "Kofi Annan downplays claims of Myanmar genocide," *BBC*, December 6, 2016, http://www.bbc.com/news/world-asia-38223055.

67. "Exclusive: Success is determined by how dispensable I can make myself, says Suu Kyi."

68. Rodion Ebbighausen, "'No easy solution' to the Rohingya problem in Myanmar," *Deutsche Welle*, December 1, 2016, http://dw.com/p/2TYmh.

69. Saw Yan Naing, "Locals in Northern Shan State Warned to Take Precautions As Fighting Escalates," *The Irrawaddy*, November 21, 2016, http://www.irrawaddy. com/news/burma/locals-in-northern-shan-state-warned-to-take-precautions-as-fighting-escalates.html.

70. Kofi Annan, "Advisory Commission on Rakhine State: Interim Report and Recommendations (March 2017)," *Reliefweb*, March 16, 2017, https://reliefweb. int/report/myanmar/advisory-commission-rakhine-state-interim-report-and-recommendations-march-2017.

71. Video can be found at http://www.rohingyablogger.com/2017/03/statement-by-kofi-annan-chair-of.html.

72. Amnesty International, "Myanmar: Act now on Rakhine Commission report," March 17, 2017, https://www.amnesty.org/en/latest/news/2017/03/myanmar-act-now-on-rakhine-commission-report/.

73. United Nations, "Myanmar: UN welcomes final assessment of independent advisory panel on Rakhine state," *UN News Centre*, August 24, 2017, http://www. un.org/apps/news/story.asp?NewsID=57408#.Whc-vHmDO7o.

74. ARSA_The Army, Twitter post, August 25, 2017, https://twitter.com/ ARSA_Official/status/900877804425932800.

75. ARSA_The Army, Twitter post, August 25, 2017, https://twitter.com/ ARSA_Official/status/900904120076435457.

76. "Aung San Suu Kyi 2017 FULL International Speech on the Violence in Myanmar," YouTube video, 30:04, posted by zofodraz, September 19, 2017, https:// www.youtube.com/watch?v=rcksU4G4Nzw.

77. "Extremist terrorists attack on police outposts in N-Rakhine," *The Global New Light of Myanmar*, August 26, 2017, http://www.burmalibrary.org/docs23/ GNLM2017-08-26.pdf.

78. "Terrorists trying to destroy Maungtaw," *The Global New Light of Myanmar*, August 28, 2017, http://www.burmalibrary.org/docs23/NLM2017–08–28-NRS. pdf. The law passed parliament in June 2014.

79. "Myanmar Rakhine: Thousands flee to Bangladesh border," *BBC*, August 28, 2017, http://www.bbc.com/news/world-asia-41067747.

80. UNHCR, "Mission report of OHCHR rapid response mission to Cox's Bazar, Bangladesh," September 13–24, 2017, http://www.ohchr.org/Documents/Countries/MM/CXBMissionSummaryFindingsOctober2017.pdf.   Amnesty International, "'My World is finished': Rohingya Targeted in Crimes Against Humanity in Myanmar," October 11, 2017, https://www.amnestyusa.org/wp-content/uploads/2017/10/Amnesty-My-World-Is-Finished-Myanmar-18.10.20171.pdf; Amnesty International, "'Caged Without a Roof': Apartheid in Myanmar's Rakhine State," November 21, 2017, https://www.amnesty.org/en/documents/asa16/7484/2017/en/; Human Rights Watch, "All of my Body was Pain," November 16, 2017, https://www.hrw.org/report/2017/11/16/all-my-body-was-pain/sexual-violence-against-rohingya-women-and-girls-burma;   Fortify Rights, "'They tried to kill us all': Atrocity Crimes against Rohingya Muslims in Rakhine State, Myanmar," November 15, 2017, http://www.fortifyrights.org/downloads/THEY_TRIED_TO_KILL_US_ALL_Atrocity_Crimes_against_Rohingya_Muslims_Nov_2017.pdf.

81. These statements are based on the discussion of one of the authors with different people (Buddhist, Muslim, and Christian) during a three-week period in Myanmar in October 2017; see also https://coconuts.co/yangon/features/facebook-responsible-myanmars-violence-against-rohingya/.

82. "Bob Geldof says Aung San Suu Kyi has become 'one of the great ethnic cleansers'," *thejournal*, October 5, 2017, http://www.thejournal.ie/geldof-anger-leaders-3630431-Oct2017/.

83. Naaman Zhou and Michael Safi, "Desmond Tutu condemns Aung San Suu Kyi: 'Silence is too high a price'," *The Guardian*, September 8, 2017, https://www.theguardian.com/world/2017/sep/08/desmond-tutu-condemns-aung-san-suu-kyi-price-of-your-silence-is-too-steep.

84. Richard Licht, "Das Schweigen der Aung San Suu Kyi," *Der Tagesspiegel*, September 13, 2017, http://www.tagesspiegel.de/themen/reportage/rohingya-in-myanmar-das-schweigen-der-aung-san-suu-kyi/20298286.html.

85. "Speech of Daw Aung San Suu Kyi (19/9/2017)," 44:50, YouTube video, posted by Ye Myint Han, September 18, 2017, https://www.youtube.com/watch?v=OsVAAtDg-bo.

86. "Myanmar Rohingya crisis: Deal to allow return of Muslim refugees," *BBC*, November 23, 2017, http://www.bbc.com/news/world-asia-42094060.

87. John Reed, "UN questions Myanmar's Rohingya repatriation pledge," *Financial Times*, November 30, 2017, https://www.ft.com/content/071e4554-d591-11e7-8c9a-d9c0a5c8d5c9.

88. Rodion Ebbighausen, "Opinion: The gray area in Myanmar's Rohingya conflict," *Deutsche Welle*, September 6, 2017, http://p.dw.com/p/2jRkT; Rodion Ebbighausen, "Kommentar: Gegen Populismus in der Myanmar-Krise," *Deutsche Welle*, September 10, 2017, http://p.dw.com/p/2jb66.

89. Mark Farmaner, "It's Time To Talk About Min Aung Hlaing," Huffington Post, April 13, 2017, http://www.huffingtonpost.co.uk/mark-farmaner/min-aung-hlaing_b_15001514.html.

90. John Reed, "Aung San Suu Kyi looks to China as criticism over Rohingya grows," *Financial Times*, November 27, 2017, https://www.ft.com/cintent/265168ca-d361-11e7-8c9a-d9c0a5c8d5c9.

91. Médecins Sans Frontières, *10 Years for the Rohingya in Bangladesh: Past, Present and Future*, (Holland, 2002).

Epilogue

1. Maung Maung, *The 1988 Uprising in Burma*. Maung Maung splits the twenty-six years of Burmese socialism in two phases: 1962–74, the time under the Revolutionary Council; and 1974–88, the time under the new constitution.

2. "Exclusive: Success is determined by how dispensable I can make myself, says Suu Kyi," *Channel News Asia*, December 8, 2016, https://www.channelnewsasia.com/news/asiapacific/exclusive-success-is-determined-by-how-dispensable-i-can-make-my-7636558

Glossary

88 Generation Students Group or **88 Generation.** This description refers back to the 1988 demonstrations. The members include Min Ko Naing (Paw Oo Tun), Mya Aya, Ko Ko Gyi, Pyone Cho, and Min Zeya. The members of the group spent many years in prison and since their release remain active in civil society.

Anti-Fascist People's Freedom League (AFPFL). A political coalition founded by the military, as well as the communist and socialist parties in 1945. Under Aung San and U Nu, the AFPFL markedly shaped the country's history from 1945 to 1962.

Association of Southeast Asian Nations (ASEAN). An economic, security, and sociocultural union of ten Southeast Asian states, founded in Bangkok in 1967. Myanmar has been a member of the union since 1997.

Burma Socialist Programme Party (BSPP). This single party was founded in 1962 and functioned like a cadre party until 1974, when the new constitution came into place. The party's vision was to lead the country on a "Burmese Way to Socialism."

Burma Independence Army (BIA). This army was founded by the Thirty Comrades in December 1941. In the coming years it was frequently restructured and renamed (Burma Defence Army, Burma National Army, Burma Patriotic Forces).

Committee Representing the People's Parliament (CRPP). The CRPP was set up by the NLD in 1998 after the military junta had for years refused to respect the 1990 election outcome. It represented a kind of shadow parliament. It was constituted of ten members and supported by 251 parliamentarians who had been elected in 1990.

Communist Party of Burma (CPB). The CPB was involved in the independence movement beginning in 1939. Aung San had founded the first cell of the party in 1939. It was subsequently led by his brother-in-law Than Tun. In 1946, Aung San cut it off from the AFPFL. The CPB remained engaged in an armed fight against the central government until 1988.

dāna. The practice of cultivating generosity. According to the London-based Charity Aid Foundation, Myanmar is the most generous country in the world, having surpassed the USA since 2014.

Democratic Voice of Burma (DVB). A media organization based in Norway. It provides news and information on Myanmar and has been broadcasting a shortwave radio program for the country since 1992.

dhamma. This is a key Buddhist term. It may be translated as the "founding law of life." In Theravada Buddhism, the dhamma is learned from the Buddha and can only be fully understood and practiced by monks.

Dobama Asiayone (We Burmans Association). A nationalist organization founded in 1930. Aung San and other former students joined the organization in 1938. It then became the leading and most radical force in the independence struggle against Great Britain.

dukkha. This is a Buddhist term that may be best translated as "suffering." It describes the basic disposition of all human life ("all life is *dukkha*"). In Buddhism, *dukkha* is seen as one of the three aspects of existence.

The Irrawaddy. A news magazine set up by Burmese refugees in Thailand in 1992.

Kachin Independence Organisation. A political organization founded in 1961 to represent the interests of the Kachin people. For many years, it controlled Kachin State, which lies in the northeast of the country. The Kachin Independence Army (KIA) is the organization's military arm.

kamma. This Pali term (*karma* in Sanskrit) means "deed." It is Buddhism's central message: every action, every thought, and every feeling comes with good or bad consequences. The consequence may not be immediately visible and may only manifest itself after reincarnation.

Karen National Union. This union of the Karen people was founded immediately after Burma's independence. Its objective is an independent Karen state. The Karen National Liberation Army is its military arm.

kathina **ceremony** (also called *upavasatha*). An important holiday in Theravada Buddhist countries. In Myanmar, people traditionally give new robes to monks on this day.

Kayin (or **Karen**). One of the large ethnic groups in Myanmar. The Kayin speak various dialects and live mostly in the Irrawaddy Delta and in the mountainous regions bordering Thailand. Around one-third of the Kayin are Christians.

kyat. Myanmar's currency.

loka nibbein. See "worldly nirvana."

longyi. A traditional piece of clothing in Myanmar. It is a wrapping cloth that is knotted around the waist. The longyi worn by men is called *paso* and the one worn by women is called *htamein*.

Maha Sammata or **Great Elect.** The first virtuous monarch in Buddhist tradition, unanimously elected for life.

Manerplaw. A city in Karen State near the Thai border. It was a central hub for various Burmese resistance groups until the central government's military forces took over in 1995.

mettā. A key term in Buddhist moral thinking. It may be translated as friendliness, active interest in the well-being of others, love, friendship, sympathy, or loving kindness.

National Defence and Security Council. According to the 2008 constitution, this council includes the president, the two vice presidents, the speakers of the upper and lower houses of parliament, the foreign minister, the supreme commander, and the deputy supreme commander of the army, as well as three ministers (defense, internal affairs, and frontier areas). This council has the power to dissolve parliament and the government, as well as suspend the constitution.

National Democratic Force (NDF). A party that was formed in 2010 after splitting from the NLD in order to participate in the 2010 elections.

National League for Democracy (NLD). This party was formed on September 27, 1988, with Aung San Suu Kyi as its first general secretary. The party won the 1990 elections but was not allowed to take over government responsibility. In May 2010, the party was declared illegal by the government for boycotting the upcoming elections. The party reregistered in 2011 and won forty-three seats in parliament during the 2012 by-elections. Aung San Suu Kyi was elected chairperson of the party during a 2013 party congress. In 2015, the NLD obtained a majority of the total seats in both the House of Nationalities and the House of Representatives of the Assembly of the Union.

National Unity Party. This was the successor party of the dissolved BSPP. It was formed in 1988 and participated in the next elections on a socialist ticket.

The New Light of Myanmar. A state-owned newspaper published by the Ministry of Information in English and Burmese. It is the successor magazine of the *Working People's Daily.* It can be traced back to a nationalist publication from 1914.

Panglong Conference. This conference, held in Panglong, Shan State, was one of the milestones of Burmese political union. In 1947, Aung San met with leaders of the Chin, Kachin, and Shan to find a common path to navigate towards an independent Burma. The conference led to the signing of the Panglong Agreement on February 12, 1947, which made little concrete proposals and relied largely on Aung San's personal promises. The Karen, an important ethnic minority group, had observer status at the conference and did not sign the agreement.

pwe. This is a traditional Burmese festivity or party, usually involving theater performances or puppet shows.

Pyidaungsu Hluttaw. The Burmese name for the national assembly of the Union of Myanmar. The political system consists of two houses: the House of Nationalities (Amyotha Hluttaw), which has 224 seats and the House of Commons (Pyitthu Hluttaw), which has 440 seats. Together they form the national assembly, which elects the president. In addition, the 2008 constitution provides for fourteen regional parliaments, seven in the largely Bamar areas and seven in states where other ethnic identities dominate.

sada. A horoscope based on the day and hour of birth. Fortune-tellers make predictions as to the life of a newborn.

Saffron Revolution. Fuel price hikes led to demonstrations against the military government in 2007. Initially, the protesters were only monks. The military government violently put an end to the protests a week later.

saṃsāra. The eternal cycle of death and rebirth in Buddhism.

sangha. The community of monks, as opposed to the laypeople.

saya or *sayama*. An honorary title for a learned teacher.

Seven-Step Roadmap to a Discipline-Flourishing Democracy. This is the official name for the seven-step program designed by the military and announced by Khin Nyunt in 2003 as setting out the path to establishing a democratic system in Myanmar. It included, among others, the convening of a national convention, the drafting of a new constitution, free and fair elections, and the creation of a civilian government.

shin byu **ceremony.** A ritual in Theravada Buddhist countries in which male children and youth symbolically follow the path of the Buddha. They are first dressed in ornate clothing, which is then exchanged for simple monks' robes.

State Law and Order Restoration Council (SLORC). This council was founded on September 18, 1988. Shortly before, the military had quelled the 1988 Uprising, dissolved the BSPP as the single governing party, and thus taken over state control. General Saw Maung was the first chairperson.

State Peace and Development Council (SPDC). The successor to SLORC, set up in 1997 and dissolved in 2011.

stupa. A Buddhist architectural construction symbolizing the Buddha and the dhamma. This structure starts from a large, round base, narrowing to its culmination in a pointed tip.

Tatmadaw. Literally, the "main army"; the armed forces of Myanmar. It includes land, naval, and air forces. It held state power from 1958 to 1960, 1962 to 1974, and 1988 to 2011. Its leaders were Aung San (1941–45), Smith Dun (1945–49), Ne Win (1949–72), San Yu (1972–74), Tin Oo (1974–76), Kyaw Htin (1976–85), Saw Maung (1985–92), Than Shwe (1992–2011), and Min Aung Hlaing (2011–present).

thakin. A form of address used for the British colonial rulers, meaning "sir" or "master" and resembling the Indian *sahib*. The members of the Dobama Asiayone started using it as a prefix to their names, documenting their claim to leadership of the country.

Theravada Buddhism. A branch of Buddhism that is dominant in Cambodia, Laos, Myanmar, Sri Lanka, and Thailand.

Thingyan. The Burmese new year festival, which usually falls around mid-April. This is a Buddhist festival, lasting four to five days. It is often called the water festival, as the new year is welcomed with a lot of water. The water symbolizes the washing away of the debris from the past year to start the new year in purity.

Thirty Comrades. A group of thirty members of the Dobama Asiayone under Aung San's leadership who during the Second World War were trained by the Japanese. They later formed the core of a Burmese independence army. Some of the thirty comrades played an important role in the country's politics after independence.

Union Solidarity and Development Association (USDA). The mass organization of the state, set up by the SLORC in 1993 and dissolved in 2010 to form the USDP. At times its members numbered over twenty million.

Union Solidarity and Development Party (USDP). The successor of the USDA, founded before the 2010 elections with Thein Sein—who would go on to become president—as chairperson. The USDP won the most seats in parliament in the 2010 elections, which were boycotted by the NLD.

Upper and Lower Burma. These are markers for the historically, geographically, and culturally distinct parts of Burma that for hundreds of years led separate lives. Upper Burma is composed of the dry central and northern regions of the country, Lower Burma covers the coastal areas and the Ayeyarwady/Irrawaddy Delta.

vipassana. A traditional Buddhist form of meditation aimed at true insight and enlightenment. This form of meditation has spread from Burma around the world.

worldly nirvana (loka nibbein). This term was probably coined by national poet Thakin Kodaw Hmaing. He describes an ideal society where all material suffering (dukkha) is radically reduced.

Bibliographic Essay

A number of biographies have been written about Aung San Suu Kyi. They all paint the life of the Nobel laureate from childhood to the time of publication of the given book. These books include an account of Aung San Suu Kyi's political development— sometimes cursorily, sometimes in detail, but never systematically. This book aims to close this gap. We have referred to the existing biographies but have not mentioned them at every point in the text in order to add to the book's readability. In addition to the works mentioned in the notes, here we set out what we consider to be the most important sources.

Justin Wintle's biography (2007) was of special importance to us. This book, *Perfect Hostage*, remains one of the most elaborate and carefully researched portraits of Aung San Suu Kyi and the people she had contact with abroad. We also relied on the biographies by Whitney Stewart (1997), Bertil Lintner (2011), Peter Popham (2012, 2016), Aung Zaw (2013), Jesper Bengtsson (2013), Thierre Falise (2007), and Nilanjana Sengupta (2015).

Aung San Suu Kyi's own writings, notably *Freedom from Fear and Other Writings* (2nd edition 1995) and *Letters from Burma* (1997), were obviously important sources. Both collections of texts provide a good first impression of Suu Kyi's political worldview. Hans-Bernd Zöllner's *Talks over the Gate* (2014), which records her conversations with her supporters in 1995 and 1996, and the interviews Alan Clements conducted with Suu Kyi (1997) play an important role.

Two websites are invaluable in understanding events in Myanmar and their international perception: www.burmanet.org and www.burmalibrary.org. The former provides an archive of news, analysis, and opinion from the Burmese press since 1994. Unfortunately, Burmanet stopped its collection in 2016 when funding from George Soros' Open Society Foundations ran out. The other website (www. burmalibrary.org) is an online database of various documents on Myanmar. The key pieces available here are the Burmese state newspaper sections from 1987 to 1996, which contain a large amount of important information.

We used additional literature for the individual chapters. The most important texts are set out below. The bibliography provides a complete list.

Chapter 1. Peacock from the Ashes

Bertil Linter's book *Outrage* (1990) is a key source on the events around the 1988 protests. The military's perspective is set out in two short volumes that were published in 1991 by Tatmadaw Researcher, a team of authors that publishes research for the Tatmadaw. We also relied on the memoirs of the last president of socialist Burma, Dr. Maung Maung (1999).

Chapter 2. The Incomplete Hero

The best German-language publication on Aung San's life is, unfortunately, difficult to access; Susanne Prager's 1998 thesis, written at Heidelberg University, can be borrowed from the university library. Besides this, we relied on Aungelene Naw's biography (2001) as well as the collection of Aung San's speeches, letters, and opinions by Josef Silverstein (1993). Aung San Suu Kyi's short biography of her father, *Aung San of Burma* (1984), was also a source.

Chapter 3. A Child of Many Worlds

Here, we largely relied on the biographies published by other authors and mentioned above. For the statements on Aung San Suu Kyi's mother's family, we relied on information collected through various conversations with people who have had contact with the family.

Chapter 4. The Struggle for the Right Path to Democracy

This chapter and the next one rely heavily on Hans-Bernd Zöllner's work (2012) on the conflict between the military and Aung San Suu Kyi after 1988. Robert Taylor's *The State in Myanmar* (2009) and his biography *General Ne Win* (2015) are also referred to. In addition, Ma Thanegi's (2013) and Ma Thida's (2016) books were helpful.

Chapter 5. Birth of a Global Icon

The iconizing of Aung San Suu Kyi was first studied critically in one of Bertil Lintner's books, which he published in 1991, the year that Aung San Suu Kyi was awarded the Nobel Peace Prize. He revised his assessment to a large extent twenty years later and criticized the "deification" of Aung San Suu Kyi. Zöllner's book (2012) about her conflict with the military includes a chapter that illustrates Aung San Suu Kyi's iconography through numerous images.

Chapter 6. The People's Voice

This chapter draws primarily on Aung San Suu Kyi's speeches and interviews, and on conversations with citizens of Myanmar.

Chapter 7. Revolution of the Spirit

The statements in relation to the meditation movement of laypeople in Myanmar, which included Aung San Suu Kyi's teacher, U Pandita, are based on Ingrid Jordt's book (2007). Jordt herself lived in a meditation center as part of the research for the book. Keiko Tosa's article (2009) and other research papers were used to understand the workings of Thamanya Sayadaw. Gustaaf Houtman's book (1999) is the source of the idea that there is a connection between the *vipassana* meditation practiced by Aung San Suu Kyi and other NLD members, and the democracy movement.

Chapter 8. One Country, Two Governments

Both Callahan (2003) and Zöllner (2010) authored helpful books for understanding the historical backgrounds on the emergence of "two Burmas."

Chapter 9. A Victory Parade Cut Short

The events that occurred towards the end of Aung San Suu Kyi's trips in 2002 and 2003 still remain unclear. The same is true for the removal of Khin Nyunt from his government post after his announcement of a roadmap to a disciplined democracy. The main sources for this chapter are web-based and must be used with caution as they may be biased.

Chapter 10. Course Correction or U-turn?

The presentation of events since March 2011 is based on a number of internet sources, newspaper articles, reports, and the authors' own research in Myanmar.

Chapter 11. The Vagaries of Realpolitik

The story of the Letpadaung Mine has only been inadequately told so far. Jacques Leider's important work in French on Rakhine State (2004) was used for the history of that region. He is the most knowledgeable source on this region and its complexities. Another source—albeit not up-to-date—is Klaus Fleischmann's book in German (1981). Up-to-date and well-researched overviews on the state of Muslims in Myanmar are published by the International Crisis Group in its Asia Reports no. 251 (2013), no. 261 (2014), and no. 283 (2016).

Chapter 12. Dual Rule

This chapter is based on the authors' insights and assessments. The information used in this chapter stems primarily from conversations in Myanmar but also from various media sources.

Bibliography

Acemoglu, Daron, and James Robinson. *Why Nations Fail: The Origins of Power, Prosperity, and Poverty*. New York: Random House, 2012.

All Burma Students' Democratic Front, ed. *Letters to a Dictator: Official correspondence from NLD chairman U Aung Shwe to the SLORC's Senior General Than Shwe, from December 1995 to March 1997*. Translated and edited by Naing Luu Aung, Aung Moe Htet and Sit Nyein Aung. Bangkok: All Burma Students' Democratic Front, 1997.

Amnesty International. "'Caged Without a Roof': Apartheid in Myanmar's Rakhine State," November 21, 2017. https://www.amnesty.org/en/documents/asa16/7484/2017/en/.

———. "'My World is Finished': Rohingya Targeted in Crimes Against Humanity in Myanmar." October 11, 2017. https://www.amnestyusa.org/wp-content/uploads/2017/10/Amnesty-My-World-Is-Finished-Myanmar-18.10.20171.pdf.

———. "Myanmar: Serious risk of further human rights abuses at controversial Letpadaung mine." November 27, 2014. https://www.amnesty.org/en/documents/asa16/0003/2015/en/.

———. "Open for Business? Corporate Crime and Abuses at Myanmar Copper Mine." May 10, 2015. http://www.amnesty.org/en/documents/asa16/0003/2015/en/.

Ang Chin Geok. *Aung San Suu Kyi: Towards a New Freedom*. Sidney: Prentice Hall, 1998.

Aris, Michael. *Hidden Treasures and Secret Lives: Study of Pemalingpa (1450–1521) and the Sixth Dalai Lama (1683–1706)*. London: Kegan Paul International, 1989.

Asian Development Bank. *Myanmar: Unlocking the Potential*. Country diagnostc study. Mandaluyong City, Philippines: Asian Development Bank, 2014. https://www.adb.org/sites/default/files/publication/42870/myanmar-unlocking-potential.pdf.

Aung San Suu Kyi. *Aung San of Burma*. Edinburgh: Kiscadale, 1984.

———. *Freedom from Fear and Other Writings*. Edited by Michael Aris. London: Penguin, 1995.

———. *Letters from Burma*. London: Penguin, 1997.

———. *Let's Visit Bhutan*. London: Burke Book, 1985.

Aung Zaw. *The Face of Resistance: Aung San Suu Kyi and Burma's Fight for Freedom*. Chiang Mai: Mekong Press, 2013.

Bengtsson, Jasper. *Aung San Suu Kyi: A Biography*. New Delhi: Amaryllis, 2012.

———. *Ikone der Freiheit: Aung San Suu Kyi; Eine Biographie*. Berlin: Rotbuch-Verlag, 2013.

Blum, Franziska. *Teaching Democracy: The Program and Practice of Aung San Suu Kyi's Concept of People's Education*. Berlin: regiospectra, 2012.

Callahan, Mary P. *Making Enemies: War and State Building in Burma*. Ithaca, NY: Cornell University Press, 2003.

Carey, Peter, ed. *Burma: The Challenge of Change in a Divided Society*. London: Macmillan, 1997.

Clements, Alan. *The Voice of Hope: Aung San Suu Kyi; Conversations with Alan Clements*. New York: Seven Stories Press, 1997.

Connelly, Karen. *Burmese Lessons: A True Love Story*. 2nd ed. New York: Doubleday, 2009.

Croissant, Aurel. *Die politischen Systeme Südostasiens: Eine Einführung*. Wiesbaden: Springer VS, 2016.

Dreifus, Claudia. "Interview: Aung San Suu Kyi" (1995). In *Interview*, 32–52. New York: Seven Stories Press, 1997.

Fahrion, Georg. "Myanmars Wirtschaft: Ein ewiges Versprechen." In *Handbuch Myanmar*, edited by Ute Köster, Phuong Le Trong, and Christina Grein, 253–65. Berlin: Horlemann, 2014.

Falise, Thierry. *Aung San Suu Kyi: Le Jasmin ou la lune*. Paris: Florent Massot, 2007.

Fleischmann, Klaus. Arakan. *Konfliktregion zwischen Birma und Bangladesch: Vorgeschichte und Folgen des Flüchtlingsstroms von 1978*. Hamburg: Institut für Asienkunde, 1981.

Fukuyama, Francis. *The End of History and the Last Man*. New York: Free Press, 1992.

Gärtner, Uta. "Nay Pyi Taw: The Reality and Myths of Capitals in Myanmar." In *Southeast Asian Historiography: Unravelling the Myths; Essays in Honour of*

Barend Jan Terwiel, edited by Volker Grabowsky, 258–67. Bangkok: River Books, 2011.

Goore-Both, Paul. *With Great Truth and Respect*. London: Constable, 1974.

Ghosh, Amitav. "54 University Avenue, Yangon." *The Kenyon Review* 23, no. 2 (2001): 158–65.

Handley, Paul M. *The King Never Smiles: A Biography of Thailand's Bhumibol Adulyadej*. New Haven, CT: Yale University Press, 2006.

Heine-Gelder, Robert. *Conceptions of State and Kingship in Southeast Asia*. Ithaca, NY: Cornell University Press, 1956.

Houtman, Gustaaf. *Mental Culture in Burmese Crisis Politics: Aung San Suu Kyi and the National League for Democracy*. Tokyo: Tokyo University of Foreign Studies, 1999.

Human Rights Watch. "'All You Can Do is Pray': Crimes Against Humanity and Ethnic Cleansing of Rohingya Muslims in Burma's Arakan State." 2013, http://www.hrw.org/news/2013/04/22/burma-end-ethnic-cleansing-rohingya-muslims.

———. "'The Government Could Have Stopped This': Sectarian Violence and Ensuing Abuses in Burma's Arakan State." 2012, http://www.hrw.org/sites/default/files/reports/burma0812webwcover_0.pdf.

Huntington, Samuel P. *The Third Wave: Democratization in the Late 20th Century*. Norman, OK: University of Oklahoma Press, 2012.

International Crisis Group. "The Dark Side of Transition: Violence Against Muslims in Myanmar." Asia Report No. 251. 2013. http://www.crisisgroup.org/~/media/Files/asia/south-east-asia/burma-myanmar/251-the-dark-side-of-transition-violence-against-muslims-in-myanmar.

———. "Myanmar: A New Muslim Insurgency in Rakhine State." Asia Report No. 283. 2016. https://d2071andvipowj.cloudfront.net/283-myanmar-a-new-muslim-insurgency-in-rakhine-state.pdf.

International Crisis Group. "Myanmar: The Politics of Rakhine State." Asia Report No. 261. 2014. http://www.crisisgroup.org/~/media/Files/asia/south-east-asia/burma-myanmar/261-myanmar-the-politics-of-rakhine-state.pdf.

Jordt, Ingrid. *Burma's Mass Meditation Movement: Buddhism and the Cultural Construction of Power*. Athens, OH: Ohio University Press, 2007.

Khin Yi. *The Dobama Movement in Burma (1930–1938)*. Ithaca, NY: Cornell University Press, 1988.

Kin Oung. *Who Killed Aung San?* Bangkok: White Lotus, 1993.

Kyaw Yin Hlaing. "Political Impasse in Myanmar." Working paper series, no 111. University of Hong Kong, 2011.

———. *Prisms on the Golden Pagoda: Perspectives on National Reconciliation in Myanmar.* Singapore: NUS Press, 2014.

Kyo Van. *The 1947 Constitution and the Nationalities.* 2 vols. Yangon: Universities Historical Research Centre and Inwa Publishing House, 1999.

Leider, Jacques. *Le Royaume d'Arakan, Birmanie: Son histoire politique entre le début du XVe et la fin du XVIIe siècle.* Paris: EFEO, 2004.

Lintner, Bertil. *Aung San Suu Kyi and Burma's Struggle for Independence.* Chiang Mai: Silkworm Books, 2011.

———. *Aung San Suu Kyi and Burma's Unfinished Renaissance.* Bangkok: White Lotus, 1991.

———. *Outrage: Burma's Struggle for Democracy.* 2nd ed. Bangkok: White Lotus, 1990.

Ma Thanegi. *Nor Iron Bars a Cage.* San Francisco: Thingsasian Press, 2013.

———. *The Native Tourist: A Holiday Pilgrimage in Myanmar.* Chang Mai: Silkworm Books, 2000.

Ma Thida. *Prisoner of Conscience: My Steps through Insein.* Foreword by U Win Tin. Chiang Mai: Silkworm Books, 2016.

Magnusson, Anna, and Morton B. Pedersen. *A Good Office? Twenty Years of UN Meditation in Myanmar.* New York: International Peace Institute, 2012. http://www.ipinst.org/images/pdfs/ipi_ebook_good_offices.pdf.

Maung Maung, Dr. *The 1988 Uprising in Burma.* Yale Southeast Asia Studies 49. New Haven, CT: Yale University, 1999.

———, ed. *Aung San of Burma.* Den Haag: Martinus Nijhoff, 1962.

Maung Maung, U. *From Sangha to Laity. National Movements of Burma, 1920–1940.* Delhi: Manohar, 1980.

Médecins Sans Frontières. *10 Years for the Rohingya in Bangladesh: Past, Present and Future.* 2002 http://www.rna-press.com/data/itemfiles/5ae98e43d068cb7 49b3060b002601b95.pdf.

Ministry of Information. *Daw Suu Kyi, the NLD Party, and Our Ray of Hope and Selected Articles.* Rangoon: News and Periodicals Enterprise, 2003.

Myint Kyi, Naw Angeline, Tun Tint, eds. Hla Tein, trans. *Myanmar Politics 1958–1962.* Vol. 2. Yangon: Ministry of Culture, Historical Research Center, 2007.

Nemoto, Kei. "The Concepts of Dobama (Our Burma) and Thudobama (Their Burma) in Burmese Nationalism: 1930–1948." *Journal of Burma Studies* 5 (2000): 1–16.

Nietzsche, Friedrich. *Morgenröthe: Idyllen aus Messina; Die fröhliche Wissenschaft. Kritische Studienausgabe.* Vol. 3. Edited by Giorgio Colli and Mazzino Montinari. Berlin/New York: dtv/de Gruyter, 1999.

Pandita Bivamsa, U. *In This Very Life: The Liberation Teachings of the Buddha*. Boston: Wisdom Publication, 1992.

Popham, Peter. *The Lady and the Generals: Aung San Suu Kyi and Burma's Struggle for Freedom*. London: Rider, 2016.

———. *The Lady and the Peacock: The Life of Aung San Suu Kyi*. New York: Experiment, 2013.

Prager, Susanne. "Nationalismus als kulturelle Reproduktion: Aung San und die Entstehung des postkolonialen Birma." PhD diss., University of Heidelberg, 1998.

Richardson, Bill. *Burma's Aung San Suu Kyi*. Congressional Record Volume 140, Number 19, February 28, 1994. http://www.gpo.gov/fdsys/pkg/CREC-1994–02–28/html/CREC-1994-02-28-pt1-PgH16.htm.

Roewer, Richard. "Myanmar's National League for Democracy at a Crossroads." *GIGA Focus Asia*, no. 1 (April 2017). https://www.giga-hamburg.de/de/system/files/publications/gf_asien_1701_en.pdf.

Schütte, Heinz. *Yangon: Ein historischer Versuch*. Berlin: regiospectra, 2017.

Schwepcke, Barbara. *Aung San Suu Kyi—Heldin von Burma: Das mutige Leben der Nobelpreisträgerin*. Freiburg: Herder, 1999.

Seekins, Donald M. *State and Society in Modern Rangoon*. Abingdon: Routledge, 2011.

Sengupta, Nilanjana. *The Female Voice of Myanmar: Khin Myo Chit to Aung San Suu Kyi*. New Delhi: Cambridge University Press, 2015.

Silverstein, Josef, ed. *The Political Legacy of Aung San*. Revised ed. with introductory essay. Ithaca, NY: Cornell University, 1993.

Spiro, Melford E. *Buddhism and Society: A Great Tradition and Its Burmese Vicissitudes*. Berkeley: University of California Press, 1982.

Stalin, Josef. *Nation and Nationalism*. Moscow: Foreign Languages Publishing House, 1953.

Steward, Whitney. *Aung San Suu Kyi: Fearless Voice of Burma*. Minneapolis: Lerner, 1997.

Tatmadaw Researcher. *A Concise History of Myanmar and the Tatmadaw's Role*. 2 vols. Yangon: Ministry of Information, 1991.

Taylor, Robert H. *General Ne Win: A Political Biography*. Singapore: ISEAS, 2015.

———. *The State in Myanmar*. Singapore: NUS Press, 2009.

Thant Myint-U. *Where China Meets India: Burma and the New Crossroads of Asia*. New York: Farrar, Straus and Giroux, 2012.

Thomas, William. *Aung San Suu Kyi*. Milwaukee: World Almanac Library 2005.

Thompson, Mark R., and Claudia Derichs, eds. *Frauen an der Macht: Dynastien und politische Führerinnen in Asien*. Passau: Universität Passau, 2005.

Tinker, Hugh. *The Union of Burma: A Study of the First Years of Independence*. London: Oxford University Press, 1957.

Tonkin, Derek. "The 1990 Elections: Broken Promises or a Failure of Communication?" *Contemporary Southeast Asia* 29, no. 1 (2007): 33–54.

Tosa, Keiko. "The Cult of Thamanya Sayadaw: The Social Dynamism of a Formulating Pilgrimage Site." *Asian Ethnology* 68, no. 2 (2009): 139–64.

Victor, Barbara. *The Lady: Aung San Suu Kyi; Nobel Laureate and Burma's Prisoner*. New York: Faber & Faber, 1998.

Wade, Francis. *Myanmar's Enemy Within: Buddhist Violence and the Making of a Muslim "Other."* London: Zed Books, 2017.

Walton, Matthew J. "Ethnicity, Conflict, and History in Burma: The Myths of Panglong." *Asian Survey* 48, no. 6 (2008): 889–910.

Wintle, Justin. *Perfect Hostage: Aung San Suu Kyi, Burma and the Generals*. London: Hutchinson, 2007.

World Bank. *Myanmar Economic Monitor: Anchoring Economic Expectations*. Washington, DC: World Bank Group, 2016.

Zöllner, Hans-Bernd. *The Beast and the Beauty: The Conflict between the Military and Aung San Suu Kyi, 1988–2011, Set in a Global Context*. Berlin: regiospectra, 2012.

———. *Fetisch Demokratie: Der Arabische Frühling, von außen betrachtet*. Hamburg: Abera Verlag, 2014.

———. *Konflikt der Welt-Anschauungen: Die "Zwei Birmas" seit Beginn der Kolonialzeit*. Berlin: regiospectra, 2011.

———. *Neither Saffron nor Revolution: A Commented and Documented Chronology of the Monks' Demonstrations in Myanmar in 2007 and their Background*. Berlin: Humboldt University /Department of Southeast Asian Studies, 2009.

———, ed. *Talks over the Gate: Aung San Suu Kyi's Dialogues with the People, 1995 and 1996*. Hamburg: Abera Verlag, 2014.

———. *Von Birma nach Myanmar: Ein Zeit-Reise-Führer*. Hamburg: Abera Verlag, 2014.

———. *Weder Safran noch Revolution: Eine kommentierte Chronologie der Demonstration von Mönchen in Myanmar/Birma im September 2007*. Hamburg: Abera Verlag, 2008.

Index